GENEALOGY ONLINE

Genealogy Online

Researching Your Roots

Elizabeth Powell Crowe

Web Edition

McGraw-Hill
New York • San Francisco • Washington, D.C. • Auckland • Bogotá
Caracas • Lisbon • London • Madrid • Mexico City • Milan
Montreal • New Delhi • San Juan • Singapore
Sydney • Tokyo • Toronto

Library of Congress Cataloging-in-Publication Data

Crowe, Elizabeth Powell.
   Genealogy online : researching your roots / Elizabeth Powell
Crowe.—Web ed.
      p.   cm.
   Includes index.
   ISBN 0-07-014722-1 (alk. paper)
    1. United States—Genealogy—Computer network resources.
   2. Genealogy—Computer network resources. I. Title.
CS49.C76 1998
929′.1′0285—dc21   97-33669
                                                       CIP

McGraw-Hill

*A Division of The **McGraw·Hill** Companies*

ISBN 0-07-014722-1

*The sponsoring editor for this book was John Wyzalek, and the production supervisor was
Sherri Souffrance. It was set in Vendome by North Market Street Graphics.*

Printed and bound by R. R. Donnelley & Sons Company.

McGraw-Hill books are available at special quantity discounts to use as premiums
and sales promotions, or for use in corporate training programs. For more information, please write to the Director of Special Sales, McGraw-Hill, 11 West 19th Street,
New York, NY 10011. Or contact your local bookstore.

CONTENTS

Contents

Contents

ACKNOWLEDGMENTS

As with any book, this one was made possible by the efforts of many people besides the author. First, I'd like to thank each and every person mentioned in this book, as I obviously couldn't have done it without all of you.

Very special thanks to Jeri Steele and Cliff Manis, who pointed the way out of many a dead end. Special thanks to John Wyzalek and Brad Schepp for helping me through this edition. I'm grateful as well to Christina Palaia and the staff at North Market Street Graphics.

Great gratitude is due to all my family and friends, who were more than patient with me while I was writing this book.

But most of all I want to thank my mother, Frances Spencer Powell, who urged and encouraged me, babysat and researched for me, and traveled and travailed with me throughout the entire process from initial idea to final galleys. This book is dedicated to her.

INTRODUCTION

"I've gotten more genealogy done in one year on Prodigy than I did in 20 years on my own!" my mother exclaimed. This quote, from a 30-year genealogy veteran, shows how technology has changed even this popular hobby. The mind-boggling deluge of data needed to trace one's family tree has finally found a knife to whittle it down to size: the computer.

This book will help you understand that there's a rich community of information out there—information that can help you find where those missing ancestors are lurking. Some of the sources are free, some cheap, some dear. However, until you know about them, they're worthless to you. Once you know, you can decide for yourself whether to use them.

This book does not intend to teach you how to do genealogy, but how to use the tools of the online world to help you do it better. Still, I feel I should at least touch on how and why we do genealogy.

For Those New to Genealogy

Genealogy is the study of ancestry, or family bloodlines. Genealogists trace lines of family ancestry and usually show their findings by means of pedigree charts, or genealogical trees. Professional genealogists' studies can be relevant to history, law, sociology, and eugenics. To an amateur, the appeal is usually more limited and personal, such as finding out about family history.

Almost any self-respecting public library, no matter how small, has a local history and genealogy section. Some even have entire floors dedicated to those subjects. The desire to make history personal is a long-standing tradition.

Ancestor worship is a factor of most cultural history. Tribes or clans often sought to trace their clan's ancestry to gods, legendary heroes, or animals. This gave them a sense of identity and perhaps divine protection. Genealogy was originally transmitted by oral tradition, but later literate societies began to write theirs down. Notable early Western examples include the genealogies of the tribes of Israel (recorded in the Bible), the Greeks, and the Romans.

Genealogies assumed special importance concerning inheritance of power, rank, and property. Lists of hereditary kings were compiled by the ancient Sumerians, Babylonians, Egyptians, Indians, and Chinese. To this day, one reason for hiring a genealogist is to contest a will or prove right to an inheritance.

In medieval Europe, feudal landholders kept relationship records for transferring rank and land. Concern with kinship, and thus rank, was also reflected in heraldic developments; a single coat of arms can incorporate considerable genealogical information. With the Domesday Book now being put on CD-ROM, genealogists will have access to records heretofore too expensive or too rare to use.

Pedigree doesn't do what it used to for social status, but genealogy remains of interest to many people other than scholars. The United States, for example, has numerous genealogical societies that trace people's descent. Some of these are national, but many more are local or regional, such as the Tennessee Valley Genealogical Society or the New England Historical Society. Others are specific to certain names. Many patriotic organizations, such as the Daughters of the Confederacy, limit membership to descendants of a particular historical group.

The Mormon Church has collected an extensive bank of genealogical data (official registers of births, marriages, and deaths, and related documents), probably the greatest such collection in existence. Church members use these records in order to bring their ancestors posthumously into the church.

The federal government has recently started to put much of its data, such as death records, veterans' records, and so on, in machine-readable databases, which could then be accessible via an internet. This has genealogists everywhere excited.

Popular interest in genealogy was increased by the television miniseries of Alex Haley's *Roots* (1976); in researching this book, Haley traced his ancestry back to his African forebears. A major appeal of genealogy is that it provides people with a sense of continuity and of belonging, for the hobby teaches you one thing very quickly: mathematically, we all must be kin somehow. This sense of belonging extends to other genealogists, for it is almost impossible to research any family line by yourself.

A recent cover article in *CompuServe* magazine highlighted the uses of the magazine's online forum for genealogy. "We get several thousand users per week on this forum," says forum leader Dick Eastman. The article then proceeded to describe how the forum helped one woman find her natural father, how stories about ancestors are swapped, and the sort of informational files uploaded to the library.

Genealogy is a popular hobby and it's becoming a popular home business. It's a way to learn history that makes it personally meaningful.

Where Computers Come In

Databases, online services, online card catalogs, and bulletin boards are changing the *brick wall syndrome,* that frustrating phase of any lineage search where the information needed seems unavailable. Genealogists who have faced the challenges and triumphed are online, helping others.

There's no denying that the computer has changed just about everything in our lives, and the avocation and vocation of genealogical research is no exception. Further, a wonderful new resource for computers, the Internet, has come into being and is still developing at a pace that's dizzying. This book will explore many different networks, services, and bulletin boards that can help you in your pursuit of your ancestry.

Stories about how online communities have helped people in their genealogical research abound. Here is just one example:

Ten or twelve years ago, I was doing my research partly by mail, and partly by phone. I was searching for all of the descendants of Samuel Cousins, who settled in Alma, Wellington County, Ontario. There were five sons and four daughters, and since I had information on only one son, I had a long way to go. I contacted a gentleman in Aurora Ontario who was my fourth or fifth cousin (through number 3 son). He gave me the address in Weston Ontario of another cousin who had 'a family tree from someone in California.' I wrote to this lady, but she would not send me the information, could not copy it, and I could not visit her. Four or five years later, when I lived in Alberta, I interviewed a lady about the Cousins family there, and collected family group sheets on about 130 individuals who, as far as I could determine, where not related to me. Last spring, when I first got onto this echo, I noticed a lot of messages from a lady in San Diego (Mary Ferguson—thanks Mary), who seemed to know everything. On a hunch, I asked her if there was anyone in her local club/association named Cousins, hoping to contact the individual who had supplied my cousin with the information previously mentioned. Mary wrote back that there was no one named Cousins, but that a gentleman named Weidenheimer had done a book, and his family connected to the Cousins family. Could that be it? I dug out the letter from Weston, and sure enough, the man's name was Weidenheimer! Mary sent me photocopies of the FGS from her library, and lo! The Weidenheimer connection showed the descendants of number 1 son, and guess what? The Alberta bunch were all descended from him! Mary and the echo had supplied me with over 190 Cousins descendants in one fell swoop!
Sincerely,
Roger

Some Conceptual Background

Genealogists have had publications to turn to for many years. From local/regional publications such as the Tennessee Valley Genealogical Society's *Valley Leaves* to the venerated *Genealogical Helper*, a wealth of information has been printed to help genealogists find others working on the same ancestral lines, publish interesting tidbits, and help each other with vexing research problems.

For not quite so long, but for some time now, they have also had computers and genealogical database programs to help them track, organize, analyze, and share their genealogical information. For a while there was a dearth of such programs, then a widening choice of formats, and then finally a standard in the GEDCOM. Everyone was plugging away, gathering and storing information. They all had more information than they could use, some of it germane to their own lineages, some of it not, but surely useful to someone, so why throw it away?

So, here were all these collections of data, and all these users wanting to share that data. Now how to transfer it, for example, from a CP/M to DOS-based machine to a Mac?

In other fields, people were faced with the same problems. Astronomers, teachers, and the military were all doing the same thing genealogists were on different subjects. Electronic mail systems (e-mail), bulletin board systems (BBS), and the Internet came into being to solve the problem of getting data from one place to another using phone lines and protocols, regardless of the machinery and proprietary software involved.

Electronic Mail

Electronic mail systems are simply a way to send text from one place to another, just as regular mail does. Through a variety of different programs, that text can be private messages, public postings of articles, text files, graphics, even sounds.

However, please take that "private messages" phrase with a grain of salt. I'll make this point several times in this book: posting something to a list, echo, or board means that many, many people will read it. Posting something to a certain person at his or her e-mail address means you and that person will read it, but so will the people who run the system to which you posted the text. As of this writing, no law or court case has established that electronic mail is as private as first-class mail. One or two court cases, indeed, have held the opposite: when something is posted to a company-owned, company-run, electronic mail system, the text is considered the property of the company.

An e-mail system might be a part of an internet, a bulletin board, or a pay-per-use commercial service; it might even be part of a combination of these. Alternatively, it might stand alone, as a company-run e-mail service does. You need to check out any e-mail service you use, its costs and distribution, carefully.

Bulletin Boards

A *bulletin board*, as the name implies, is a place to post messages and information that anyone with access to that board is free to read and retrieve. Most bulletin boards have several functions, including games, but the two most genealogists will want to know about are messages (or mail) and files.

To continue the image, you would have a big cork bulletin board with messages tacked to it. On many systems, the messages are allowed to stay for only a few days or weeks, then they're replaced with new ones. The old ones are either filed or just thrown away, depending on the system operator's (sysop's) preference. Picture in your mind several of these boards, each one devoted to a specific topic. On a typical BBS, there are many of these.

Next to these boards are corresponding file cabinets. In the drawers are libraries of files, generally longer than the messages. They might even be collections of certain threads of messages, if a topic was interesting and informative enough. (A *thread*, in e-mail parlance, is a series of messages on a topic from several different people. Typically, such a discussion lasts only a few days, and the issue is resolved in a few dozen messages. However, there are exceptions!)

In the file cabinets concerning genealogy, you'll find programs, help files, ahentafels and tiny tafels, GEDCOMs, and so on (see App. C). You can go in the file drawer and get a copy for your own computer, or you can leave one from your computer for others to see and use. Generally, you cannot modify the files you find there.

Networks and Echoes

Connections of computers are called *networks*. The connection may be constant, or intermittent, but the point is that computers that are in different places can share information. This book is concerned with bulletin board system (BBS) networks and the Internet.

The BBS networks are called FidoNet, RIME, and so on. To send messages to someone on one of these echoes, you must use a bulletin board on that echo. Then when you post a message, you flag it as either local or echo. If it's *echoed,* then the BBS you used will get and receive messages from all the other BBSs connected to the same echo or network.

In general usage, *network* refers to the overall exchange regardless of subject matter, and *echo* refers to a specific message subject category on that network. However, sometimes you'll see the terms used interchangeably, which is a sloppy practice. Occasionally, files are also sent this way.

At least one of these echoes, FidoNet, is "gatewayed" to the Internet. That means that if you use the proper addressing scheme, you can send a message from a FidoNet BBS through a computer somewhere to an Internet address. It's trickier than it sounds, but quite useful once you get the knack.

These networks are not unlike the Internet in purpose. However, when you get to the Internet, the functions and services are unimaginably expanded, and ever changing.

The Internet

The Internet, with a capital *I,* is more of a concept than an entity. The concept is hook up lots of computers running the same protocol (way of communicating digital data) and let people communicate over their computers with pictures, words, sounds, and whatever else they can digitize. The Internet is a network of networks to implement that idea. There are several smaller internets with government, educational, or research purposes that connect to the Internet at certain points.

A network is a group of computers working together through some connection, intermittent or continuous. The connection can be phone wires (most common) but also can be cables, or radio, satellite, or other wireless connections. The Internet is a set of computers connected all the time, (the *backbone*) to which your computer can connect any time and through which your data can travel. The data is sent with a protocol called *TCP/IP.* It makes sure the data goes in the most efficient (not necessarily the shortest) route available at the moment.

The backbone consists of companies such as America Online, MCI and AT&T, universities, research institutions, and government organizations, all running computers connected with the Internet protocols. Every facet of the communications industry, in other words, gives some support to the Internet.

At first, you couldn't use the Internet unless you were an employee or student at one of those places, and your connection was probably free, supported by tax and research dollars. There were a few exceptions to this. Some entrepreneurs paid for an Internet connection at one of those places and then sold access: they are Internet Service Providers. Then the government decided it had done enough to get the information super-highway paved, and bowed out. The infrastructure was opened to commercial use, and the number of Internet Service Providers went from a few dozen to about a thousand.

Today, a great deal of scientific, educational, and technical research still goes on over the Internet, but entertainment and hobby use has grown phenomenally. The Internet is a resource, a method of research, and a "place" called cyberspace, all at the same time.

Much more is involved in how the Internet developed and works today than this book can cover. For the genealogy hobbyist, it's enough to understand that the Internet is a worldwide connection of computers; you can connect to it; and it has a wealth of information and many people willing to share on it.

How to Use the Internet

To use the Internet, you use different services. All of these services started out as text-based programs. Most of them are now available in some Windows or Macintosh graphical user interface. The main Internet services are as follows:

Chat—typing conversations, real time, over a network with someone. If you liked CB radio, you'll like online chat. Though it's popular, I haven't found much use for it in genealogy, except on the commercial online services. The chapters dealing with CIS, AOL, Prodigy, and MSN note the genealogy chat services (sometimes called *conference*) they offer.

E-mail—sending and receiving messages at your individual Internet account's address.

Finger—sending a test signal to a person's e-mail address. If that person has written a text file to respond to a finger command, the file will be returned to you. Some systems will also tell you if that person is logged on to the Internet right now or the last time that person logged on to the system.

FTP—file transfer protocol is how you get files, programs, pictures, and other data from another site to yours or how you send those things to another site. *Anonymous ftp* is a system where a lot of files are stored at a certain computer, and anyone is welcome to download them. You simply log in as "anonymous" or "ftp" and give your e-mail address as the password.

Ping—sending a test signal to a specific computer on the Internet. Useful for when you cannot connect to a WWW, telnet, or other Internet site; ping will tell you if the computer is down or running but busy. Windows 95 comes with a ping program, but you have to drop to the MSDOS prompt to use it.

Telnet—a text-based system of running a distant computer from your own. Once you log in, you must know and use the commands at that remote computer, but you can run programs and services such as ftp from telnet connections. The most common use for genealogists is to look at library card catalogs. Windows 95 comes with a telnet program, but there are graphical user interface ones that are better.

Usenet—also called *Internet bulletin boards*, Usenet newsgroups number in the thousands. They are organized by topic, and when you post a message to one, you are talking to the whole world, usually. Usenet is not e-mail; it's many-to-many or one-to-many communication.

World Wide Web—an interface called a browser ties together all these services except ping and finger. It's the easiest way to use the Internet.

A Quick Look at This Book

This book will give you a basic education in the online world. Nevertheless, please be aware that what is written here was current as of late 1997. Since that time, commercial online services, BBS, and the Internet will have added, expanded, revised, and changed what they offer, as well as how and when they offer it. The only constant in the online world for the last five years has been change, and at an exponential rate. So, be prepared for adventures!

Section 1: The Basics

1. What you need—A quick look at the basics you need to get connected.

Section 2: The Internet

2. Usenet—A short treatise on Usenet's use will be followed by a discussion of using a GUI newsreader and a text-based one.

3. Mail lists—Have genealogical information and discussions delivered to your virtual mailbox!

4. World Wide Web—The main place Internet things are happening. Fifty great genealogy sites to get you going.

Section 3: Other Online Resources

5. Local BBS and their nets—The concept of the local bulletin board system and the message networks will be discussed, with examples of good genealogical boards to visit.

6. FidoNet and friends—The lively genealogical discussion groups on FidoNet and other BBS message networks are discussed, with how to find a local board that carries these.

7. The National Genealogical Society BBS—This BBS is at the center of what's happening in American genealogy.

8. Everton Publisher's BBS—This BBS is a dial-up, searchable database. Some use is free, some is for subscription.

9. Online library card catalogs—How to find books through the Internet.

10. The Library of Congress Online—Available through telnet, ftp, WWW, and commercial services such as AOL, this is an invaluable resource.

11. The Church of Jesus Christ of Latter-Day Saints—The first question concerning online genealogy is always, "Can I get to the Mormon database?" No, but they still have lots of good stuff to help!

Section 4: Commercial Online Services

12. America Online's Genealogy Club

13. CompuServe's Roots Forum and Genealogy Support Forum

14. Prodigy's Genealogy BBS

15. MSN Genealogy SIG

Appendix A: The Genserv Project—Details on how this GEDCOM database can be searched via e-mail.

Appendix B: Tiny Tafel Matching System—How to use this FidoNet service, a searchable database over several different BBSs.

Appendix C: Forms of Genealogical Data—Gedcoms, Ahetafels, and Tiny Tafels: how to share what you have.

Appendix D: Internet Error Messages—When things go wrong on the Internet, here's the code.

Glossary

CHAPTER 1

What You Need

People speak of online services and the Internet as a place: cyberspace, or the information superhighway. If you like to envision it that way, think of the modem as your car and the software you use as the engine.

Modem (the Car)

The car you'll take on this electronic road is your modem. To the average user, this box sits on your computer or a card in the expansion slot, connected to a phone line and your computer.

Note that telephone lines have very little electrical resistance. If lightning strikes a telephone wire outside near your home, the electricity can travel right into your home's phone lines. The stories you've heard about people who were killed while talking on the phone in a thunderstorm are true. Therefore, if you have a modem you should always disconnect it from the wall during a thunderstorm. If you don't, your modem, computer, and even printer could be irreparably damaged by a lightning strike. The added measure of installing a surge protector on your phone lines wouldn't hurt, but it's no substitute for unplugging during electrical storms.

A modem is a gadget that converts the data of your computer system into sounds, which are sent out on a phone line (or a cable physically connecting two computers) to another computer. That's modulation. The other computer, with its modem, translates these sounds back into computer-readable signals. That's demodulation. The modulator/demodulator, or *modem*, makes it possible for computers to "talk to each other."

Unfortunately, the phone lines we have in much of the country were never made to carry this sort of signal, and some of them have a hard time doing it at a reasonable speed. So, standards of translation came into being to help the phone lines carry this data faster and faster. The bad news is that, unlike fax machines which all use a standard way of sending data to one another, modems come in a plethora of standards and speeds. (How fast a modem can transmit data is commonly called its *baud rate* and is measured in *bits per second*, or *bps*.) In addition, compression methods (more about that in a minute). And error correction. Let's look at how all of this came about.

A Little History

In the beginning, modems had switches to enable them to talk to different systems, and they were used to set stop bits, set parity, and so on. You had to use a paper clip or ballpoint pen to set those switches. In addition, if you needed to change them for dialing up a different place than you did last time, this was a real pain.

Then Hayes created modems with a set of software commands to control these settings without touching the switches. This set of commands became the Hayes standard, which led other modem manufacturers to emulate Hayes and produce Hayes-compatible modems.

If noisy phone lines introduced errors in transmission, then telecommunications software took care of it. If the data was compressed for faster transmission, decompression software took care of it (programs such as StuffIt for Macintosh, PKZip for PCs, uuencode for UNIX systems).

Then manufacturers began designing modems with compression and error correction built into their wiring. This helped with the transmission of data, but it meant that both modems had to be using the same kind of compression and error detection. The standards wars went on for a while, but have settled somewhat, into names like V.32.

I started out with a little old 300-bps Hayes Smart Modem in 1982, and I now find the speed and variety of modems available today can be quite confusing. Many articles and even books are out there to help you choose from today's models, so I won't try to get detailed here. You have to decide what you want based on these two criteria:

Cost. The older, slower models can be found in second-hand shops, flea markets, and so forth. The fastest, fanciest ones can set you back several hundred dollars. However, remember that, on almost every online service or system you'll use, time is money. Spending a little more up front might very well save you money over the life of the modem.

Speed. Get at least a 14.4-kilobyte-per-second, or even 56-kilobyte-per-second, modem. The prices on these are dropping rapidly. Many systems won't let you log on at less than 9600 bps because they want as many users as possible to get on, get what they want, and get off again. Other places might let you, but they charge by the minute. Uploading or downloading a large file of genealogical data will be painfully slow and painfully expensive at less than 9600 bps.

Communications Software (the Engine)

What makes a modem work is your communications software, which can be likened to the engine in a car (your modem is the car). There are two basic types: serial communications programs and TCP/IP stacks. The first will be just fine for dialing into bulletin board systems and some commercial online services. Such software is most commonly bundled with a modem or another software package.

TCP/IP is the standard communications format for the Internet. Because so many of the commercial online systems are now offering Internet connectivity, the software you get with a CompuServe or America Online membership is probably TCP/IP now. Windows 95 with the Plus! package has a TCP/IP stack built into it; there are versions for DOS, Macintosh, and many other platforms, too. First, let's look at the common serial program.

Serial Programs

The selection of programs for standard serial communications is wide and diverse. Many modems come with a communications package included, and it's usually enough to get you started. Eventually you'll want more than a stripped-down, basic program. However, before you can effectively choose one, you must learn and understand the several functions of communications software packages.

First, and most important, is which modems the program supports. Most commercial communications programs come with more than 100 configurations, and you can almost count on most popular models of modems being included. If your modem isn't listed, chances are the combination of your modem and the program will work with one of the generic configurations; you just might not get to use every bell and whistle your modem has. Nevertheless, if you've purchased a just-released model, *especially on the high-performance end,* make sure it's supported by the program you have in mind. Be especially careful with the Hayes program SmartCom; it provides configurations only for Hayes modems.

The supported file-transfer protocols are also important. At first glance, this seems easy, because it's a rare program that doesn't come with all the major transfer protocols (XModem, ZModem, and YModem). Though XModem is probably the most typically used protocol, especially on the systems you'll explore in this book, I personally prefer ZModem. This protocol allows you to resume an interrupted file transfer instead of starting again, a blessing if you're uploading and downloading large files on unreliable phone lines. YModem's advantage is that it allows you to batch a number of files for sending in sequence.

A typical serial communications program will have a capture feature and a scroll-back buffer. The first allows you to save every character and keystroke to a file as you proceed with a session. This is useful for scripting, which I'll explain in a moment. The second allows you to use page up and page down to see what's happened so far, but the buffer isn't usually written to disk for later reference. You should check how large a screen buffer the program offers. For many online sessions on the Internet and with some bulletin board programs, it's useful to scroll back to see something that has already moved off the screen.

If you have a multitasking environment, you should look at the communication program's resource handling. Does the program adjust its share of processor time depending on whether it's running in the foreground or background? If not, you'll have annoying interruptions when transferring files in the background and working in the foreground.

Many modems today come with a fax function as well. If yours has this, you'll need a communications program that can send and receive faxes. However, some of these programs hog the serial port, something that can be annoying if you have the fax program in memory and need to call an online service. To avoid this, you need a feature called *TAPI*, which allows the fax receive and send function to be active, yet shares the communications port.

Now let's talk about scripts. This is one feature of data communications programs that's developing rapidly. However, while many features are useful, others seem to be there just to impress you. Be certain the program offers a scripting language you can live with. Learning any of these scripting languages takes considerable time, so many users rely instead on scripts written by others, editing them to suit their needs. Also, bear in mind that, in general, the more commands, the more powerful the scripting language, but the harder it is to learn and understand.

The best thing to do is look for a program that comes with a library of predefined scripts for such operations as logging on to the most popular online services and setting the program and modem in answer mode to receive calls. When you log on to popular online services such as CompuServe, you might find that the forums there have member-written scripts for you to download. Check how many scripts are available on the software company's bulletin boards, too. These scripts are generally set up to let you provide your user name and password the first time you use the script, and from then on the script carries out your session automatically.

If you plan to write your own scripts, having a capture-to-file feature is a big help because you can record your first session and turn it into a script for future use. In addition, it's nice if the program offers a built-in script editor, because it's faster and easier to open script files using a built-in editor from the communications program itself. The editor often includes extras such as help screens, which list the available script commands, and step-through debuggers for locating problems; these make writing scripts easier. Determine whether the program will let you import scripts from other communications programs or platforms. This can save you some work if you're switching from one program to another, or even from DOS to Windows.

A feature that has become almost standard is a *phonebook* where you can store the names, numbers, speed, and modem settings for your favorite places to call. This should be easy to set up, edit, and sort according to your current whim: alphabetically, by phone number, by entry last dialed, whatever.

Another feature to consider is called *queuing.* When you want to call a lot of bulletin boards or commercial online services, particularly if you experience busy signals repeatedly, you'll want to make sure the program can queue calls. This feature has the program continually dial the numbers until it's able to connect with one of them. Queuing saves you the tiresome task of cycling through the calls manually.

You might want to be able to have multiple sessions open at the same time. (A *session* is a configuration file within the program's phonebook for placing a call to a certain service or bulletin board, including name, phone number, modem speed, and the appropriate modem parameters.) Multiple sessions mean you can open a new session without closing a previous one, especially helpful if the preceding session was busy and you want to retry it. A session that remains open also serves as a reminder to try the call again. Some programs even let you run multiple sessions simultaneously, say one on a modem and another through a direct connection or network gateway. Many businesses find this handy, but a genealogist probably won't need it.

Many genealogists will want a program that gives the user remote access. If you're interested in calling your home computer from a library or a convention to download or upload files, you'll want to look at the communications program's remote-access features. Can you assign a password so you can log on from a remote location? Can anyone else log on without your permission or can you lock people out? Once logged on, can you allow or deny access to directories on your hard drive? Can you set the program to call you back to continue the session? This feature would be worthwhile if it's a toll call, but would be most useful if you regularly call in from the same phone number, since the callback number has to be preset on the host computer before you leave home.

In addition, if you plan to communicate via modem, one on one, with other genealogists regularly, you'll want to look at the chat utilities. These allow users on both ends to carry on a typed conversation. While any communications program lets you type messages back and forth in the terminal window, chat utilities separate your typing and the other person's typing into two windows, making it much easier to follow the conversation. This is most useful when you're running a BBS yourself, but if you and another genealogist are exchanging tiny tafels (see App. C) directly, chatting might be helpful.

Lastly, if you get serious about this way of doing your genealogy, you might want network support. Many homes now have more than one computer, and some people like to connect them. If you plan to share a network modem or modems, you'll need a program with network support. Several programs can be used to access modem pools with NetWare's NASI protocol, while other programs support NetBIOS networks. Match your communications program to your network program if you plan to set up something like this.

In looking for a communications program, by all means consider the commercial programs, and read the ads and reviews. Also, look into the many fine shareware programs—Telix, CILink, and so on. They're usually good buys, have good support for registered users, are powerful programs, and have most of the features discussed here. Ask at your local computer users' group to find out about these, or sign on to a local bulletin board and ask the sysop for a recommendation.

Whichever communications program you choose, you can fine-tune your engine (i.e., communications software) for error-free, high-speed file transfers. Look for a chip inside your computer near your main processor, called the UART. It's both a transmitter and a receiver. Your *universal asynchronous receiver and transmitter (UART)* simplifies terminal, printer, and computer interfaces by being fully programmable, including the bps, number of data bits, number of start bits, number of stop bits, type of parity, manipulation of output handshaking lines, and sending of input handshaking lines. If a UART is too old, it can't keep up with the new modems when it tries to speak "modemese," RS232 protocol. If you need help with this, you can read technical manuals or ask your local computer shop.

If your modem can operate at 9600 bps or higher, be sure your serial port uses a UART 16550 chip; if it was made in the last three years, it probably does. If it doesn't, you can buy an I/O board that has one for as little as $40. Use the communications program to turn off the software flow control for connections at 9600 bps or faster. Xon/Xoff uses characters inserted in transmitted data to instruct the modem to pause when the transmitted data exceeds the capacity of the receiving modem's buffers. Unfortunately, this method really slows high-speed transfers. Set the program to use RTS/CTS, a hardware-based flow control, and let the modem decide how fast it can take it.

You can use other engines besides your main communications program. Many of the commercial services have front-end software, which is a communications and script program to connect to their services. CompuServe Information Manager, Aladdin, D-Lite, and so on can make your sessions on these pay-by-the-minute services faster and less painful. Some of the front-end programs have the features I've mentioned, and some can be used as very limited, general-purpose communications software to log on to other systems.

TCP/IP Stacks

TCP/IP works a little differently from standard communications programs. Instead of sending bits of data serially down the wire, IP bundles it up into discrete packages and TCP routes them around the Internet in the fastest way. At the other end, the packages of data are reassembled by IP.

Getting a TCP/IP program is not nearly as hard as it used to be. Windows 95 comes with an inherent TCP/IP stack that works great; it's called Dial-Up Networking and is found in the "My Computer" window. Your Internet Service Provider should be able to tell you how to set it up to connect.

Furthermore, all the major online services (Microsoft Network, CompuServe, Prodigy, America Online, and GNN) have front-end software now that connects to the service with TCP/IP. So, you can use World Wide Web browsers (see Chap. 4) with any of these.

In addition, in many bookstores you can now find Internet connection packages. These run from $19 to over $100, depending on how much software and documentation is included. Netscape Navigator, for about $30 for PCs and Macs, is an excellent package that gives you not only the TCP/IP but also several programs you need to use the Internet effectively. Many times such packages come with a trial subscription to an Internet Service Provider (ISP).

Which brings me to the final way to get Internet software before you're on the Internet: find a good Internet Service Provider. The best ones will include a package of software, manuals, and handholding to get you started.

Choosing an ISP

Why go the direct route? Although commercial online services such as America Online and MSN offer lots of non-Internet goodies, dedicated Internet providers can offer a cheaper, faster, and more comprehensive entrée to the Internet. For example, AOL's Internet programs are slow and sometimes clunky, and not well integrated; Delphi features lots of Internet services, but they're all text-based. With a dedicated Internet provider, you can use a graphical front end such as Netscape Navigator, access every Internet service in existence via 28,800-bps or faster lines, and pay as little as $20 a month.

Like choosing a mate, you should know what you want before you start looking. Your choice isn't final, of course—but you don't want to hopscotch from one e-mail address to another. So, go into this knowing that Internet providers are as different as dog breeds. All of them will get you onto the Net, but access speeds, services, software, and other goodies will vary. Before you lay down any cash, ask yourself some basic questions:

- What services do I need?
- How often do I need them?
- How fast do I need them?
- How many hassles am I willing to put up with to save money?
- How much am I willing to pay?

Just keep in mind that there are trade-offs no matter what provider you finally choose. For example, you may find there is a price break for slower and less direct connections, or a premium to be able to dial into your account from various places in the country. In addition, you may find that companies consider support extremely expensive to provide, so if you sign up with a full-service provider it will cost a bit more.

You may save money by choosing only what you need. However, in the end you will find you need the whole shebang: while some users are happy with just electronic mail, to find all the genealogical treasures out there you will need more features, such as a WWW browser to fetch sound, pictures, and animation. If you're to use them, you'll need a provider who can offer a high-speed connection.

When it comes to services, you should insist on the whole range: e-mail, telnet, Usenet newsgroups, ftp, gopher, and more—in short, everything that the Internet has to offer. Even if the ISP service is austere, you should get at least a little support with that, too.

Baby Steps

As I mentioned, the commercial online services now offer Internet access, and for your first online forays they are probably your best bet. Once you are online with CompuServe, America Online, or a similar service, you'll learn the ropes and get familiar with what's out there. Then, you may decide you want an Internet Service Provider (ISP) instead. To find one, before you sign off the commercial online service, use the Web browser to go to the searchable page *http://www.commerce.net/directories/products/isp/isp.html.* You can choose to search either by area code or by region; use this list to find a local Internet Service Provider or a remote one that offers access via a local number. Make a list of two or three and contact them. Ask these questions and listen for these answers:

■ *Do you offer 14.4 Kbps and faster access?* The answer should be yes. The faster, the better, because the genealogical information out there is immense.

■ *Will I get busy signals if I call during prime time in the evening?* In other words, how many high-speed lines does the provider have? How many customers log in on average during prime time? (And test them on their answer: dial them up just after supper!) The answer should be that you can get on any time you want; they have enough lines or enough ISDN capability to handle their current customer base.

■ *Do you offer anything else besides Internet access, such as BBS echoes and file collections?* The answer should be yes; this is part of support.

■ *Can I use a graphical third-party front end like Netscape to access your system? Do you provide this software?* Both answers should be yes. If the first answer is no, then you have to deal with a text-oriented UNIX system, and the provider should supply a written manual. If there's no manual or menu system, this should be a *really* cheap service.

■ *Which message readers can I use with Usenet newsgroups?* The answer should be a client that runs on your machine, that they can provide you. If the answer is *rn* or *nn*, beware! These are arcane UNIX newsreaders, text-based and a real pain to use. Windows and Mac-based user-friendly readers such as Free Agent are better; new browsers such as Microsoft Internet Explorer and Netscape Navigator include news readers as part of the program.

■ *What's the capacity of private e-mail boxes?* Here, the answer should be at least 100K of space. Bigger is better. If you subscribe to even a few genealogical mail lists and newsgroups, your mailbox could be stuffed quickly. If your mailbox is limited to 100 messages, you might miss important mail.

■ *Will my connection be SLIP or PPP?* PPP is better: it's newer, faster, and more reliable than SLIP, but if SLIP is all you can get, take it.

■ *Do you provide access to all Usenet newsgroups, or just a selection?* The answer should be all. This is very important for some of the more arcane genealogical ones.

■ *When do you schedule downtime for maintenance? How heavily loaded is the system?* Good luck getting straight answers to either question, but they should at least reassure you that downtimes will be announced in advance somehow. For the real answer, nose around Internet discussion areas and ask users of the service for the real poop.

■ *Do you have points of presence (POPs) across the country, so if I'm on the road I can still reach you with a local (or toll-free) call?* You hope the answer is yes. But reality may dictate that you get Internet accounts from two different providers—one for home, and one for the road.

■ *How do you charge?* A flat monthly fee for unlimited connect time is the ideal answer. Second best: a flat fee with a generous allotment of online time and a low hourly fee ($1 to $3) for use beyond that allotment. Beware of hourly based connect charges, which can add up in a hurry.

According to Michael Fraase, author of *The Internet Tour Guide,* an excellent book/disk set to get you started on the Internet, really smart Internet Service Providers offer a complete manual, training classes, and online news featuring phone number changes, service enhancements, and other information of interest to users.

With prices ranging from $10 a month for telnet access to $260 a month for an always-open direct line, there's something out there for everyone. The trick is knowing what you want, asking tough questions of prospective Internet providers, and finding a company that will give you what you need. Don't forget to compare the answers to these questions with the commercial online services and to check up on how prices have changed every few months.

Inoculations

No journey is without risk. Whenever you enter the realm of file transfer, the dreaded microorganism, the computer virus, might be lurking. A *virus* is a program hidden on a disk or within a file that can damage your data or your computer in some way. Some simply display a message. Others will wipe out your entire hard drive. I strongly recommend that you inoculate your computer before using this mode of electronic travel. Programs to detect and remove viruses are available on BBS, in your computer store, and on various online services. Some are shareware, others more costly, but if the program ever deletes a virus before it harms your system, it's worth the price.

Generally, when you download, ask the sysop specifically if he or she checks all files on the system for viruses. If not, reconsider downloading from there. If someone mails or hands you a diskette with data, always run a virus checker on the disk before you do anything else. Once a virus is copied onto your hard disk, getting it off of there is a headache. In addition, run the virus checker on your hard drive at least twice a month, just to be certain. This should be part of your regular tune-up and maintenance.

Mail-Reading Software

Reading mail is the biggest part of online life. Whether you're using a local BBS, Delphi, or the Internet, a mail reader makes life much easier. If you send and receive e-mail from a number of online services you need an electronic Labrador that can fetch your messages from anywhere: commercial online services, BBS, and the Internet. Here, I'll describe four basic types: general purpose, BBS-oriented, Internet-oriented, and front ends for specific online services. There will be some overlap: some programs such as QmodemPro come with features for all four types.

GENERAL PURPOSE. E-Mail Connection, RFD Mail, and Robo-Comm are three programs that will do this. RFD mail is very typical of this type of program.

RFD Mail is a Windows-based communications program that grabs your e-mail from a number of services: CompuServe, GEnie, MCI Mail, World Unix, The Direct Connection, and even TCP/IP networks. You can also add BBS and other text-based services to RFD's list by writing scripts. When you first install RFD, you supply your name and password for each service, the numbers to dial, and other parameters. If you go by different names on different systems, you can store these *e-mail signatures* as well. Built-in binary file-transfer features let you upload and download files attached to messages. Once everything is recorded, click an icon and RFD trots off to get the mail. RFD gathers all your mail in one place and makes reading and answering messages a one-click job. There's a single electronic address book for all the services you use, and the program keeps track of what service a message came from. The only downside: RFD Mail calls only systems that use ASCII characters (it turns off any ANSI environment), so you can't use it with Prodigy or America Online. However, this is a quibble. As one satisfied customer wrote, "RFD mail pays for itself in about three months in reduced charges."

BBS-ORIENTED. For BBS systems, investigate programs that use the QWK format. More than 75 percent of the BBS software out there, including PCBoard, RBBS, Remote Access, and Wildcat BBS, use the QWK packet format.

If you're new to the online world, you're probably scratching your head at that last paragraph, so here are some definitions:

QWK is a program/format for retrieving a lot of messages at once, quickly, to be read later after you've logged off. The BBS selects the messages you want according to what you input. It gathers them all into one file, then compresses them with a program such as PKZip, ARC, or StuffIt. That file is then downloaded to you, and you sign off.

It's assumed that you have the program to uncompress the file on your machine. Your mail reader will use that program, then let you look at all the messages, one by one, answer the ones you want, delete whatever you don't want, and so on.

Many programs allow you to sort the messages several different ways: by date, subject, sender, or receiver. Some have what's called a *twit filter,* a feature that excludes messages from a certain name if you've found that person to be offensive or otherwise unhelpful. A mail reader will usually save and compress your answers, including any changes in your preferred subject categories of messages, and then upload the answer file to the board the next time you sign on. This saves you time and, on certain systems, money. It frees up your phone line while you read and answer messages. Best of all, it organizes things!

My favorite BBS mail QWK reader is Off-line Xpress because it comes with an editor, a great interface, and even a spell checker. (There are other popular ones, such as Blue Wave, and you should certainly try them.) OLX, as it's called, is now included in Mustang Software's QmodemPro communications software. This is an outstanding, feature-packed communications program that was shareware and is now commercial, although there are still thousands of copies of the shareware version out there on BBS. OLX is now a module of the communications program. Fax, CompuServe, MCI Mail, or a BBS that uses .QWK mail doors can send messages prepared in OLX. QmodemPro can even function as a BBS host. Another nice feature is that the whole QmodemPro package requires only two megabytes of disk space.

INTERNET-ORIENTED. There are two very good Internet mail programs with free versions that the new user should consider.

EUDORA. Eudora is a mail program named for author Eudora Welty, and it's as simple and powerful as her stories. If all you need is simple mail management, Eudora Pro, or its free version called Eudora Light, will take care of it with ease. If you lack a TCP/IP stack or Winsock software, you can use the one supplied in the package of the Eudora Pro version. If you do have a provider, you simply enter the mail server's address (a painless task) and log on.

After you've logged on to your mail server, sending and receiving messages are one click. You can log off to read the mail, then log on to post your replies, using Eudora Pro's spelling checker to help prevent embarrassing mistakes. Eudora also lets you set up a timer for retrieves—anywhere from every few seconds to once a day. Both Eudora Pro and Eudora Light offer configuration options stored in one easy-to-navigate settings window; for example, you can set the program so it won't retrieve messages larger than, say, 20K.

Eudora Light puts all received mail in the "new" box, and lets you sort the messages into others by hand, but Eudora Pro lets you filter messages as they come in, route them to specific mailboxes, and sort messages by various criteria. You can also search all message headers and bodies for text strings in both versions. The Macintosh and Windows versions of Eudora Pro are nearly identical in capabilities, except that the Mac version lacks support for multiple mailboxes. Eudora Light works perfectly under Windows 95, as well. On either platform, Eudora is so simple to install and configure that you'll be sending and collecting e-mail less than 30 minutes after opening the box.

To get Eudora Pro, call Qualcomm at 800-238-3672 or 619-658-1292. The list price is $89. To get the slightly less functional version called Eudora Light, check your local BBS or log on to http://cwsapps.texas.net/smail

.html#eudora to download it. The price of Eudora Light is to send the author a postcard!

PEGASUS. Pegasus Mail has all the features of Eudora Light and more. Because it has so many more features, it's a little harder to learn at first, but once you get the hang of it, Pegasus Mail is just wonderful. It is an extremely intuitive, great-looking mail program with integrated address books and mailing lists.

Extensive drag and drop capabilities also help to make Pegasus Mail easy to use. You can attach or include a file in a message with Pegasus Mail but there are so many wonderful options for how to do that, you may have to do it a few times to get the hang of it. Pegasus also includes a spelling checker, advanced filtering controls for incoming messages, and a feature that lets you minimize Pegasus and have it check the mail at regular intervals and play a sound file when it finds new mail. Most functions are one click off the menu bar, and you can change your setting easily from the Configuration menu. One of the best features of Pegasus Mail is how wonderful it is to use offline: you only have to connect to post and retrieve. In addition, in sending or replying to a message, you have the option of sending a copy to both the recipient and yourself or just to the recipient, and you can review or delete queued mail. The price is nice too...it's free!

To download Pegasus Mail, use ftp to get it from risc.ua.edu/pub/network/pegasus, from ftp.let.rug.nl/pub/pmail, from the CompuServe system in the NOVUSER area, or via Gopher from ftp.cuslm.ca.

ISDN. The modem isn't the only way to connect to all these services, nor is it the fastest. The alternative, ISDN, is so innovative and expensive I hesitate to mention it, but in the interest of completeness I feel I must. This will be a very short introduction; if you want to try to jump into ISDN, you'll have to read much more than this brief section before you're ready.

The phone companies currently marketing ISDN (Integrated Services Digital Networks) to their customers would like you to believe that faster is better and that's all there is to it. ISDN is a new kind of connection that has three channels—A, B, and Data—to carry your signals. Phone companies have been promising for years that ISDN would replace our old (and reliable) analog phone lines. With an ISDN line hooked up to your PC, phone, fax, and what-have-you, you can send and receive just about any kind of data—voice, documents, graphics, sound, the full-motion video necessary for movies or teleconferencing—over the line at speeds up to 64,000 bits per second (bps).

Another selling point is versatility. With the right equipment and software on your end, a single ISDN line can support two phone numbers. In effect, you could get a video phone call from Grandma on one line, while transmitting a report to your company on the other. ISDN also lets your phone be a little smarter, because the ring sent down an ISDN line could tell your phone who's calling, the type of call (data or speech), the number dialed, and so on. Your intelligent phone could analyze this information and act appropriately. For example, your phone could be programmed to answer calls from certain numbers only or to answer specific calls on specific lines, such as all fax calls on line two.

Unfortunately, ISDN isn't cheap, and there are times when it seems like a solution in search of a problem. Although you'd treat an ISDN line like your old analog phone line—you would be billed for long-distance charges, you could have call waiting features, and so on—it comes with a passel of complications. Cost, for one thing.

Although an ISDN line costs as little as $20 a month in California, it's considerably more expensive in the East. Moreover, installation runs about $200. An ISDN line would eliminate the need for a modem—after all, a *mod*ulator-*dem*odulator is designed to turn digital data into analog and back again, and ISDN is all digital. Yet, hooking up your PC to an ISDN line would require a special adapter that can cost up to $1000 or more, depending on the application. Moreover, using your existing fax machine, telephone, and so on, requires buying bridging devices and still more software. The alternative is to buy all new, ISDN-smart equipment.

Another consideration: the ISDN system is powered by your household current, not the phone company's. If the power to your ISDN system goes out, you're unreachable. This is why many businesses that have jumped on the ISDN bandwagon also buy a separate power source for their ISDN system—and keep an old analog line around, just in case of thunderstorms, brownouts, and earthquakes.

The price tag for your local telephone company is also steep, and no doubt some of that cost will find its way onto your monthly bill. For starters, all the switches in your phone company's central office have to be replaced with digital switches that can recognize ISDN. The new switches also have to be within $3\frac{1}{2}$ miles of your house. Therefore, the cost on both sides of the ISDN connection is high.

Consequently, communities that have adopted ISDN have found themselves isolated digital islands in an analog sea. But the Baby Bells have been selling ISDN hard the last year or two, so many major cities in the United States have it, as well as smaller communities, such as Chapel Hill, North Carolina, and Huntsville, Alabama. The web of ISDN communities is growing, so that sending and receiving data at blinding speeds from point A to point B across the country may be possible fairly soon. But not just yet.

Criticizing ISDN is easy—after all, adopting it involves more than a few leaps of faith. A lot of companies that you'd expect to be taking the ISDN leap, such as commercial online services, haven't budged. You're lucky if you can find an Internet Service Provider that has an ISDN link. Nevertheless, ISDN may be coming to a town near you.

The idea of high-speed, multichannel phone lines is appealing. But like most cutting-edge technologies that don't offer immediate, quantum gains in productivity, ISDN won't make serious inroads until it's as ubiquitous, invisible, and cheap as cable TV—when ISDN support is built into PCs, phones, and faxes and can be accessed via a plug in the wall. Personally, I'm waiting until then.

Attitudes and Etiquette

I've already noted that the online world has definite communities, and none are friendlier and more helpful than the genealogical ones. Nevertheless, as with any community, there are customs and etiquette you're expected to follow. Some of these you should know before you sign on.

One good idea is to lurk first, read a list or echo without posting messages yourself. It's sort of like sitting in the corner at a party without introducing yourself, except it's not considered rude online; in some places you're expected to lurk until you get the feel of the place. Read the messages for a while, find out who's interested in what. If the board or service has a help or information file, read it well, understand what's allowed and not allowed with this particular group. Then introduce yourself with your first message.

When you post a query, which should be your second message, never make the subject line (called the title in some places) something vague and general such as *query* or *searching my family.* Some people choose what messages to download based on the subject line; if yours isn't specific enough, it might not get read at all. Your subject line should have the surnames mentioned in the messages, such as *SPENCER, POWELL, CRIPPEN, BEEMAN.* If it's a general information request, don't use *general informa-*

tion as your subject line, but rather *is the IGI on CD-ROM?* or similar specific phrase. Respect people's time (and lack thereof) by being quite clear about the subject matter in your title.

If you can avoid it, don't ask over the Net what can be more easily, efficiently, and quickly done over the phone or at your own library. Sometimes your local sources don't have an answer that to others seems simple; in that case, ask. Nevertheless, you might get flamed (I'll deal with that in a minute).

Another commonly accepted practice is to target your messages. When posting a message, you have a choice of how wide the distribution will be on most systems; sometimes you can flag it to a subcategory, as on CompuServe and Prodigy. In other places, you can aim it to go only to those who read a certain subject, as on FidoNet, or only to those who use that certain BBS. On the other hand, it can go over the whole Internet. Choose wisely, for the same reasons you want to use descriptive titles. It's considered bad form to post a message to the wrong subject heading on the BBS nets; certain groups have rules about what can be posted and how it must be worded. You may inadvertently break some rules by posting it to the wrong heading. In addition, post a message only once, especially to groups where all the messages are stored somewhere. This doesn't mean you can't repeat a query once in a while; just don't do it so often that you become annoying. This is an obvious courtesy to those trying to control the traffic.

It's considered tacky to test out a system with a message like "this is a test" to a forum. The software works. Trust it.

Many people store a signature, which serves the same purpose as a return address label. This should be a pure ASCII file with the details of how to reach you, which is inserted at the end of a message. Try not to make yours overly long and complicated, but do try to update it often as it helps someone contacting you directly. (Surnames in the signature are discouraged on the Internet, due to the archiving of the messages.) In addition, sometimes a *tagline* is added, some pithy or humorous statement of 10 words or less. Some examples:

> I'm in shape ... round's a shape isn't it?
> If this were an actual tagline, it would be funny.
> It's only a hobby ... only a hobby ...
> Libbi's Law: You cannot do just one thing ...

These are used just as signatures are. Again, they're fine if not overdone. Lurk a while to see whether taglines are accepted before using them in a certain group. *Note:* Don't take seriously or execute any code mentioned in a tagline like "<Ctrl><Alt><Del> to read the next message." On the Internet, a most vicious code has appeared in taglines, for example, one that a Bourne shell would eventually interpret as RM * (a command to remove all files on the current disk, like DEL .), and there are no recovery tools like Norton on UNIX. Sadly, vandalism has followed us into the virtual world.

Eventually, you'll see a message you want to answer. Great! However, remember that there are customs to be followed in this case, too. First, look at the top of the message. Several lines will tell you who posted the message, from where and when, and how it traveled. This is the header. Use it to direct your answer.

Be as brief as possible. Everyone is busy. Postings on some networks are huge in number. With so many going so far, only the most important bytes of information should be included. Also, remember that somewhere, someone down the line is paying a long-distance charge to send your postings on. The briefer the article, the more likely it is that people will take the time to read it.

When you see something you want to answer, comment on, or discuss, it's traditional to summarize the message in the following format:

Joe Usenetter said in the title or subject line:
>what he said, with one arrow for each quoted line.
>>two arrows for information Joe quoted.
My answer to this is:

and so on. Some mail readers will take care of this quoting the original for you. This way, if someone didn't see the beginning of the message he or she can take the time to look up the original or take your word for the direct quote. However, don't directly quote the whole article! Only truly pertinent parts, at most four or five lines, should be repeated.

Use e-mail to answer a question posted at large. Instead of posting an article that everyone reads, post a mail response only to the person who asked the question. Also, check to be sure no follow-ups have already been posted; someone might have already given your answer. The questioner is then expected to post all the answers received in an edited, summarized form. *Editing* means stripping the headers and signatures, combining duplicate responses, and briefly quoting only the original question.

As mentioned earlier, you might get *flamed*. This is when someone sends an insulting or offensive message. It's usually a personal attack in response to an opinion on an issue. If you're flamed, the best, easiest, and safest thing to do is ignore the flaming message. Forget it. Put the sender on your twit filter and go on. The optimum course of action is not to start or get involved in a flame.

Rule no. 1, indeed, could be stated as "Never forget that the person on the other side is human." You're using machines to upload and download, so your interaction with the online world at first might seem pretty dry and impersonal. But the whole point of the Net is to connect people. Don't treat the people out there as machines. Remember they have feelings.

Also, be aware how your postings reflect on you. Never write anything you wouldn't say at a party or in a crowded room. Those postings are all many, many people will know about you. And, you never know who's out there reading. The world is in constant motion today; no matter where they are right now, people online now might someday be clients or work with you or meet you in other circumstances. In addition, they could remember your postings. In the end, you can't really hide behind the modem.

Let me repeat my warning about privacy of e-mail. It all depends on your system administrator and the other person's. Generally, yes, something posted to someone's e-mail box will be seen only by you two. System operators have been held responsible for what goes over their boards and nets, so they have good reason to spot-check messages. Be aware of that.

Humor and sarcasm are best used cautiously. Subtle humor, especially satire, is hard to get across with no facial expressions, body language, or hand signals. Well-done sarcasm so closely resembles the attitude it belittles that it's sometimes taken for a genuine attitude when delivered only in written form. Therefore, it's polite to clearly label all humor. How? Well, some conventions are (tilt your head to the left):

:-) or :-]	A smiley face
:-D or HAHAHA	A laugh
;-)	A wink
LOL	Laughing out loud
ROTF	Rolling on the floor

Other expressions besides humor are as follows:

IMHO	In my humble opinion
TAFN	That's all for now
TTYL	Talk to you later

There are more smileys in the glossary.

It might seem silly, but these symbols can help prevent misunderstandings. Moreover, should you be tempted to become incensed over something you've read, remember that some people on the Net consider themselves above using these silly symbols. Don't flame the author unless you're sure he or she was serious.

Also, be aware that in many cases a network or echo stretches across oceans and borders. Don't criticize someone's spelling or grammar; that person might be using English as a second language.

Be careful about copyrights and licenses, and cite appropriate references. Copyright law is complicated and no clear-cut case has defined the use of copyright in electronic versions of text. Further, no one owns some of these networks. You could be personally guilty of plagiarism unless copyright laws and rules are carefully followed. Posting licensed software anywhere is another good way to get flamed, if not sued.

It's also important to cite references. If you give statistics, quotes, or a legal citation to support your position, you'll be much more believable if you give full credit to the source.

Finally, on the subject of rights, be aware that because of the powerful editing programs that come with mail readers it's possible to post a message from one net to another, either in its original form or altered in some way. For this reason, some nets have a rule against posting something from another net; it's very possible to misquote a message, accidentally or deliberately, with the originator's signature still attached. Be sure you're quoting accurately and that the forum or net you're using allows quotes from other sources.

So now, you're ready to go. Let's look at some specific systems.

2

The Usenet Newsgroups

Usenet has been called *Internet bulletin boards, Internet news,* and many other similes and metaphors over the years. My definition of Usenet is this: an Internet service where messages to the world are posted.

It isn't an organization per se, nor is it in any one place. Lots of machines carry the messages, receiving them and sending them on down the line. Your Usenet feed comes from your Internet Service Provider.

Gene Spafford, a kind and wise man at Purdue University, regularly posts several files about Usenet to misc.news. If you find them on your ISP's help page, especially one called WHATIS_UZIP, be sure to read them. However, for now I'll try to give you some pointers.

Complicated, But Useful

The first thing to understand about Usenet is that it's hard to understand. Don't be discouraged about that. It has been said that many Usenet flame wars arise because the users don't comprehend the nature of the network. And these flames, of necessity, come from people who are actually using Usenet. Imagine, then, how hard it is for those unfamiliar with Usenet to understand it! On the other hand, it should be comforting to the novice that so many people are successfully using Usenet without fully understanding it.

One reason for the confusion is that Usenet is a part of the Internet, and for some people it's the only part they use. Yet it isn't the Internet, any more than Boston is Massachusetts.

Usenet's messages are sorted into thousands of *newsgroups,* which are sort of like magazines (you subscribe), sort of like late-night dorm discussions, and sort of like a symposium. A newsgroup is supposed to be a set of messages on a certain subject, although abuses abound. Usenet's flavor depends on the newsgroups you subscribe to. Some newsgroups are wild, some very dull, most are in between.

A *moderated* newsgroup has a referee who decides what messages get to go on that newsgroup. An *unmoderated* one isn't edited in any way, except you'll get flamed (insulted) if you post a message off the proper topic. Most Usenet newsgroups are unmoderated.

There are eight major categories of newsgroups:

- ALT for alternative topics
- COMP for computer-science—related topics
- SCI for science not related to computers

- NEWS for topics about Usenet itself
- REC for recreation
- SOC for social interaction and hobbies
- TALK for general conversation, usually to no purpose at all
- MISC for miscellaneous items

Tom Czarnik, who is a Usenet guru from way back, says, "And let's make a distinction between the Internet and Usenet. The Internet has come to mean the sum of the regional nets, while Usenet is a system for the exchange of Newsgroups, mostly via UUCP." (*UUCP* is a program that runs under a system called UNIX and was the first program for Usenet; nowadays, most people read Usenet with a graphical newsreader such as Free Agent.)

Despite this clear separation, you'll often hear of "pictures sent over the Internet" or "messages on the Internet" when Usenet, a particular part of the Internet, is meant.

No person or group has control of Usenet as a whole. No one person authorizes who gets news feeds, which articles are propagated where, who can post articles, or anything else. These things are handled one newsgroup at a time. You won't find a Usenet Incorporated or even a Usenet User's Group. This means that, although the freedoms of expression and association are almost absolute, Usenet is not a democracy. It's anarchy, that is, something with little or no control except as exerted by the social pressures of those participating.

Therefore, sometimes Usenet is not fair—in part because it's hard to get everyone to agree to what's fair, and in part because it's hard to stop people from proving themselves foolish.

Usenet History

It got started, according to legend, in 1979, when a group at Duke University in North Carolina wanted to exchange data on research with some other universities. This group was in on the ground floor of the development of UNIX, an operating system. Soon the group members had written programs in UNIX to allow them to exchange data and analysis back and forth to other universities running the same programs. The neat part was that they could send programs that had been changed into plain text (encoded) and could be changed back into their digital form (decoded) so that they could send anything without using up the very limited bandwidth of the time.

Then they began to use the program to send each other messages to discuss hardware, problems, industry gossip, and how to fix certain bugs. Then messages started about current events. And jokes. And dreams. And chatting about their hobbies.

Then they began routing the more interesting stuff through an automated program. This program's duty was calling other UNIX sites while people slept, leaving off packets of data and programs and messages, picking up others destined for other places, and calling another site. More than 5000 articles a day are routed this way today. Having so much information to route meant that some sort of categorizing became necessary. So, messages were labeled according to their newsgroup and people signed up for them the same way you subscribe to a newspaper. Your subscribed newsgroups were presented to you in your *newsreader,* which at this time was a text interface.

Meanwhile, nonuniversity types who also ran UNIX got in on the newsgroup loop from colleges, research centers, and high-tech corporations connected with those to government agencies, and with their interests, which just happened to include genealogy.

So, today, you have commercial connections to the whole thing. In fact, there are more business connections than educational. A list of free Usenet sites is available from Phil Eschallier, in the pubnet.nixpub newsgroup. Since he updates it every month, any list printed here would be outdated before the book went to press. Nevertheless, if you have an Internet Service Provider (whether an independent or a service such as Netcom), you probably have access to a news server already.

Because all of this happens largely on a volunteer basis, you must understand that access to Usenet is not a right. (Although someone in Dallas recently filed a court case claiming it was just that! He kept stirring up flames on Mid-East politics and UTD pulled his student account. He was suing to get it back based on free speech. The case was unresolved as of this writing.)

Usenet is not a public utility, at least not yet; there's no government monopoly and little or no government control, so far. Some Usenet sites are publicly funded or subsidized, but most of them aren't. Lots of universities are connected, and often the hard work of keeping Usenet going is done on campus, but it's not an academic network.

Moreover, although many people are connected through and because of their work, Usenet is not to be used for advertising. Commercials are tolerated only when they're infrequent, informative, low-key, and preferably in direct response to a specific question. The only exception is the .biz groups, where advertisements are accepted.

Usenet is not a strictly U.S. network. Many, many correspondents are from around the globe, so be polite about grammar and spelling. The heaviest concentrations of Usenet sites outside the United States are in Canada, Europe, Australia, and Japan.

Prices

To read any Usenet newsgroup, you need some sort of Internet connection.

America Online, Netcom, CompuServe, Delphi, Microsoft Network, Portal, PSI, The Well, and many other commercial services offer Usenet connections. Many local BBSs, as well, are getting Usenet connections. There are Usenet-only connections, too. One is UUNET. UUNET is not free, although it is affordable. One way to hook up is to subscribe by writing to the following address:

UUNET Communications Services
3110 Fairview Park Dr.
Suite 570
Falls Church, VA 22042
703-876-5050 voice
703-876-5059 fax
Net Domain address: *info@uunet.uu.net*

Freenets are a good source of Usenet feeds, if there's one in your local dialing area. The original one is the Cleveland freenet (telnet freenet-in-a.cwru.edu). This is like National Public Radio adapted to the online experience. As of February 1992, *Communications Week* reported that 10 were in operation across the United States. For additional information on NPTN and freenet activities or programs, you can contact the following:

Dr. Tom Grundner
President, NPTN
Box 1987
Cleveland, Ohio 44106
aa001@cleveland.freeneg.edu (Internet)
72135,1536 (CompuServe)

Supported by volunteers, corporations, and sometimes quasi-governmental agencies, freenets are for everything from support groups to hobby groups. AIDS information and guinea pig raising, community events, and private friendships abound on these.

The Software

In the old days (the first edition of this book!), we had to learn disagreeable, arcane UNIX commands and use unfriendly UNIX news readers to obtain the wonders of the Usenet. You may still have to do that, and text-based newsreaders are explained in the following discussion. But, happily, times have changed. We now have a plethora of graphical newsreaders for any platform, be it Windows, Mac, UNIX, Xwindows, or whatever. The online commercial services have all integrated newsreaders into their front-end software, too.

Newsreaders

However, you may want to use a dedicated newsreader. Figure 2.1 shows Free Agent, a free Windows newsreader from Forte Software. You can download it from the company's site at http://www.forteinc.com/getfa/download.htm. Alternatively, you can try the full-fledged, $29.00 Forte Agent reader with more features. However, Free Agent does quite well for a free program, so let's look at it.

After the program is installed in Windows, you have to tell the newsreader your news server. Your Internet Service Provider tech support people should tell you what it is. It will be something like news.yourISP.com. For example, the news server at CompuServe is news.compuserve.com. Generally, you have to be a signed-in customer to use a system's news server: You can't get into CompuServe's server logged in to another Internet Service Provider, for example.

Agent's layout is very typical. The default is three panes of the window showing you information from your Usenet site. The upper-left pane shows the names of the newsgroups. The upper-right shows the message headers of a selected newsgroup. The lower pane shows the body of the message. If you don't like this particular layout, use the menu item Options, Window Layout and choose another one.

Figure 2.1

Free Agent, a free
newsreader, is fun
to use.

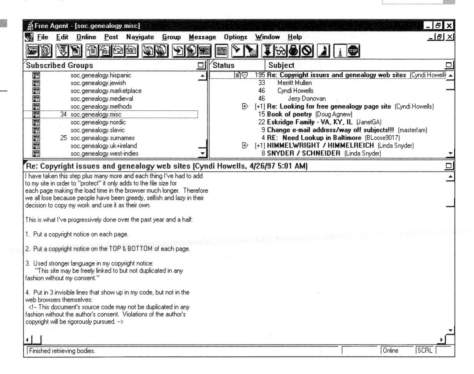

Figure 2.1

Free Agent, a free
newsreader, is fun
to use.

The Newsgroups pane can be set to show you all newsgroups or only the ones to which you have *subscribed* (that is, told the program you want to read regularly).

A nice feature of this reader is the search feature. Under Edit, Search on the menu, or with the flashlight on the toolbar, you can search this list of all newsgroups for *genealogy.* When you have clicked in the pane showing the list of message subject lines, you can use the same tool to search them, say for a surname or a state. In addition, when your cursor is in the body of a message itself, you can search that message as well. A newsreader with a search function can save you tons of time and online charges.

A simple click in the box next to the name of a newsgroup in the group's pane subscribes you. Then you can click on the "all groups" bar to turn it into "subscribed groups" in order to view only the names of the newsgroups you have subscribed; the rest don't appear until you decide to look at the whole list again.

The upper-right pane is where information about the current messages (*articles,* in Usenet parlance) in the newsgroup highlighted in the upper-left pane can be found. Double-clicking on one of these lines brings up the message itself in the lower pane You can choose what colors mean what, but the default is that red subject lines are unread, black ones are ones you have seen.

Replying and posting are accomplished by simply clicking on icons on the toolbar at the top. You can reply by e-mail to just the person who posted the message or to the whole Usenet group.

Free Agent is a good newsreader. Its commercial sibling, Forte Agent, has even more features:

- Filters for subjects and senders you do or don't want to be sure to see
- Sorting by thread, subject, author, date, or size
- Launching your browser when you click on URLs, integration with other Internet applications
- Customizable toolbar
- Folders for mail and news
- Address book
- E-mail as well as Usenet send and receive
- Ability to skip or sample long e-mail messages
- Automatic filing of e-mail messages in folders by rules you decide
- Import e-mail messages from Pegasus and Eudora
- Spellchecker

Any newsreader you buy should have these features; for a free one, Free Agent is very good.

Although I don't own a Mac, and so couldn't test it, three different sites on the Web recommended John Norstad's NewsWatcher for the Mac-connected. NewsWatcher does everything you'd want a newsreader to do, except filtering by keywords, but there's an add-on called Value Added Newswatcher if you need filtering. It gets updated and improved so often that you'll sometimes find a new version every week. You can find it at http://src.doc.ic.ac.uk/public/packages/mac/newswatcher/ and ftp://ftp.tidbits.com/pub/tidbits/select/newswatcher.hqx.

Browsers

Reading newsgroups with a Web browser (see Chap. 3) is another way to go. Netscape Navigator 3.0 comes with a newsreader window. Microsoft Internet Explorer 3.0 can use any newsreader program registered with the Windows system.

In Netscape Navigator 3.0, this means clicking on Options, Mail, and News Preferences and choosing the Servers tab as in Fig. 2.2. Now Netscape Navigator is ready to read news for you.

In Microsoft Internet Explorer 3.0, you use the menu item View, Options, and choose the Programs tab, as in Fig. 2.3. If you have installed Microsoft Internet News, Forte Agent, or some other Windows newsreader, you can choose one of those to be the default newsreader.

In some other browsers, you may have to find the Helper Programs dialog window and put in the news server and newsreader information.

Commercial Online Services

Microsoft Network, CompuServe, America Online, and the other major online services also have ways for you to read Usenet. Most of them involve reading online, while the meter is ticking.

AOL, however, has an option to let you retrieve newsgroup articles when you retrieve e-mail for offline reading. First, you use the keyword *USENET* to go choose your newsgroups. Simply click on the Search Newsgroup button, search for genealogy, groups you want, and then close the

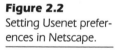

Figure 2.2
Setting Usenet preferences in Netscape.

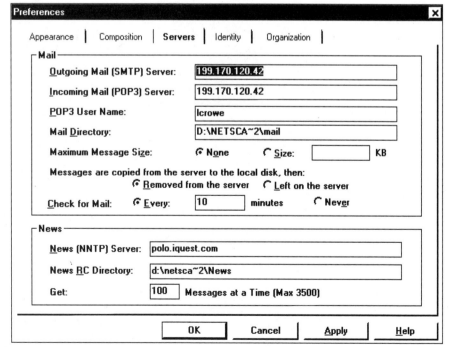

Figure 2.3

Setting Usenet prefer-
ences in Microsoft
Internet Explorer.

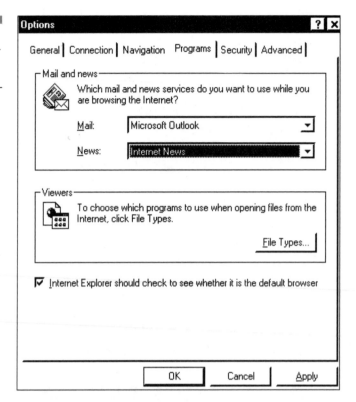

window. Back at the AOL Usenet window, click on the Read Offline button. Those that you would like to read offline, put in the right-hand pane
of the window (see Fig. 2.4).

Close that window and click on the menu in Mail, Set Up FlashSessions.
Put checkmarks in the boxes about sending and receiving newsgroup messages. Now, whenever you run a FlashSession to retrieve your AOL mail,
you'll get the genealogy newsgroups you chose, too. This will make the sessions longer but it's less online time than reading the newsgroups live.

On Prodigy, CompuServe, and MSN you have to read Usenet online, as
of this writing.

Text-Based Readers

Some Internet Service Providers offer only the old, text-based UNIX
newsreaders. They're not much fun. Sometimes, though, that's all you can
go with.

Let's say you want to go read a day's worth of soc.genealogy.surnames
on Usenet. Remember that your connection determines how you pro-

Figure 2.4
You can choose
newsgroups to be
downloaded with
your e-mail on AOL.

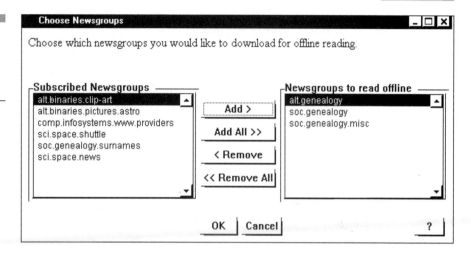

ceed. But let's pretend your Usenet connection is on my Internet Service
Provider, InterQuest.

Signing on, I choose Usenet resources from the menu. I'm then given a
choice of several UNIX newsreaders: Tin, NN, and Trn. Tin is the most
popular, so I'll choose it. After a moment, Tin shows me the current subscribed newsgroups (see Fig. 2.5). Tin also shows me the commands I can
use to unsubscribe, move around the messages, and so on.

Figure 2.5
In the text news-
reader Tin, reading
messages is very
slow.

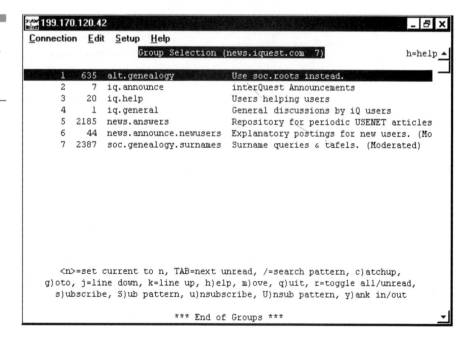

In Tin, *catchup* means mark the newsgroup as read. *Yank* means list all the available newsgroups. / means search the current list. You can search the list for the genealogy newsgroups you want to subscribe to. Then you can press *Y* again to yank the "all newsgroups" list away again.

As you choose a group, you are shown the topic lines of the messages. Choose a message and you can read that one, reply to it if you want, or move on to the next one. *Q* quits the current screen; you just keep pressing *Q* until you are back to the sign-in prompt and then you type *bye* to log off.

The Genealogy Newsgroups

Once upon a time, we had one online genealogy Usenet newsgroup for genealogy: soc.roots. But it became unwieldy to try to discuss beginners' questions, software, history, specific regions, specific family name queries, and the joy we get from our hobby all in one newsgroup. After much discussion, soul-searching, argument, pleading, and finally reconciliation, we now have an embarrassment of riches in genealogical newsgroups:

alt.genealogy	An older genealogy group, very general, and mostly people who don't want to use soc.genealogy.misc for some reason.
alt.culture.cajun	Cajun history, genealogy, culture, and events.
fido.eur.genealogy	A FidoNet echo copied to Usenet; for those searching in Europe.
fido.ger.genealogy	Same as the previous newsgroup, but for Germany research; most messages in German.
pnet.rec.genealogy.announce	A Prodigy-only newsgroup, this one for announcements about its genealogy area.
pnet.rec.genealogy.talk	A Prodigy-only newsgroup for discussion of genealogy.
soc.genealogy.african	For those tracing roots of African-Americans and other African genealogies.

soc.genealogy.australia+nz	Australia and New Zealand, only.
soc.genealogy.benelux	Luxembourg, Belgium, and the Netherlands.
soc.genealogy.computing	Programs, bugs, how-tos. Mostly software, some hardware discussions.
soc.genealogy.french	France only, in French mainly.
soc.genealogy.german	Germany only, in German mainly.
soc.genealogy.hispanic	Spanish, including Central and South America, many messages in Spanish.
soc.genealogy.jewish	Judaic genealogy, moderated.
soc.genealogy.marketplace	Buy, sell, trade books, programs, seminars, and the like related to genealogy.
soc.genealogy.medieval	Ancient genealogy, mostly European.
soc.genealogy.methods	How-tos, what works, tips and tricks in genealogy, moderated.
soc.genealogy.misc	This is what became of soc.roots.
soc.genealogy.nordic	Scandinavian genealogy.
soc.genealogy.slavic	Slavic genealogy. Some messages in Slavic languages.
soc.genealogy.uk+ireland	The United Kingdom and Ireland, only.
soc.genealogy.west-indies	Caribbean genealogy, mostly in English but not all.

In addition, there are several groups in the soc.history.* hierarchy that discuss areas touching on issues genealogists face: records, sources, and so on. Be aware, however, that not every genealogy newsgroup will be available on every new server; the Prodigy Net groups, for example, are available only to Prodigy users signed on to their Prodigy accounts.

Several of these groups post files of information called *Frequently Asked Questions* (*FAQs*) to their own newsgroups and to the newsgroup soc.answers, about once a month. Look for a message called the Meta Genealogy FAQ, posted about the 22nd of each month to most of the soc.genealogy newsgroups; this message will show you how to get the FAQ files for the individual genealogy newsgroups.

Net Etiquette and Tips on Usenet

Try to stay on topic in a newsgroup, or you might receive insulting messages, called flames. In general, these topics are welcomed in the genealogy newsgroups:

- Your own family history information and requests for others to help you find information. Tiny tafels are often posted for this.
- Information on upcoming genealogical meetings, workshops, symposia, reunions, and so forth.
- Reviews, criticisms, and comments for software or hardware you've used about genealogy/family history.
- Telling others about book shops around the world that contain books or information about this subject.
- Almost any message about genealogy in general.

Remember what you send is posted as you sent it, unless it is to a moderated group such as soc.genealogy.surnames, where all messages must pass the moderator's muster.

The basics of etiquette in this group aren't very different from general online etiquette discussed in the introduction. The participants in this forum want the topics of discussion to relate to genealogy or family history, however, and it's held that anything a subscriber thinks is appropriate is appropriate if it relates to genealogy.

Assume an attitude of courtesy among subscribers and readers. Remember that your postings and comments might be seen by as many as 20,000 readers on different networks in many different countries throughout the world. Remember the rules I mentioned earlier:

Read carefully what you receive to be certain that you understand the message before you reply.

Read carefully what you send, to ensure your message won't be misunderstood. As a matter of fact, routinely let a reply sit overnight, then read it again before sending. It prevents that sinking feeling of regret when you realize what you posted is not what you meant.

Avoid sarcasm. If humor seems appropriate, clearly label it as such. A smiley face should indicate humor. It's easy to misunderstand what's being said when there's no tone of voice, facial expressions, or body language to go by.

Know your audience and double-check addresses. Make sure that the person or list of people to whom you're sending your message are the appropriate one(s) with whom to communicate.

Be tolerant of newcomers, as you will expect others to be tolerant of you. None of us were born knowing all about the Internet or Usenet. Do not abuse new users of computer networks for their lack of knowledge. As you become more expert, be patient as others first learn to paddle, then swim, then surf the Net. And, be an active participant in teaching them.

Avoid cluttering your messages with excessive emphasis (**, !!, >>, and so on). It can make the message hard to follow.

When you respond to a message, either include the relevant part of the original message or explicitly refer to the original's contents. People will commonly read your reply to the message before they read the original. (Remember the convention to precede each quoted line of the original message you include with the > character.) Do not quote more than necessary to make your point clear, and please don't quote the entire message. Learn what happens on your particular system when you reply to messages. Is the message sent to the originator of the message or to the list, and when is it sent? When responding to another message, your subject line should be the same, with RE: at the beginning.

Always include a precise subject line in your message. It should get attention and the only way to do that is to make sure it describes the main point of your message.

If you're seeking information about a family, include the surname in uppercase in the message subject. Many readers don't have time to read the contents of all messages.

Bad sample subject line:
Wondering if anyone is looking for JONES

Good samples:

Researching surname JONES
SPENCER: England>MA>NY>OH>IN>MS
Delaware BLIZZARDs pre-1845
? Civil War Records

In the good samples, note these conventions: surnames are in all caps, but nothing else. An arrow is used to denote migration from one place to another. A date is always helpful. If your message is a question, indicate that in the subject line. Although passages in all uppercase are considered shouting, the exception to this rule in the case of genealogy echoes is that surnames should be in uppercase, just as in any query.

Keep messages to only one subject. This allows readers to quickly decide whether they need to read the message in full. Second subjects within a single message are often missed. Questions are often the exception to this rule. When you ask a question, end it with a ? and press the Return key. That should be the end of that line. This makes it much easier for people to reply, because most newsreaders will quote the original message line by line.

Some other rules about questions that apply only to the genealogy messages: all questions concerning the possibility of access to the LDS database from Usenet or any other technique will be answered *no*, so please don't ask. No one has electronic access to the LDS (Latter-Day Saints) database. Period. Please see Chap. 11.

Be specific, especially when asking questions. If you ask about a person, identify when and where the person might have lived. In questions concerning specific genealogical software, make it clear what sort of computer (PC/MS-DOS, PC/Windows, Apple Macintosh, etc.) is involved. The folks reading these newsgroups are very helpful but very busy, and are more likely to answer if they don't have to ask what you mean.

Always, always put your name in the text of your message, and your best e-mail address for a reply. The end of the message is a good place for your name and e-mail address. Furthermore, this newsgroup is read by many people who have read-only privileges; they cannot reply by e-mail. So, it's a good idea to also put your postal address in your messages so anyone can reply to you.

Whenever any newsgroup posts a FAQ, *read it*. If you can't find a FAQ message or file, make one of your first questions on the group, "Where and when can I get the Frequently Asked Questions for this group?"

Sometimes (as when, in early 1994, rotten weather, an earthquake, and a national holiday all converged on a certain Monday) you'll find the Usenet newsfeed absolutely clogged with messages, because so many people found themselves unable or not required to go to work. In that case, you must choose what to read based on subject line or sender, because it's impossible to read everything posted to the group that day. This is when a newsreader that lets you search the subject headings is invaluable!

Searching Usenet Newsgroups

You don't always have to read the whole newsgroup to find what you want. There are several places where you can search Usenet newsgroups, one or several or all at a time. Two of them use the Web:

InfoSeek has the last two weeks of all Usenet newsgroups in a searchable database. Using a Web browser (see Chap. 4), go to http://www.infoseek.com. Use the drop-down box on the page to choose Usenet Newsgroups, and type in the surnames you want and +genealogy. InfoSeek Guide will return a list of the messages. Each message title is a link; click on it to read it. However, this guide won't let you choose which groups to search!

That's why DejaNews is my favorite way to do this. DejaNews has more like a month's worth of messages. Using a Web browser (see Chap. 4), go to http://www.deja.news.com. At the top of the page, there's a graphic called Power Search. Click on that, then choose Create a Query Filter. Type in soc.genealogy.* for all the groups or just the full name of the one you want (see Fig. 2.6). Click on Create Filter, and you're back to the search page. Now type in the surnames you're looking for, and within seconds DejaNews will return a list of messages that match the search! Other search engines such as http://www.lycos.com have similar features, but DejaNews is my favorite.

Figure 2.6
You can search Usenet messages at http://www.dejanews.com.

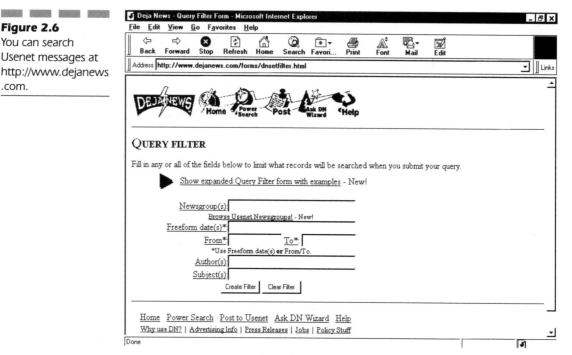

Beyond Usenet

There's more to communicating with others on the Internet beyond Usenet, of course. In addition, some people find delivery to their own mailbox more convenient than Usenet. For that, we have mail lists, the subject of the next chapter.

ROOTS-L and Other Mail Lists

There are lots of ways to get and share information on the Internet. The one almost everyone knows how to use is e-mail. For many people, just reading several dozen messages a day on Usenet is great. Yet, there's so much more on the Internet that has to do with genealogy, and Usenet is just a tiny part of it. Two ways to get genealogical information by e-mail are the newsletter and the mail list.

Just another way to interact with other Net users, *mail lists* are messages on a specific topic, delivered to your e-mail door. Unlike Usenet messages, which are stored in one central location on your ISP's computer, mail lists come directly to you. Another difference with Usenet: you don't need special software to participate. Whatever you are using to read your e-mail now will do, whether that's AOL's mail or a POP3 reader such as Eudora.

Mail lists, like Usenet, are discussion groups. Using your e-mail program, you post a message to the address of the mail list. This message is seen by everyone else on the mail list. The other members respond to the mail list with comments and answers.

The differences between mail lists and Usenet newsgroups are in how you send and receive the messages. While Usenet is sent and received mainly with newsreaders, you read messages from and post messages to a mail list with your mail program, whether that's Eudora, MicroSoft Mail, or the mail function of your favorite online commercial service such as CompuServe or America Online.

Generally, you must request to join a mailing list (to read it and post messages to it), and the messages of the list will only be sent to the other people who have also requested to join. The advantage of mailing lists over Usenet is that they tend to be more focused in subject and moderated, which means someone checks the messages to be sure they are actually on the assumed topic of the list. If you've been on Usenet any length of time, you know few newsgroups have such controls!

You can find mailing addresses and descriptions of mail lists of all descriptions in the news.announce.newusers newsgroup with the subject of *Publicly Accessible Mailing Lists*. There are several of interest to the genealogist, both specifically on family history and more general ones on historical and research topics; later in the chapter, I'll list some of them.

The concept of a mail list has been adapted somewhat to another use: online newsletters. Some, like the Journal of Online Genealogy (http://www.onlinegenealogy.com/), are posted to the World Wide Web, and you have to go get them (see Fig. 3.1). Others are *pushed* at your mailbox. The newsletters, unlike the mail lists, are not message exchanges but periodicals in e-mail form. The end of the chapter will have a few genealogy newsletters, too.

Figure 3.1
ROOTS-L defaults
to index mode; order
the interesting mes-
sages from roots-l-
request@rootsweb
.com.

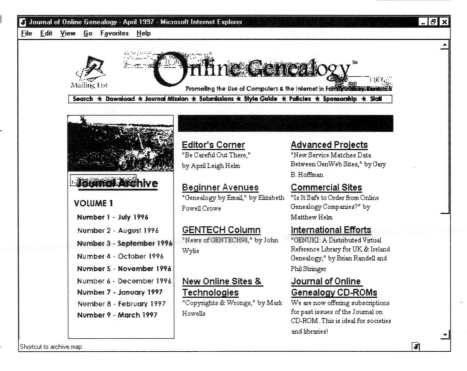

ROOTS-L

This is the grandparent of mailing lists for people who are interested in genealogy. It has spawned generations of genealogy mailing lists, large and small, but this is the original. Its home page on the Web, with an archive of old messages, is http://www.rootsweb.com/roots-l.

The people who bring you ROOTS-L with their volunteer work include the following:

- Alf Christophersen (http://www.uio.no/ãchristo/), the fearless leader
- Dan Chase (http://pobox.com/~danimal/)
- Karen Isaacson
- Sandy Myers
- Vicki Lindsay
- John Salter
- Rick Carpenter
- Cliff Manis (http://soback.kornet.nm.kr/~cmanis/genscli1.htm)

In early 1997, over 7000 people were subscribing to ROOTS-L. To subscribe, first have a large mailbox (ROOTS-L generates a lot of mail traffic). Send e-mail to ROOTS-L-request@rootsweb.com with the message

subscribe

Don't include your signature block, your name, or your address; don't include anything but that single word.

To later unsubscribe (yes, not everyone chooses to stay with us), just send to that same address the message

unsubscribe

ROOTS-L also has loads of files and databases, and you can get these by sending e-mail commands to the listserv program that runs ROOTS-L. You can get files such as:

ROOTS-L Library: Everything from a fabulous collection devoted to obtaining vital records, to useful tips for beginners, to book lists from the Library of Congress, and the like.

The Roots Surname List or RSL: A list of over 200,000 surnames and contact information for the 25,000+ people researching them. The RSL may be interactively searched. See FAMILY.README for more information and FAMILY.INDEX for a listing of all the related files.

The Roots Location List or RLL: A list of locations of special interest to individual researchers, along with contact information for those researchers.

The U.S. Civil War Units file.

The Irish-Canadian List: A list of Irish immigrants who settled in Canada, including (if available) dates and locations.

Books We Own: Books and other genealogical resources owned by Internet genealogists, in which, under certain restrictions, they are willing to do lookups.

And much more. When you subscribe, you'll get a long HELP message that tells you just how to retrieve the list of available files, and then how to have the files delivered to your mailbox. If you want, you can also retrieve them from the ROOTS-L Web site previously listed.

ROOTS-L has undergone many changes since the first edition of this book: it's no longer echoed in a Usenet newsgroup, and it's no longer at North Dakota University. But the number one rule still holds: everyone is welcome, and any message pertinent to genealogy is gladly received.

The list has clearly established purposes:

1. To provide subscribers a way to communicate and request information about genealogy (family history). Not to refight old wars or discuss religion or politics.

2. To provide a forum for communication, since we have no campus on which we can regularly congregate and exchange ideas. This means it is open to people from all over the world, as well as all over North America.

3. A means of keeping informed of activities taking place in the genealogical community. However, be aware that rumors spread as fast as news!

4. A meeting place for those who wish to learn about finding information concerning their own family history, as well as share what they have learned.

5. To help people learn to spell the word *genealogy!* Spell it correctly in your messages!

Advertising of or selling a product is not in general regarded as acceptable on this list. The posting of an announcement of a product is acceptable. ROOTS-L, the mail list, did correspond to soc.roots: each echoed the other and the only difference was how you retrieved the message. That connection was severed June 1994 and new newsgroups and mail lists resulted.

There is something at this point you must master in using ROOTS-L. Stop a moment, now, and memorize this:

Messages to people go to ROOTS-L@rootsweb.com

Commands to programs go to ROOTS-L-request@rootsweb.com

This is true of any listserver: the messages go to the address of the list. The commands to use the list in various ways must go to the listserver, even though everything after the @ is identical. But if you send the UNSUBSCRIBE message to the request address, you will be signed off. If you send it to the ROOTS-L address, you won't be signed off and you will annoy the rest of the members of the list.

It's possible that for some reason you stop receiving ROOTS- L when you did *not* send any of these commands. In this case, it may be your subscription to ROOTS-L was deleted. This can happen if

■ Your site is not receiving the mail sent to you, and if so you probably will not even receive the message saying that your subscription has been deleted. If you don't receive any mail for two days, then simply subscribe again when your system is working again.

■ Your e-mail address changed. In that case, you must resubscribe from your new e-mail address.

Taking Control

When you are subscribed to ROOTS-L, you will receive a helpful file with information on how to make the list work best for you. Fortunately, the listserver supports more commands than SUBSCRIBE and UNSUB-SCRIBE. You can control your subscription from your e-mail program. Note, however, you must be sending your command from the same e-mail address from which you subscribed, in order to make adjustments to your subscription. These commands will be handled automatically by the list processor. Just remember to use the request address when you send one of these commands.

By default, all subscriptions are set to *index*. This means that once or twice a day, you'll get a list of messages that have been posted to ROOTS-L. This list will have a message number, a subject line, how long the message is, and who posted it (see Fig. 3.2). If you see one that interests you, send a message to ROOTS-L-request@rootsweb.com. The subject line of your request message should contain the word *archive*. Suppose you wanted messages 51597 and 51598. There would then be two lines in the message itself:

    get messages/51597
    get messages/51598

Important: Don't include anything else in the message, such as your signature! The commands have to be in lowercase, and you must use the slash that leans to the right (/), not the left (\). You can't ask for a range of messages as you could in the old days when ROOTS-L was housed at the university. You can only have one request per line.

Put all together, it might look like the following:

    To: ROOTS-L-request@rootsweb.com
    Subject: archive
    ─────────
    get messages/51597
    get messages/51598

Figure 3.2
The Journal of Online Genealogy is a newsletter online. You can be notified of new issues by e-mail.

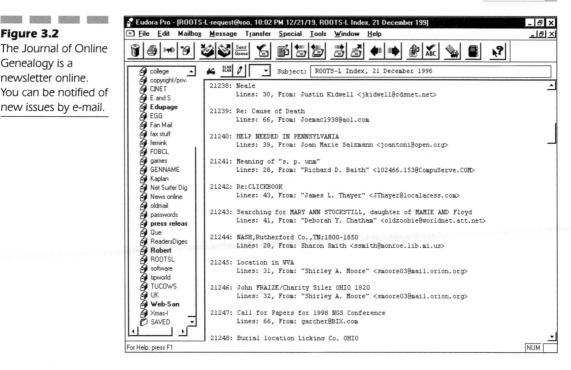

Remember, if you would like to send a message to the 7000+ readers of ROOTS-L, just address it to ROOTS-L@rootsweb.com. This means you can't *reply* to the index message and expect others to see it.

You may also receive each and every posting individually, a setting called *mail mode*. To change to this mode, first send a message that says

unsubscribe to *ROOTS-L-request@rootsweb.com*

Then send a message that says

subscribe
to ROOTS-M-request@rootsweb.com.

Unlike many mail servers, this one has no NOMAIL mode. If you want messages to stop, you have to UNSUBSCRIBE to the appropriate address (if in digest mode, ROOTS-L-request@rootsweb.com; if in mail mode, ROOTS-M-request@rootsweb.com; and if in index mode, ROOTS-I-request@rootsweb.com). When you want messages to begin again, send the message SUBSCRIBE to the same address.

Other Mail Lists

Once you've mastered how ROOTS-L works, you're ready to sample other mailing lists, and here I'll list just a few. Where noted, the messages are copied to the specified newsgroup on Usenet.

Not all mail lists run on a listserver. Some are done *by hand,* so to speak, by a person who receives the messages and then forwards them to all the subscribers. Such lists are subscribed to by sending a politely worded message to an address such as *afrigeneas-request@drum.ncsc.org.* It will go to the list owner, who will read it when he or she can and add you as soon as possible. When the subscription information in the list below shows an address including the word *request,* assume your message is going to a real, live person, not a machine, and complete sentences are advised. If the subscription message is to a *listserv,* assume you are talking to a machine, and use the commands described.

Generally, you will get a welcome message when you subscribe, telling you about the group, the server, and the associated files. Sometimes a list is aimed at particular countries and areas of the world. While these lists are not devoted to genealogy, the list owners have indicated that genealogy is an acceptable, though in some cases unusual, subject for the list.

Lists come in many subjects, some only tangentially touching genealogy. Some will touch on heritage, culture, and genealogy of particular ethnic groups, some on specific family names, some on specific historical periods, some on research in specific regions, regardless of ethnic background, some on software and other computer-related topics, and some strictly on general genealogy topics. Here's a list to get you started; you'll find one list often has messages referring to another and it just snowballs!

Ethnic Groups

These lists often are not specifically genealogy, but about culture, history, and current events in a particular ethnic group; still most of them will accept an occasional genealogy query, and most also are good to lurk on, just to glean information you perhaps didn't know.

- AFRIGENEAS.   A private mailing list created as a place to discuss and promote family history research. This is a place for the African Ancestors, in particular, and others to communicate their genealogical interests, needs, concerns, history, culture, and resources. Discussion areas include, but are not limited to, queries on surnames, records/ events, how do I start, census, locations, people and places, and resources. Mailing address for postings is *afrigeneas@drum.ncsc.org.* To subscribe, send e-mail to *afrigeneas-request@drum.ncsc.org* with the subject of: Add Me.

- AFROAM-L. A discussion group focusing on the pivotal issues which confront the everyday life of African Americans; an extremely busy list (up to 25 messages an hour!). Postings of specific genealogical queries are not considered appropriate; however, postings regarding the broader areas of interest to genealogists are acceptable. The mailing address for postings is *afroam-l@harvarda.harvard.edu.* To subscribe, send e-mail to *listserv@harvarda.harvard.edu* with the following message: SUBSCRIBE AFROAM-L firstname lastname.

- ALBANIAN. A mailing list dedicated to the exchange of news and discussion of issues on Albania, the Albanian people in Albania and other areas in the Balkans (Kosova, Macedonia, Montenegro), and Albanians living around the world. The language of the news and discussions is Albanian and English. Mailing address for postings is *albanian@ubvm.cc.buffalo.edu.* To subscribe, send the following to *listserv@ubvm.cc.buffalo.edu:* SUBSCRIBE ALBANIAN firstname lastname.

- APSA-L. A list devoted to the subject of literature and cultures of the Portuguese-speaking world, especially Brazil and Portugal. Although associated with the American Portuguese Studies Association (APSA), the list is not restricted to members of the association. Mailing address for postings is *majordomo@beacon.bryant.edu:* SUBSCRIBE APSA-L.

- ARAB-AMERICAN. A moderated list geared toward fostering and building community among North Americans of Arabic descent. Arab-Canadians, Arab-Mexicans, and Arabs in the United States may find this list of interest. Any topic directly relating to the experience of Arab-Americans is welcome. Mailing address for postings is *arab-american@carleton.edu.* To subscribe, send the following to *mailserv@carleton.edu:* SUBSCRIBE ARAB-AMERICAN firstname lastname.

- ARGENTINA. General discussion and information on Argentine and Latin-American social/political issues (list contents are almost exclusively in Spanish). Mailing address for postings is *argentina@journal.math.indiana.edu.* This is the main list; there are several sublists concerning more specialized aspects of Argentina. To subscribe, send name, e-mail address, phone number, address, and topics of interest to *argentina-requests@journal.math.indiana.edu.*

- BALT-L. Online forum devoted to communications to and about the Baltic Republics of Lithuania, Latvia, and Estonia. Subscription to this list is welcomed from anyone with skills or interests relevant to the Baltics or anyone who just wants to know what's going on. Short requests to help locate families or villages are carried in general-interest digest messages. Mailing address for postings is *balt-l@ubvm.cc .buffalo.edu*. To subscribe, send the following to *listserv@ubvm.cc.buffalo .edu:* SUBSCRIBE BALT-L firstname lastname.

- BANAT. A mailing list for those doing research in the Banat region of what was formerly Hungary. Mailing address for postings is *banat@sierra.net*. To subscribe, send the following to *majordomo@ sierra.net:* SUBSCRIBE BANAT.

- BASQUE-L. A forum for the dissemination and exchange of information on Basque culture. Genealogy-related issues are often discussed on the list though the main topics of discussion are sociopolitical current affairs, gastronomy, Basque music, poetry, anthropology (e.g., origin of Basques), and such. Basque, Spanish, French, and English languages are used and any other languages are welcome. Mailing address for postings is *basque-l@cunyvm.cuny.edu*. To subscribe, send the following to *listserv@cunyvm.cuny.edu:* SUBSCRIBE BASQUE-L firstname lastname.

- BRAS-NET. Mailing list for Brazilians, conducted in Portuguese, with no specific subject orientation. Mailing address for postings is *bras-net@cs.columbia.edu*. To subscribe, send the following to *bras-net-request@cs.columbia.edu:* SUBSCRIBE BRAS-NET firstname lastname.

- CANADA-L. Discussion forum for political, social, cultural, and economic issues in Canada. Mailing address for postings is *canada-l@vm1 .mcgill.ca*. To subscribe, send the following to *listserv@vm1.mcgill.ca:* SUBSCRIBE CANADA-L firstname lastname.

- CATRACHOS. A list that unites Hondurans and people interested in topics related to Honduras throughout the world. The languages of preference are English and Spanish. The topics of discussion range from local interests to politics. Mailing address for postings is *catrachos@andrew.cmu.edu*. To subscribe, send a politely worded request to *stanmarder@aol.com* (Stanley Marder).

- CENTAM-L. This list is intended to provide students from Central America and those interested in discussing issues concerning these countries (Guatemala, Belize, Honduras, El Salvador, Nicaragua, Costa Rica, and Panama) with a discussion list conducive to the interchange of ideas. Mailing address for postings is *centam-l@ubvm.cc.buffalo.edu*.

To subscribe, send the following to *listserv@ubvm.cc.buffalo.edu:* SUB-SCRIBE CENTAM-L firstname lastname.

- E-LIST. A moderated news and discussion list for Estonia-related matters. Primary readership is Estonians abroad and home. Estonian and English languages are used. The typical content is Estonian and English language news and news reviews from some of the news agencies and Foreign Ministry of Estonia. Also includes material from Estonian universities and other Estonian lists. Sometimes discussions on important subjects are held, and questions and requests from subscribers to the public are passed. All subjects can be covered, provided they might be interesting to current readership. Mailing address for postings is *jaak.vilo@cs.helsinki.fi.* To subscribe, send a politely worded request to *jaak.vilo@cs.helsinki.fi.*

- EC-CHARLA. This list is a forum for discussion of Ecuadorian society, politics, culture, and so forth. List activities are conducted mostly in Spanish; however, any language is welcome. Mailing address for postings is *ec-charla@lac.net.* To subscribe, send the following to *listproc@lac.net:* SUBSCRIBE EC-CHARLA firstname lastname.

- ESPANA-L. A mailing list to facilitate general discussion and exchange of information regarding Spain. All interested in Spain and Spanish culture are invited to join. Mailing address for postings is *espana-l@uacsc2.albany.edu.* To subscribe, send the following to *listserv@vm.stlawu.edu:* SUBSCRIBE ESPANA-L firstname lastname.

- GEN-DE-L. Gatewayed with the soc.genealogy.german newsgroup for the discussion of German genealogy. Mailing address for postings is *gen-de-l@rz.uni-karlsruhe.de.* To subscribe, send the following to *listserv@rz.uni-karlsruhe.de:* SUB GEN-DE-L firstname lastname.

- GEN-FF-L. Gatewayed with the fr.rec.genealogie newsgroup for the discussion of Francophone genealogy—the genealogy of French-speaking people (traffic mainly in French). Mailing address for postings is *gen-ff-l@mail.eWorld.com.* To subscribe, send the following to *listserv@mail.eWorld.com:* SUB GEN-FF-L firstname lastname.

- GEN-FR-L. Gatewayed with the soc.genealogy.french newsgroup for the discussion of Francophone genealogy—the genealogy of French-speaking people. Mailing address for postings is *gen-fr-l@mail.eWorld .com.* To subscribe, send the following to *listserv@mail.eWorld.com:* SUBSCRIBE GEN-FR-L firstname lastname.

- GENPOL. A mailing list for discussions of Polish genealogy. Postings are made in both English and Polish; however, there is no guarantee that postings in English will receive replies in English. Mailing address for postings is *genpol@chem.uw.edu.pl.* To subscribe, send the following to *listproc@chem.uw.edu.pl:subscribe* genpol firstname lastname.

- GENUKI-L.   Gatewayed with the soc.genealogy.uk+ireland newsgroup for the discussion of genealogy and family history discussion among people researching ancestors, family members, or others who have a genealogical connection to any people in any part of the British Isles (England, Wales, Ireland, Scotland, the Channel Isles, and the Isle of Man). Mailing address for postings is *GENUKI-L@postman.essex.ac.uk.* To subscribe, send one of the following to *listproc@herald.co.uk:* SUBSCRIBE GENUKI-INDEX or GENUKI-DIGEST.

- GER-RUS.   Germans from Russia. Mailing address for postings is *ger-rus@vm1.nodak.edu.* To subscribe, send the following to *listserv@vm1.nodak.edu:* SUBSCRIBE GER-RUS firstname lastname.

- HUNGARY.   Discussion of Hungarian issues. The list is open to scholars and students from all disciplines. Although the working language of the group is English, contributions in other languages will be accepted and posted; however, they may not be understood by a significant proportion of the membership. Mailing list for postings is *hungary@gwuvm.gwu.edu.* To subscribe, send the following to *listserv@gwuvm.gwu.edu:* SUBSCRIBE HUNGARY firstname lastname.

- INDIAN-ROOTS.   Discussions of Native American genealogical and historical research. Mailing address for postings is *indian-roots@rmgate.pop.indiana.edu.* To subscribe, send the following to *maiser@rmgate.pop.indiana.edu:* SUB INDIAN-ROOTS.

- INROOTS.   Discussions of Indiana genealogical and historical research. Mailing address for postings is *inroots@rmgate.pop.indiana.edu.* To subscribe, send the following to *maiser@rmgate.pop.indiana.edu:* SUB INROOTS.

- JEWISHGEN.   Discussions of Jewish genealogy. Gatewayed with the soc.genealogy.jewish newsgroup (JEWGEN is a synonym for JEWISHGEN and postings to both will just give subscribers two copies of the same message). Mailing address for postings is *jewishgen@mail.eWorld.com.* To subscribe, send the following to *listserv@mail.eWorld.com:* SUBSCRIBE JEWISHGEN firstname lastname.

- LLAJTA.   Discussion of any and all topics relating to Bolivia. The principal language for discussions is Spanish although English, Quechua, and Portuguese language messages have appeared. Mailing address for postings is *llajta@io.asd.litton.com.* To subscribe, send the following to *listserv@io.dsd.litton.com:* SUBSCRIBE LLAJTA firstname lastname.

- MAKEDON. A moderated mailing list for discussions of the Macedonian Republic. Every posting made to this group is also automatically posted to INFORMA—BBS in Macedonia. They may also reach the Macedonian BBS in Canada. Acceptable languages for the group are Macedonian and English, with emphasis on Macedonian. Mailing address for postings is *makedon@ubvm.cc.buffalo.edu*. To subscribe, send the following to *listserv@ubvm.cc.buffalo.edu*: SUBSCRIBE MAKEDON firstname lastname.

- NAMNET. Anything related to Namibia (as of February 1995, mainly technical stuff). Small postings preferred. Mailing address for postings is *namnet@lisse.na*. To subscribe, send the following to *namnet-request@lisse.na*: SUBSCRIBE.

- NAT-LANG. A discussion list about Native American languages. To subscribe, send the message SUB NAT-LANG to *LISTSERV@tamvm1.tamu.edu*.

- NYASANET. This list is for Malawians or people interested in discussing things Malawian. Mailing address for postings is *nyasanet@unh.edu*. To subscribe, send the following to *nyasanet-request@unh.edu*: SUBSCRIBE NYASANET firstname lastname.

- PERU. Discussion of Peruvian culture and other issues. This list is simply an echo site, so all posts get bounced from that address to all the people subscribed. Mailing address for postings is *peru@cs.sfsu.edu* (you have to be subscribed to post to this list). To subscribe, send the following message with no subject to *listproc@cs.sfsu.edu*: SUBSCRIBE PERU firstname lastname.

- PIE. A mailing list for people interested in topics related to Italian genealogy (over 160 people from around the world as of February 1995). Mailing address for postings is *pie@jsoft.com*. To subscribe, send the following to *PIE-REQUEST@jsoft.com*: subscribe pie firstname lastname or *PIE-DIGEST@JSOFT.COM* subscrib pie-digest firstname lastname.

- POLAND-L. Discussions of Polish culture and events including all subjects related to Poland, Polish Americans, and Eastern Europe (related to Poland). Mailing address for postings is *poland-l@vm1.nodak.edu*. To subscribe, send the following to *listserv@ubvm.cc.buffalo.edu*: SUBSCRIBE POLAND-L firstname lastname.

- RUSSIAN-JEWS. Dedicated to sharing information, discussions of history, announcements of upcoming events, and so forth. Mailing address for postings is *russian-jews@shamash.nysernet.org*. To subscribe, send the following to *listproc@shamash.nysernet.org:* sub russian-jews firstname lastname.

■ SEPHARD SIG.   A special interest group of JewishGen, the Jewish Genealogy discussion group, established to develop resource lists for researchers of Sephardic genealogy. The definition of *Sephardim* is Jews who, after the expulsion from Spain in 1492, settled in northern Africa, Italy, Egypt, Palestine, Syria, the Balkans, and the Turkish Empire. Subsequently, these communities were reinforced by refugees from Portugal who later established congregations in Amsterdam, London, Hamburg, Bordeaux, Bayonne, western Europe, and North America. Mailing address for postings is *sephard@cgsg.com.* To subscribe, send the following to *listserv@cgsg.com:* subscribe sephard firstname lastname.

■ SLOVAK-L.   A mailing list for anyone interested in Slovak history, culture, politics, social life, economy, and anything else concerning the Republic of Slovakia and its people or their descendants in other countries. The list is unmoderated and unlimited in scope. Mailing address for postings is *slovak-l@ubvm.cc.buffalo.edu* or *slovak-l@ubvm.bitnet.* To subscribe, send the following to *listserv@ubvm.cc.buffalo.edu* or *listserv@ubvm.bitnet:* subscribe slovak-l firstname lastname.

■ SLOVAK-WORLD.   An unmoderated mailing list which can be used to contact Slovaks around the world to help find lost contacts, join relatives, meet new friends, and so forth. It is not limited to territory or to language and is open for all who have something in common with Slovaks and Slovakia. Mailing address for postings is *slovak-world@fris.sk.* To subscribe, send the following to *listproc@fris.sk:* SUBSCRIBE SLOVAK-WORLD firstname lastname.

■ SUDAN-L.   A forum for sharing experience, ideas, thoughts, comments, and sources of information on issues concerning Sudan. Mailing address for postings is *sudan-l@emuvm1.cc.emory.edu* (you have to be subscribed to post to this list). To subscribe, send the following to *listserv@emuvm1.cc.emory.edu:* SUBSCRIBE SUDAN-L firstname lastname.

■ SUGUSELTS.   An Estonian-language genealogy list (English and other languages such as German, French, and Finnish are acceptable). Mailing address for postings is *suguselts@lists.ut.ee.* To subscribe, send the following to *lisproc@lists.ut.ee:* SUBSCRIBEsuguselts firstname lastname.

■ WELSH-L.   Aims to foster the amicable discussion of questions of the Welsh language, Welsh culture, history and politics, and to offer a forum for speakers and learners of the Welsh language. Genealogical queries may be posted as long as the queries are in Welsh. (English may be used on WELSH-L to discuss questions of grammar, not questions of Grandma!) Diolch yn fawr i chi. Mailing address for postings is *welsh-l@irlearn.ucd.ie*. To subscribe, send the following to *listserv@ irlearn.ucd.ie:* SUBSCRIBE WELSH-L firstname lastname.

Family Name Lists

These are lists for specific surnames or families. You usually have to ask to join.

- CAMPBELL-L.   A mailing list for Campbell descendants to discuss their possible kinship and for the various Campbell Societies to discuss membership. Mailing address for postings is *campbell-l@genealogy .emcee.com*. To subscribe, send e-mail to *campbell-l-request@genealogy .emcee.com* with the subject *subscribe.* No message is necessary. Queries are welcome; you should include your snail mail address so the Clan can contact you.

- CLAFLIN.   Researchers of the surname *CLAFLIN*—also MACK-CLOTHLAN, MACLACHLAN, MACLACHLAN, MAKCLACHLANE, MAKLAUCHLANE, M'CLACHLENE, MAKCLAUCHLANE, MCLAUCHLANE, M'LAUCHLANE, M'CLAUCHLANE, M'LAUCHAN, MCCLAUCHLAN, MCLAUCHLANE, M'CLACH-LANE, M'CLAICHLANE, MACLAUGHLIN, and any other variation of the name you might be researching. Also, unless there is a mail list covering another surname, you are free to use this service to discuss those as well, as long as they are related to a CLAFLIN. (But please try to limit it to Claflins.) Mailing address for postings is *claflin-l@ genealogy.emcee.com*. To subscribe, send a message to *claflin-l-request@ genealogy.emcee.com* with the following in the subject line: Subscribe.

- CLAN-HENDERSON.   Researchers of the surname *HENDERSON* and variant spellings. To subscribe, send e-mail to *ancanach@uabdpo .dpo.uab.edu* with no message.

- CLAN-MCCALLUM.   A list for the discussion of the MACCALLUM/ MALCOLM clan, chief, its gatherings, and genealogical research in the surnames MALCOLM, MCCALLUM, MCCOLLUM, COLLUM, and other variants. Mailing address for postings is *clan-mccallum@csn.net*. To subscribe, send the following to *majordomo@csn.org:* subscribe clan-mccallum your_email_address.

- COOLEY-L.   Researchers of the surname *COOLEY.* Mailing address for postings is *cooley-1@genealogy.emcee.com.* To subscribe, send a request to be added to the list to *cooley-1-request@genealogy.emcee.com.*

- CULP/KOLB.   Researchers of the surname *CULP* or *KOLB* families. To subscribe, send e-mail to John Culp at *aa101932@midnet.csd.scarolina.edu.*

- MARJORIBANKS.   Researchers of the surname *MARJORIBANKS* family (a Border Scots family) and variants (MARCHBANKS, MARSHBANKS, BANKS, etc.). Regardless of how spelled, all who claim Marjoribanks/Marchbanks descent or who have an interest in the family are eligible for membership. Persons desiring further information may contact the honorary secretary by e-mail at *an770@ freenet.carleton.ca* or the vice president at *ranslaw@dgs.dgsys.com.*

- MOBLEY.   A small e-mail group (about 30 to 35 in the forward) for discussions of the genealogy and history of the MOBLEY family. To subscribe or to post, send e-mail to *Moberley@Freenet.FSU.Edu.*

- MOORE-L.   A mailing list for researchers of the surname *MOORE,* anywhere, anytime. Mailing address for postings is *moore-1@xx.zko.dec .com.* To subscribe, send the following to *majordomo@xx.zko.dec.com:* subscribe moore-1 (this listserver is case-sensitive; use lowercase).

- PETTIT-L.   Researchers of the surname *PETTIT.* Mailing address for postings is *pettit-1@genealogy.emcee.com.* To subscribe, send a request to be added to the list to *pettit-1-request@genealogy.emcee.com.*

- SCOL.   An informal group used to establish contact with people who have the name SUTFIN/SUTPHEN/SUTPHIN/ZUTPHEN (or people doing research on those families) in order to share information on their heritage. To subscribe, send e-mail to *msutphin@fred.net* with no message.

- WHITE-L.   Researchers of the surname *WHITE.* Mailing address for postings is *white-1@genealogy.emcee.com.* To subscribe, send a message to *white-1-request@genealogy.emcee.com* with *subscribe* as the subject and no message.

General Genealogy Lists

These are lists with general genealogy in mind, apart from region and specific names. These are the ones a beginner should check out first.

- ADOPTEES.   The discussion here is among people who have been adopted or have a family member who is adopted. Mailing address for postings is *adoptees@ucsd.edu.* If you have access to a WWW browser such as Mosaic, the preferred method to subscribe is to use the form linked to the Adoptees Mailing List Home Page, located at *http://psy.ucsd.edu/jhartung/adoptees.html*. Otherwise, send the following to *listserv@ucsd.edu:* subscribe [YOUR E-MAIL address] adoptees.

■ ADOPTION.   Discussions of anything and everything connected with adoption. Mailing address for postings is *adoption@listserv.law .cornell.edu*. To subscribe, send the following to *adoption-request@ listserv.law.cornell.edu:* SUBSCRIBE ADOPTION firstname lastname.

■ BRTHPRNT.   Mailing list open to anyone wanting to discuss birth-family issues. Mailing address for postings is *bras-net-request@cs .columbia.edu*. To subscribe, send the following to *listserv@indycms .iupui.edu:* SUB BRTHPRNT firstname lastname

■ ELIJAH-L.   A list for believing members of the Church of Jesus Christ of Latter-Day Saints to discuss their ideas and experiences relating with genealogy in the LDS Church (individuals not of the LDS faith are welcome to join as long as they respect the beliefs of the LDS faith and do not deliberately offend these beliefs). To subscribe, send a message to *Elijah-L-Request@genealogy.emcee.com* with *archive* as the subject and the following message: get charter. After reading and approving the charter, follow the instructions in the charter to subscribe. This list is to be used specifically for sharing LDS-related genealogy ideas, tools, and approaches; sharing LDS-related genealogy experiences and testimonies; and discussing answers to LDS-related genealogy questions and scriptures relating to genealogy. Members also share LDS-related genealogy news from throughout the world as well as other LDS-related genealogical topics.

■ GENMSC-L.   A general discussion of genealogy for questions that don't fit the preceding categories. *Note:* This list usually subscribes you in digest mode. If you want mail mode you must send a message to the listserver: SET GENMSC-L MAIL ; SUB GENMSC-L ; *LISTSERV@mail.eworld.com*.

■ GENMSC-L.   Gatewayed with the soc.genealogy.misc newsgroup for general genealogical discussions that don't fit within one of the other soc.genealogy.* newsgroups. Mailing address for postings is *genmsc-l@ mail.eWorld.com*. To subscribe, send the following to *listserv@mail .eWorld.com:* SUBSCRIBE GENMSC-L firstname lastname.

■ GENMTD-L.   A general discussion of genealogy and methods of genealogical research. *Note:* This list usually subscribes you in digest mode. If you want mail mode you must send a message to the list-server: SET GENMTD-L MAIL Gatewayed with the soc.genealogy

.methods newsgroup for the discussion of genealogy methods and resources. Mailing address for postings is *genmtd-l@mail.eWorld.com*. To subscribe, send the following to *listserv@mail.eWorld.com:* SUBSCRIBE GENMTD-L firstname lastname.

■ GENNAM-L. Gatewayed with the soc.genealogy.surnames newsgroup for surname queries and tafels. Mailing address for postings is *gennam-l@mail.eWorld.com*. To subscribe, send the following to *listserv@mail.eWorld.com:* SUBSCRIBE GENNAM-L firstname lastname.

■ GEN-NEWBIE-L (*www.rootsweb.com/~newbie*). A message-exchange mail list for the beginner, where the most basic questions are answered. Send a new message to *gen-newbie-l-request@rootsweb.com* with the word *subscribe* and nothing else in the body of the message (unsubscribe by sending *unsubscribe*). Gen-Newbie-L describes itself as "like a bouncing ball, with someone asking a question and others suggesting answers, or asking more questions." The group will discuss genealogy, family history, and computer applications, but there's a lot of leeway for off-topic exchanges. This tolerant group is willing to assist anyone who wants "community coaching" about the Internet, genealogy, computers, or whatever. The membership is international and everyone is welcome. Unlike many other genealogy-related groups, however, it is not OK to use *surname signatures*. These are those signatures at the bottom of someone's e-mail message that list all the surnames (last names) the author is researching. The computer cannot distinguish between the surname signature and the message. Turn off your signature when posting to this group.

■ GENWEB. Discussions of the implementation of a genealogical information exchange system using the World Wide Web. Mailing address for postings is *genweb@uscd.edu*. To subscribe, send the following to *listserv@ucsd.edu:* ADD GENWEB.

■ ROOTS-L. The best-known genealogy mailing list with over 4000 subscribers from around the world. Mailing address for postings is *roots-l@vm1.nodak.edu*. To subscribe, send the following to *listserv@ vm1.nodak.edu:* SUBSCRIBE ROOTS-L firstname lastname.

Historical Groups

■ MENNOLINK. A mailing list for and about Mennonites including a fair bit of genealogy. Mailing address for postings is *menno@uci.com*.

To subscribe to the complete list which includes a great deal of discussion, send the following to *listserv@uci.com:* sub menno.d firstname lastname (to receive mail once a day in digest mode, include a second line with the command: set memmo.d mail digest). To subscribe to an abbreviated form of menno.d that includes informational messages but not the discussion, send the following to *listserv@uci.com:* sub menno firstname lastname.

- QUAKER-L. Moderated, online discussion of all aspects of Quakerism/the Religious Society of Friends. Such discussion may include (but is not limited to) Quaker worship, decision making, publications, and so forth. Social and activist Quaker issues such as peace, justice, ecology, and others are discussed on QUAKER-P. Mailing address for postings is *Quaker-L@vmd.cso.uiuc.edu.* You must be subscribed to post to Quaker-L. To subscribe, send the following to *listserv@vmd.cso.uiuc .edu:* SUBSCRIBE QUAKER-L firstname lastname.

- HISTORICAL GEN-MEDIEVAL. Gatewayed with the soc.genealogy .medieval newsgroup for genealogy and family history discussion among people researching individuals living during medieval times (loosely defined as the period from the breakup of the Western Roman Empire until the time public records relating to the general population began to be kept and extending roughly from AD 500 to AD 1600). Mailing address for postings is *gen-medieval@mail.eWorld.com.* To subscribe, send the following to *listserv@mail.eWorld.com:* SUBSCRIBE GEN-MEDIEVAL firstname lastname.

- RUSHIST. A forum for the reasonable discussion of any aspect of the history of Russia from the reign of Ivan III (1462–1505) to the end of the Romanov dynasty in the person of Nicholas II (1894–1917). Any element of this period is discussable. Mailing address for postings is *rushist@vm.usc.edu.* To subscribe, send the following to *listserv@vm .usc.edu:* SUBSCRIBE RUSHIST firstname lastname.

- Overland-Trails. Devoted to discussions concerning the history, preservation, and promotion of the Oregon, California, Sante Fe, and other historic trails in the Western United States. One project particularly interesting to genealogists is that all of the names inscribed as graffiti on the various rocks along the trails have been put into a database. Therefore, if someone's ancestor was suspected to have traveled the trail, there is a possibility that the route and dates can be pinpointed. Mailing address for postings (you have to be subscribed) is *overland-trails@hipp.etsu.edu.* To subscribe, send the following to *listserv@hipp.etsu.edu:* subscribe overland-trails firstname lastname.

Regional Groups

- **4CORNERS-ROOTS.** A genealogy discussion list for the Colorado-Utah-Arizona-New Mexico area. To subscribe, send a message that says SUB 4CORNERS-ROOTS to *MAISER@rmgate.pop.indiana.edu.*

- **CANADIAN-ROOTS.** A discussion list for Canadian genealogy. To subscribe, send a message that says SUB CANADIAN-ROOTS to *MAISER@rmgate.pop.indiana.edu.*

- **CAPITOL-ROOTS.** A discussion of genealogy for the New Jersey-Maryland-Delaware, District of Columbia region. To subscribe, send a message that says SUB CAPITOL-ROOTS to *MAISER@rmgate.pop .indiana.edu.*

- **DEEP-SOUTH-ROOTS.** A discussion of genealogy for the Mississippi-Alabama-Georgia-Florida region. To subscribe, send a message that says SUB DEEP-SOUTH-ROOTS to *MAISER@rmgate.pop.indiana.edu.*

- **ERIE-ROOTS.** A discussion of genealogy for the New York-Pennsylvania-Ohio region. To subscribe, send a message that says SUB ERIE-ROOTS to *MAISER@rmgate.pop.indiana.edu.*

- **FAR-WEST-ROOTS.** A discussion list for the California-Nevada-Hawaii region. To subscribe, send a message that says SUB FAR-WEST-ROOTS to *MAISER@rmgate.pop.indiana.edu.*

- **KANSAS-L.** Announcements and activities of the Kansas State Historical Society, a clearinghouse for announcements by other organizations, and a public forum for the discussion of Kansas heritage, both past and present. Mailing address for postings is *kansas-l@ukanaix .cc.ukans.edu.* To subscribe, send the following to *listserv@ukanaix .cc.ukans.edu:* SUBSCRIBE KANSAS-L firstname lastname.

- **KYROOTS.** Discussions of Kentucky genealogical and historical research. Mailing address for postings is *kyroots@ukcc.uky.edu.* To subscribe, send the following to *listserv@ukcc.uky.edu:* SUBSCRIBE KYROOTS firstname lastname.

- **LA-CAJUN-ROOTS.** A discussion of genealogy in Louisiana and for those of Cajun heritage. To subscribe, send the message SUB LA-CAJUN-ROOTS to *MAISER@rmgate.pop.indiana.edu.*

- **MI/WI-ROOTS.** A discussion of genealogy for the Michigan-Wisconsin area. To subscribe, send the message SUB MI/WI-ROOTS to *MAISER@rmgate.pop.indiana.edu.*

- MID-PLAINS-ROOTS.   A discussion of genealogy for the Arkansas-Missouri-Iowa-Illinois-Nebraska area. To subscribe, send the message SUB MID-PLAINS-ROOTS to *MAISER@rmgate.pop.indiana.edu.*

- NC/SC-ROOTS.   A discussion of genealogy for the North Carolina–South Carolina area. (*Note:* References to NCROOTS or SCROOTS are identical to NC/SC-ROOTS. NCROOTS and SCROOTS are synonyms for NC/SC-ROOTS.) To subscribe, send the message SUB NC/SC-ROOTS to *MAISER@rmgate.pop.indiana.edu.* Mailing address for postings is *nc/sc-roots@rmgate.pop.indiana.edu.*

- NDSDMN-L.   A genealogy discussion list for North and South Dakota and Minnesota. To subscribe, send the message SUBSCRIBE to *NDSDMN-L-REQUEST@genealogy.emcee.com.*

- NDSDMN-L.   Discussions of genealogical and historical research for the North Dakota, South Dakota, and Minnesota region. To subscribe send a message with SUBSCRIBE as the Subject to *ndsdmn-l-request@genealogy.emcee.com.* Mailing address for postings is *ndsdmn-l@genealogy.emcee.com.*

- NO.SLEKT.   Norwegian genealogy conference called SLEKT (family) on NordicNET (a PCBoard BBS network connected to Internet Net-News via Thunderball Cave and distributed on NetNews as no.slekt). To subscribe, send the following to *majordomo@news.uninett.no:* SUBSCRIBE no.slekt.

- NORTHEAST-ROOTS.   A genealogy discussion list for Maine, Vermont, New Hampshire, Rhode Island, Massachusetts, and Connecticut. To subscribe, send the message SUB NORTHEAST-ROOTS to *MAISER@rmgate.pop.indiana.edu.*

- NORTHWEST-ROOTS.   A genealogy discussion list for Washington, Oregon, Alaska, Idaho, Montana, and Wyoming. To subscribe, send the message SUB NORTHWEST-ROOTS to *MAISER@rmgate.pop.indiana.edu.*

- SOC.GENEALOGY.BENELUX or SOC.GENEALOGY.DUTCH or GENBNL-L (aliases).   Research in the Benelux region (Belgium, the Netherlands, and Luxembourg). For details on usage, send e-mail to *maiser@omega.ufsia.ac.be* with *help* in the message body. Mailing address for postings is *genbnl-l@omega.ufsia.ac.be.* To subscribe, send the message SUB SOC.GENEALOGY.BENELUX to *maiser@omega.ufsia.ac.be.*

- TEXAHOMA-ROOTS.   A discussion list of genealogy for the Texas-Oklahoma area. Send the message SUB TEXAHOMA-ROOTS to *MAISER@rmgate.pop.indiana.edu* to subscribe.

- TNROOTS. A discussion of genealogy for the Tennessee area. Send the message SUB TNROOTS to *MAISER@rmgate.pop.indiana.edu* to subscribe.

- TNROOTS. Discussions of Tennessee genealogical and historical research. Mailing address for postings is *tnroots@rmgate.pop.indiana.edu*. To subscribe, send the following to *maiser@rmgate.pop.indiana.edu:* SUB TNROOTS.

- VA-ROOTS. A discussion of Virginia genealogy. This is *not* the same as VAROOTS. Send the message SUB VA-ROOTS to *LISTSERVER@leo .vsla.edu* to subscribe. (*Note:* LISTSERVER not LISTSERV.)

- VA-ROOTS. This group will provide the opportunity for researchers in the field of Virginia family history to share information about current work, pose queries to list members, share information about resources, debate issues, and discuss the techniques of genealogical research. Mailing address for postings is *va-roots@leo.vsla.edu*. To subscribe, send the following to *listserver@leo.vsla.edu:* subscribe va-roots firstname lastname.

- VA/WVA-ROOTS. Discussions of genealogical and historical research for the Virginia—West Virginia region. Mailing address for postings is *va/wvaroots@rmgate.pop.indiana.edu*. To subscribe, send the following to *maiser@rmgate.pop.indiana.edu:* SUB VA/WVA-ROOTS.

- WVA-L. West Virginia Discussion List. Mailing address for postings is *wva-l@world.std.com*. To subscribe, send the following to *majordomo@ world.std.com:* SUBSCRIBE WVA-L.

- WVA-LA. This is for discussion of anything and everything related to West Virginia. Not genealogical, per se, but another good list to lurk on. This is *not* the same as WVROOTS. To subscribe, send the message SUB WVA-L to *MAJORDOMO@world.std.com*.

Software Lists

- GENCMP-L. A general discussion of genealogy and its relation to computing and computers. *Note:* This list usually subscribes you in digest mode. If you want mail mode, you must send a message to the listserver: SET GENCMP-L MAIL; SUB GENCMP-L; *LISTSERV@mail .eworld.com*.

- NO.SLEKT.PROGRAMMER. Norwegian genealogy conference called SLEKTsPROGRAM (family) on NordicNET (a PCBoard BBS network connected to Internet NetNews via Thunderball Cave and distributed on NetNews as no.slekt.programmer). To subscribe, send the following to *majordomo@news.uninett.no:* SUBSCRIBE no.slekt .programmer.

■ SOFTWARE .FTMTECH-L.   A mailing list maintained by Banner Blue Software for the discussion and technical support of the Family Tree Maker genealogy program and the Family Archive CDs. Paul Burchfield, one of Banner Blue's technical support representatives, answers technical questions posted to this list. Mailing address for postings is *ftmtech-l@best.com.* To subscribe, send the following to *majordomo@best.com:* subscribe ftmtech-l.

■ SOFTWARE BBANNOUNCE-L.   A mailing list maintained by Banner Blue Software for product announcements (10 to 15 postings a year). To subscribe, send the following to *majordomo@best.com:* subscribe bbannounce-l.

■ SOFTWARE BK.   An experience-exchange platform for the Brother's Keeper genealogical program. Mailing address for postings is *bk@ omega.ufsia.ac.be.* To subscribe, send the following to *maiser@omega.ufsia .ac.be:* sub bk.

■ SOFTWARE BK5-L.   A mailing list for the discussion of the Brother's Keeper genealogy program. Mailing address for postings is *bk5-l@ genealogy.emcee.com.* To subscribe, send e-mail to *bk5-l-request@genealogy .emcee.com* with *SUBSCRIBE* as the subject and no message.

■ SOFTWARE LINES-L.   Serves as a vehicle for topics related to the enhancement of LifeLines Genealogical Database and Report Generator (an experimental, second-generation genealogical system). Don't subscribe unless your computer runs on UNIX, you know who Tom Wetmore is, and you run LifeLines. Mailing address for postings is *lines-l@vm1.nodak.edu.* To subscribe, send the following to *listserv@vm1 .nodak.edu:* SUBSCRIBE LINES-L firstname lastname.

■ SOFTWARE PROGEN.   An experience-exchange group for the Progen genealogical program. Mailing address for postings is *progen@omega.ufsia.ac.be.* To subscribe, send the following to *maiser@omega.ufsia.ac.be:* sub progren.

■ SOFTWARE TMG-L.   A mailing list for those interested in The Master Genealogist software program. Mailing address for postings is *tmg-l@netcom.com.* To subscribe, send the following to *listserv@netcom.com:* subscribe tmg-l.

■ SOFTWARE.GEDCOM-L.   A technical mailing list to discuss the GEDCOM specifications. If you are not a computer programmer, a serious genealogical computer user, or haven't read the GEDCOM specification, then this list is definitely not for you. Mailing address for postings is *gedcom-l@vm1.nodak.edu*. To subscribe, send the following to *listserv@vm1.nodak.edu:* SUB GEDCOM-L firstname lastname.

- SOFTWARE.GENCMP-L.   Gatewayed with the soc.genealogy .computing newsgroup for the discussion of genealogical computing and Net resources. Mailing address for postings is *gencmp-l@mail .eWorld.com*. To subscribe, send the following to *listserv@mail.eWorld .com:* SUBSCRIBE GENCMP-L firstname lastname.

- SOFTWARE.PAF-L.   Mailing list for discussion of issues relating to the Personal Ancestral File genealogy program. Mailing address for postings is *paf-l@genesplicer.org*. To subscribe, send the following to *listserv@genesplicer.org:* SUBSCRIBE PAF-L firstname lastname.

- GENWEB.   A discussion list for ROOTSBOOK. A project to link genealogy trees on a mass basis. To subscribe, send the message SUB GENWEB to *LISTSERV@ucsd.edu*.

Newsletters

Another resource by e-mail is the newsletter. Unlike interactive mail lists, newsletters are meant to be read like a magazine. You can write letters to the editor if you like, but you won't see it in the newsletter often.

Three that are worth your notice:

Journal of Online Genealogy (http://www.onlinegenealogy.com/).   This monthly *e-zine* covers aspects of doing genealogy with computers. It is published on the Internet and you have to use your Web browser to read it. If you can't remember to do it each month, you might want to sign up for its e-mail reminder. Simply click on the mail list icon on the Journal's home page, enter your e-mail address, and when the new issues are published, you'll receive an e-mail notice.

The Journal has several regular features: Editor's Column, Advanced Features, Beginner's Avenues, New Online Sites, and others. The articles are written by amateur and professional genealogists with experience in online research.

You can look at a low-graphics version for faster loading or a high-graphics version for pretty pictures.

Eastman's Genealogy Newsletter (http://www.rootscomputing.com/ newsletter/index.htm).   This newsletter is by e-mail, all text. The editor, Dick Eastman (http://ourworld.compuserve.com/homepages/ eastman/) is the sysop of CompuServe's Roots Forum, a genealogist, and an author. Using all these skills and talents, he publishes a weekly newsletter on genealogy topics. A typical issue will cover reviews of genealogy computer programs; news items of note to the genealogist; a list of World Wide Web sites to visit; book, CD-ROM, and television program reviews; and a computer-related Rumor of the Week. All of this comes to your e-mail box, and it's totally free.

Eastman is a veteran online genealogist with a sharp eye for what is worth your time. His reviews are specific, without being overly verbose, and honest. Each issue, besides being sent to your mail box, is posted online at the preceding URL. Back issues, if you'd like to read them, are on CompuServe's Roots Forum (GO ROOTS).

To subscribe, send an e-mail message to the following address: subscribe@rootscomputing.com. Your message title must be SUBSCRIBE.

To cancel your subscription, send an e-mail message to the following address: unsubscribe@rootscomputing.com. Your message title must be UNSUBSCRIBE.

Don't put anything in the body of these messages, because no human being will read them. The computer takes care of everything.

Treasure Maps Newsletter (http://www.firstct.com/fv/sub.html). Treasure Maps is one of the best sites on the Web for newcomers. It is a site aimed at hands-on, how-to information to help you actually do research. To be sure you're up to date on the latest on Treasure Maps, you might want to subscribe to its newsletter, a monthly update. It also has genealogy information not yet available on the Web site. To subscribe, send a message with the subject *Subscribe TM* to the e-mail address ragan@southeast.net. Within 24 hours, you'll get an issue and a help file on how to make the newsletter work best for you.

Be sure to switch off any "skip large messages" toggle on your mail reader; this newsletter is chock full of stuff every month and can run over 30 kilobytes.

The World Wide Web

At the beginning of this decade, the Internet was a lot harder to use. For each function (or *Internet service*), you needed to know about a different program, with a different set of arcane commands. Once you got the hang of it, it wasn't hard to use the Internet, just clumsy, switching from one program to another.

To transfer a file, you used file transfer protocol or *ftp*. To search for where the file was that you wanted to get by ftp, you might use a search program called *archie*. To run a computer on the Internet by remote control, you used *telnet*. To look at documents on a system, say a university's information system, you might use a menu-based display system called a *gopher*. To search the gophers for a specific document you might use *veronica* to search all the gophers in the world, or *jughead* to search just one gopher.

Finally, a Swiss research group, CERN, decided to try to pull all these different services into one interface, with a single protocol. At first, its new program, called a *browser*, was text-based, too, just as the entire Internet was. Very soon, however, graphic interfaces were added, making the browsers even easier to use.

So now, for most people the *Internet* is the *World Wide Web*, an attempt to link information all over the world on the Internet. Of course, genealogists are involved in this, too!

How Browsers Work

The World Wide Web has its own lexicon of terminology. These terms can be confusing. Here are a few terms you should know before you get going:

HTML is the language that turns a text document into a WWW-browseable one. Many shareware and commercial products have popped up in the past year to help you create HTML documents, but if you get a good book on the subject you can create HTML code in any word or text processor.

URL is *uniform resource locator*. It's an address on the WWW. The format of a URL is accessmethod://machine.name/directory/file. *Access method* can be ftp, http, gopher, or any other Internet service. The *machine name* is the computer that holds what you are after. The *directory* and *file* are where on that computer the object is. You type the URL in your browser's address box to get there.

A *page* is a file presented to you in the browser. The file will be simple ASCII text, with embedded commands to tell the browser how things should look to you. Some text will be designated a *headline,* other text might tell the browser to show a picture in a certain place. The most important part of this coding scheme, called *HTTP* for *HyperText Transfer Protocol,* is the link.

A *link* is a pointer to another file. The term for linking files is *hypertext.* Hypertext is a system whereby pointers are embedded in text, presented to you usually as underlined colored words or pictures that will have the browser display another file, either on that same site or somewhere else on the Internet. When the cursor changes from an arrow to a hand, you are pointing your mouse at a link.

If you click on a link, you will be taken to another document, perhaps at another site, which has information on your choice. Or given a sound bite, if you have a sound card. Or shown a picture, if you have VGA graphics. (*Warning:* Sound and pictures across the Internet are *very slow* as of this writing!)

What is wonderful about the Web is that most browsers combine many Internet services: sending and receiving e-mail, reading and posting to Usenet, transferring files with ftp and gopher—all in one program called a browser.

To use WWW, you must have a WWW browser or be able to connect to one. The best method of access to the Web is to run a browser from your own machine. Browsers are available for many platforms.

Which Browser to Use

I'm often asked, "Which is the best browser?" I can only reply that this is like asking, "Which is the best car?" It all depends on your taste, habits, and budget.

The current leaders in the browser wars are Netscape Navigator and Microsoft Internet Explorer, and entire books are devoted to helping you get the most out of them. The major online services and Internet Service Providers have lined up with one or the other for their customers to use.

Microsoft Internet Explorer is free, but it makes major changes to your operating system and therefore sometimes causes trouble with other programs. Netscape Navigator is not free (about $40 as of this writing), but it has a nice user interface, is easy to configure and is the most widely used.

Others, such as Mosaic and Ariadne, are less feature-packed, but they are free and very easy to use.

Netscape Navigator and Microsoft Internet Explorer are chock-full of features but they are also what I call "hardware hogs": they need super-duper hardware and lots of disk space to run. If you have an older or smaller machine (in terms of RAM and hard disk drive size), check out some other browsers, too. They have fewer features, but take up much less room on your hard disk and in your RAM. For a good list of them, visit *http://www.tucows.com* and search for *browser.*

My advice is to try a few of them (most of them allow you to try before you buy) and see which one suits you best.

What It Looks Like

The Genealogy Home Page is illustrated in Fig. 4.1 in Netscape Navigator. To see this page in your browser, type this in the address box: *http://www .genhomepage.com/.* You can also use the menu option FILE | Open and type the URL in the dialog box.

Now, in Fig. 4.1, you can see the browser's title bar at the top of the screen. This tells you the title of the Web page you're viewing. The title is often the same as the page's first headline, but it can be different. When you save a Web page's address (URL) in your bookmark file, the name associated with the URL is usually taken from the title. Sadly, many Web developers don't realize this and name their pages something uninformative such as My Page or Link.

Next is the browser's menu bar. Most browsers will have File, Edit, View, Go, Bookmarks (or Hotlist or Favorites), Options, and maybe a few others. Usually under File, you can save or open a page, among other commands. Edit allows you to search for a word or save something to the clipboard, generally the same sort of commands in any Edit Windows menu. View will often let you reload the page or see details of the HTML. GO is the navigation command; clicking it will give you a list of the sites you've visited today. Bookmark is for remembering the URL of good sites. The Options menu lets you decide things such as the typeface shown in the window, and so on.

Below the menu bar is the toolbar. Most browser toolbars let you move backward and forward through Web pages, reload a page, travel to a home page, print a page, stop the current load action, and so on. They are simply one-click shortcuts to the commands in the menu bar.

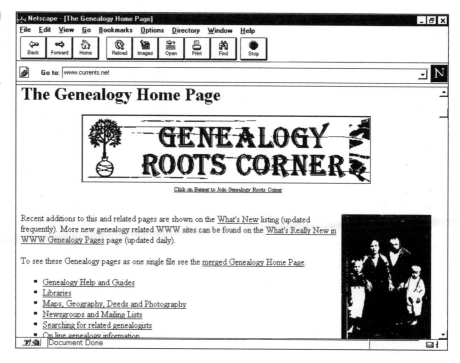

Underneath the toolbar is the URL bar. At the far left is the URL link icon. Double-click this, and the URL is saved to the Windows clipboard as text to be pasted in another document. Drag the box to Netscape's bookmarks window and a bookmark is created on the spot. Drag it to the Windows desktop in Windows 95, and you create a shortcut to that site. Double-click that shortcut and your browser starts and takes you to the page. Microsoft Internet Explorer has a similar icon that does the same thing.

Of course, what dominates this line is the Location box, where you actually enter a Web site's address. If you need to copy a URL to your clipboard, you can just double-click, press Ctrl+C, and it's ready to be pasted elsewhere. Are your fingers tired of typing http://www? Just type the unique part of the URL (such as genealogy.com) and the browser will fill in the first part. Type in an ftp site such as ftp.symantec.com, and the browser will insert the necessary ftp://. If you click the down arrow on the right side of the Location box, you'll see a list of the last 15 or so URLs typed in this way. This feature is handy if you can't remember that neat place you visited yesterday. Place the pointer in the

Location box and press the down arrow key. You'll hop to the next URL in the list.

At the end of this row is the Netscape icon. Whenever you're loading a page, you'll see an animation of comets raining down on the poor little Netscape planet. If you double-click the *N,* you'll be taken immediately to Netscape's home page at http://home.netscape.com.

The next row of directory buttons takes you to new pages that Netscape thinks are cool, worthwhile sites. For example, NetSearch takes you to a page of Web search engines. The People button jumps you to a form for searching online white pages, while Software takes you to the Navigator software site where a new version of the program is posted almost weekly! (Microsoft Internet Explorer has similar buttons.)

Below, taking up most of the screen, is Netscape's active window, where the current Web page is displayed.

Finally, let's go to the bottom of the screen. At flush left is a little broken key. In Navigator, this means the page you're viewing has no built-in security. That's not a problem in this case, because you're not filling out a form or providing any information. If the page had a form, the little broken key would indicate that your answers could be seen by someone else. When a secure site is being viewed, you'll see a solid blue line at the top of the screen and a solid key. Every browser notes security in different ways. Get to know yours well.

Down underneath the display part, you'll find the status line. This line tells you how much of a page the browser has loaded. Move your mouse pointer over links on a page and you'll see the associated URLs displayed here, too. If the site's developer is versed in Java, a message can scroll across this box like a ticker tape. Next to the status line is a thermometer bar, another visual cue that shows how long you have to wait for an operation to finish.

Finally, flush right is a little mail icon that, when clicked, launches Netscape Navigator's Mail program. The question mark means Navigator hasn't checked any mail during this session. When it has—and you can set Navigator to do this automatically at set intervals—a number will appear telling you how many messages you have.

Navigation Systems (Road Maps)

When you're cruising down the information superhighway, it's helpful to have some road maps. Here are some I recommend.

Internet Roadmap

My mother wanted to know about the ins and outs of the Internet, and she wanted to also have a "cheat sheet" by her side in case she couldn't remember the difference between an ftp site and a gopher. Just as luck would have it, Patrick Douglas Crispen of the University of Alabama was about to start the third round of his e-mail correspondence course on the Internet, "Internet Roadmap." This excellent series of messages is in clear, concise language, with definitions and examples for each concept. Your homework in the course is to carry out the steps he outlines in each lesson. In no time, Mother was off and running from Web site to WAIS, happily downloading this and that; if she forgot how to do something, she simply referred to the printed copies she had made of the lessons.

This book can't cover every detail of learning the Internet, but the Roadmap does. Crispen has had such success, he's allowed other people to post the full course at various sites on the Web, so there are copies of it in gophers, ftp sites, and even a version in Japanese. If you are already with a commerical online service, use its Internet software to go to *http://ua1vm .ua.edu/~crispen/roadmap.html,* the Roadmap's home page. There, you'll find several ways to get the course: through the Web through e-mail and by file download.

To get it by e-mail, you ask a computer to send you the lessons one by one. New courses start every two weeks. Just send an e-mail letter to *LISTSERV@LISTS.INTERNIC.NET.* The message should say SUBSCRIBE ROADMAP96 YOURFIRSTNAME YOURLASTNAME (replace YOUR FIRSTNAME and YOURLASTNAME with your first and last names).

Or you can read it on the Web at *http://rs.internic.net/roadmap96/.* Or you can download the files at *http://ua1vm.ua.edu/~helpdesk/roadmap.html.*

Hytelnet

Hytelnet (the latest as of this writing is version 6.9) was designed to assist users in reaching all of the Internet-accessible libraries, freenets, BBSs, and other information sites by telnet, and is a text-based program. There are versions for UMS, VMS, Windows, and Macintosh, too. You can link up to a version on the Internet or have a copy of it on your own system. I recommend the latter because if you have a copy of Hytelnet installed on your own system, you can easily add your favorite sites to its extensive list. I downloaded a copy from Delphi; there is also a Web page with the different versions at *http://www.lights.com/hytelnet/.* Many other sites also have copies. Charles Burchill of the University of Manitoba has written a Macintosh version of Hytelnet; his e-mail address is *burchil@ccu.umanitoba.ca.*

The program is distributed as shareware; you can find information at *http://www.lights.com/hytelnet/.* If you find it to be of use, send $20 to the author.

You can browse Hytelnet offline or connect to your Internet Service Provider and have your telnet program take you to the places you find. For the Windows version, double-click on the Hytelnet icon.

When you do, you'll get the screen in Fig. 4.2 (the appearance will change very slightly depending on the platform; the text will read the same). Be sure to read the What Is Hytelnet and Telnet Tips files.

Hytelnet's main use for genealogists is to find libraries to telnet to on the Internet (Chap. 9 will discuss how to do that). Under Options, you can tell Hytelnet where your telnet program is and click on the word *telnet* on the screen to go directly to any site on the Hytelnet screen.

Hytelnet is useful in many ways; not only does it allow you to find the exact telnet addresses of hundreds of libraries, but it has help screens

Figure 4.2

The opening screen of Hytelnet, one road map to the Internet.

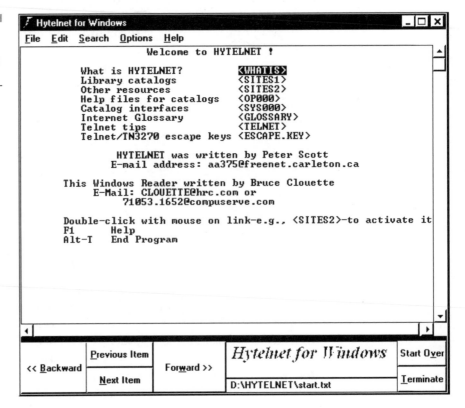

from the online public-access catalog (OPAC) program you'll encounter there, and in some cases the opening screen, too. Throughout Hytelnet, whenever you see something in pointed brackets such as <OP013>, it refers to another text file with information.

Let's step through Hytelnet to find the University of Alabama in Huntsville OPAC. From the opening screen in Fig. 4.2, you would choose Library Catalogs. (Position the cursor on the selection, and then press either Enter or the right arrow key. Moving the left cursor arrow will take you back one screen.) This will give you the screen which asks you to choose a region of the world. From this screen, highlight The Americas and press Enter. (The text within the angle brackets on the screen refers to the text file that will be called up.) From the next screen, choose the selection United States, and you'll get the screen in Fig. 4.3, where the sorting is now by type of library.

Figure 4.3

When you've chosen a continent and country, your choices are sorted into types of libraries. University of Alabama in Huntsville will be under the first choice, Academic, Research, and General Libraries.

University of Alabama in Huntsville will be under the first choice, Academic, Research, and General Libraries. Choose that item. You now have an overwhelming number of choices. By hitting Page Down, you can page through them. In this Windows version, use the Search menu item at the top to find *Huntsville,* and you'll see something like Fig. 4.4. Now highlight *University of Alabama, Huntsville,* and you'll get the screen in Fig. 4.5.

This screen tells you the address to use to telnet there, the first command you'll want to use, the type of OPAC used there, and how to exit. The screen tells you that this site has a PALS-type catalog; for an explanation of how that catalog works, highlight the <OP013> and press Enter. This screen tells you the most commonly used commands for that OPAC system.

Press Print Screen to print this out and have it handy when you sign on. Using your telnet program, you can connect as in Fig. 4.6. It's that easy. More about what to do with online card catalogs is in Chap. 9.

Figure 4.4
In the extensive list of libraries, here's the one we were looking for. In this Windows version, use the Search menu item at the top to find Huntsville.

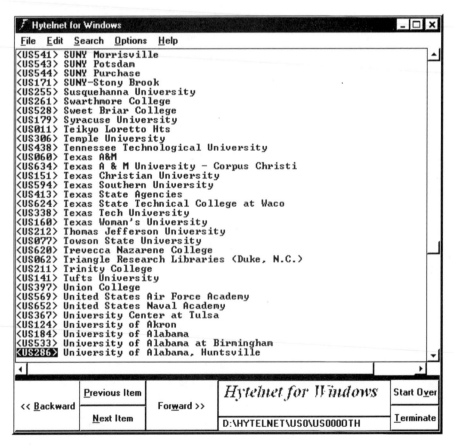

Figure 4.5
With just a few key-
strokes, you have the
specific information
on how to get to that
card catalog. Use
your telnet program
and follow the
instructions.

Figure 4.5
With just a few key-
strokes, you have the
specific information
on how to get to that
card catalog. Use
your telnet program
and follow the
instructions.

Hytelnet has much, much more information than just libraries, and it's worth the registration fee if you're going to spend much time surfing the Internet looking for files and programs.

GenBrowser

This $20 shareware program from Ripple Effect Software is designed to help you surf to genealogy pages quickly, search genealogy databases, and save what's useful. It can also keep track of what was not useful, so you don't waste time going over old ground.

If you find a Web page with ancestry information, you can use Gen-Browser to change the hypertext into a GEDCOM (see App. C). Gen-Browser can also search Web indexes, such as the Family Tree Maker site

Figure 4.6
Connected to UAH
with Hytelnet's
directions.

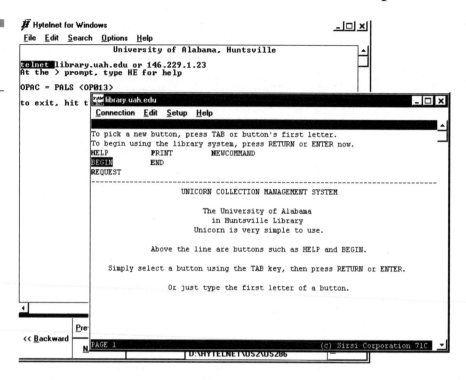

Figure 4.6
Connected to UAH with Hytelnet's directions.

or Roots Surname List for specific names and store the results on your hard drive.

It's a handy tool and worth the price.

My Top 50 Genealogy Sites to See

Since the first publication of this book, the number of genealogy-related Web pages has gone from a handful to literally thousands. You'll never be able to see them all. However, of the ones I have seen, I have found 50 that would be good starting places. They will all lead you to other pages, eventually narrowing in scope, and I hope they will lead you to what you need. This is not even close to an exhaustive list; for that, see Cyndi's List and Genealogy Resources on the Internet, which follows. These sites are listed alphabetically, not ranked.

1. Afrigeneas Home Page (*http://www.msstate.edu/Archives/History/afrigen/ index.html*) is the starting place for African-American family history. Don't miss it!

2. American Civil War Home Page (*http://funnelweb.utcc.utk.edu/ ~hoemann/warweb.html*) links to fantastic online documents from all sort of sources, from two academics who have made the Civil War their career.

3. Ancestry Inc.'s Discovering Your Heritage (*http://www.ancestry.com/ dyh/intro2.html*) is the basic beginner's how-to information source on genealogy.

4. Bob Fieg's (*http://www.getnet.com/~bfieg/*) is a typical home page, but with genealogy and pedigree chart software.

5. Canadian Genealogy Sources (*gopher://Alpha.CC.UToledo.edu:70/ 11GOPHER ROOT%3a%5b000000.RESEARCH-RESOURCES .GENEALOGY.canadian-genealogy%5d*) is a list of sources to get you started in Canada.

6. Canadian Heritage Information Network (*http://www.chin.gc.ca/*) is in French or English. Subscription service, but worth looking at.

7. Carrie's Adoptee & Genealogy Page (*http://www.mtjeff.com/~bodenst/ page3.html*) links to resources for adoptees, German heritage, general genealogy.

8. Census Bureau Home Page (*http://www.census.gov/ftp/pub/genealogy/ www/*) lists frequently occurring names in the United States, 1990, among other things.

9. CLIO—The National Archives Information Server—Genealogy (*http://www.nara.gov*) lists holdings of the National Archives.

10. Cyndi's List of Genealogy Sites on the Internet (*http://www.oz.net/ ~cyndihow/sites.htm*) is the best-organized and annotated list of WWW genealogy sites. A must see!

11. David Eppstein's home page (*http://www.ics.uci.edu/~eppstein/gene/*) has information on his shareware program Gene for Macintosh.

12. Dott's Genealogy Home Page (*http://www.electriciti.com/~dotts/*) has lots of great info on Iowa and Ohio resources.

13. Everton's Guide to Genealogy on the World Wide Web (*http://www.everton.com/*) includes an online version of the venerable *Helper.*

14. Family History, How Do I Begin (*http://www.lds.org/Family History/ How Do I Begin.html*) is the Church of Jesus Christ of Latter-Day Saints' basic tutorial.

15. GENDEX (*http://www.gendex.com/*) is an enterprise devoted to advancing the progress of family history and genealogy research on the World Wide Web. Software and surname databases.

16. Genealogy Dictionary (*http://www.electriciti.com/~dotts/diction .html#DICT*), part of Dott's Home Page listed previously, is for all those confusing terms such as *cordwainer* and *primogeniture*.

17. Genealogy for Teachers (*http://www.execpc.com/~dboals/geneo.html*) lists resources, organizations, guides, and tutorials. Aimed at educators, it would help any beginner.

18. Genealogy Resources on The Internet (*http://www.tc.umn.edu/ ~pmg/genealogy.htm*) tries to list it all. It does a good job.

19. Genealogy SF (*http://roxy.sfo.com/~genealogysf/*) has software, data, research tips, and a WWW hot list.

20. GENNAM-L Archive—Folio Infobase (*http://www.folio.com/folio.pgi/ gennam-1 archive?*); 20,000+ messages from the GENNAM-L mailing list, searchable.

21. GenServ—Genealogical Server Information (*http://soback.kornet .nm.kr/~cmanis/*) is the GenServ's home page. How to register.

22. GENUKI (*http://midas.ac.uk/genuki/*), all about genealogy in the United Kingdom and Ireland.

23. GenWeb Database Index (*http://www.doit.com/tdoyle/genweb/* or *http:// sillyg.doit.com/genweb/*) (try both) links to all known genealogical databases searchable through the Web.

24. GENWEB Discussion List (*http://demo.genweb.org/genweblist/ genweblist.html*) holds discussions about the GenWeb database.

25. GENWEB Introduction (*http://www.genweb.org*) is the WWW Genealogy Demo Page. How the GenWeb works.

26. Helm's Genealogy ToolBox (*http://www.rootscomputing.com/*) is a categorized guide to genealogy on the WWW. Great starting place; link to the *Journal of Online Genealogy*.

27. Isleuth (*http://www.isleuth.com/gene.html*) search genealogy at ISLEUTH, lots of online databases from one place!

28. Italian Genealogy Home Page (*http://www.italgen.com/*) has chat forums, databases, tips, and a toolbox for researching Italian family names.

29. Janyce's Root Diggin' Dept. (*http://www.janyce.com/gene/rootdig.html*) is a good beginner's starting place.

30. JewishGen Family Finder (*http://www1.jewishgen.org/jgff/*) is a database of towns and surnames being researched by Jewish genealogists worldwide and can be searched on the WWW or via e-mail.

31. List of Genealogy Bulletin Board Systems—Home Page (*http://genealogy.org:80/PAF/www/gbbs/*) lists every BBS that carries FIDOnet genealogy echoes, and it's searchable!

32. National Genealogical Society (*http://genealogy.org/NGS/*) is the granddaddy of all genealogical societies. Much of what's on the BBS is here, too.

33. Native American Genealogy (*http://members.aol.com/bbbenge/front.html*) is a page that tries to keep up with the latest in sites and resources for Native Americans.

34. Quick Guide to Genealogy in Ireland (*http://www.bess.tcd.ie/roots/prototyp/gguide.htm*) is a great beginner's guide to Irish genealogical resources.

35. RAND Genealogy Club Home Page (*http://www.rand.org:80/personal/Genea/*) is used to search roots surnames and locations and get soundex codes.

36. Registry of genealogists with home pages (*http://www.wolfe.net/~janyce/genealogy/gene.cgi*) is a guide to individual genealogy pages. When your page is up, register!

37. Repositories of Primary Sources (*http://www.uidaho.edu/special-collections/Other.Repositories.html*) is a listing of over 1900 Web sites describing holdings of manuscripts, archives, rare books, historical photographs, and other primary sources. It's worth a look.

38. ROOTSBOOK on the Web (*http://mlane2.inhouse.compuserve.com:8000/Search.htm*) is a big database made up of a lot of little databases; cooperative effort of lots of people.

39. ROOTS-L Page (*http://www.rootsweb.com/roots-l*) is the home page of the ROOTS-L mailing list.

40. Southern Genealogy (*http://www.traveller.com/genealogy/*) lists Southern families, Civil War pages, government Web servers, genealogy software companies, family societies and/or associations pages, books for sale, and genealogy newsgroups.

41. South Carolina Library (*http://www.sc.edu/library/socar/books.html*) is an online card catalog; extensive genealogy holdings.

42. Spanish Heritage home page (*http://www.webcom.com/shharnet*) is for getting started on Hispanic research.

43. Surnames.Com (*http://www.surnames.com/*) has genealogy in general, Arizona in particular. It has a good beginner's section.

44. Tracking Your Roots (*http://members.aol.com/genweblisa/genealog.htm*) is an absolute gold mine of Alabama genealogy information, county by county. The Tennessee River, which flows through northern Alabama, was a major westward immigration route from Tennessee, Virginia, and the Carolinas.

45. Treasure Maps, the How-to Genealogy Site (*http://www.firstct.com/fv/tmapmenu.html*) is full of tips, sources, and sites.

46. U.S. Gazetteer (*http://wings.buffalo.edu/geogw*) is where you can type in a city and/or state and a map will appear showing the location.

47. Utah State Archives (*http://www.archives.state.ut.us/*): click on the Research Center for the Archives' public services, which include research, answering questions, and sending you records. It's not all free, but over the Internet, it's very convenient!

48. Library of Virginia Digital Collections (*http://image.vtls.com/*) is where you can search Virginia newspapers, court records, and state documents online.

49. Xerox Map Server (*http://pubweb.parc.xerox.com/map*) contains interactive maps for finding any place in the world.

50. Yale Libraries Gopher (*gopher://libgopher.yale.edu/1*) is a listing of online card catalogs around the world.

Find Your Own Favorites

The World Wide Web is a big place. Many folks have devoted their careers to helping you find what you need. These are called Web searchers, and they are free. They support themselves by selling advertising. Here are the ones I like best. Put *genealogy* and your surname(s) in the search box and see what comes up!

General Search Engines

Excite Netsearch, *http://www.excite.com/*, an all-Web search, looks at the complete text of Web pages and builds a database of keywords. When you search Excite, it returns the URLs of pages that have the keywords you used. Capitalization and word order do not affect the outcome of the search, nor the ranking of the results.

InfoSeek Net Guide, *http://guide.infoseek.com/,* is the only searcher where capitalization counts, so you can search for surnames such as *Weeks* and *Fox.* Like Excite, InfoSeek (see Fig. 4.7) builds a database of commonly occurring words and compares your search terms to the database. Infoseek returns the results in order of relevance. You can use a + (plus sign) by a term to mean that it must appear and a – (minus sign) by a term to mean it must not. This makes it much easier to find surnames. It also does not ignore common terms such as *the* and *new.* Word order is considered only if the terms are in quotation marks as a phrase.

Lycos Web Search, *http://www.lycos.com/,* an all-Web search, is the most complete Web searcher, but in Lycos's search scheme, a blind Venetian is the same thing as a Venetian blind, no matter what you do. Furthermore, words such as *new* and *the* are ignored, making it impossible to search for *New York* and *New England.* However, Lycos Web also has separate databases for pictures, sounds, and programs.

Webcrawler, *http://www.webcrawler.com,* an all-Web search, is not as complete or as fast as the others are. Use it as a last resort.

Figure 4.7
Infoseek allows small words, dates, and phrases in searches.

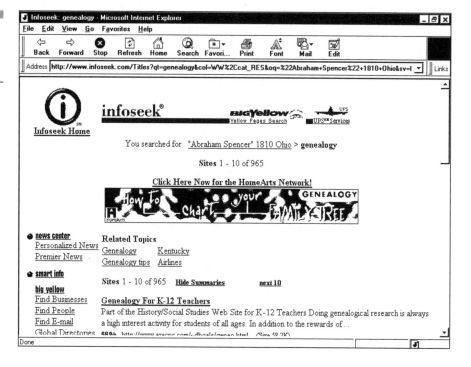

Yahoo!, *http://www.yahoo.com*, is an edited, sorted catalog of sites. It's arranged in a hierarchy of categories, but the catalog can also be searched. It's updated weekly from a search program as well as entries from people who have published Web sites. Only those deemed valuable in content or design make it into Yahoo!, so it's a good place to start for general searches such as *genealogy,* but not for very specific searches such as *Abraham Spencer 1810.*

People Search Engines

If you need to find lost, living relatives, try the following.

Four11, *http://www.four11.com*, is one of many white pages services on the Web. It's free and has the e-mail and telephone numbers of millions of people, taken from public records, searches of Internet sites such as Usenet, and other sources. If you register as a user, adding your name and addresses to the database, you can search many different ways: by city, state, college affiliation, and other keys that other Four11 members have chosen to input. Of course, if someone chooses not to put in these keys, you can only find them with a name search.

BigFoot, *http://www.bigfoot.com*, is another such effort to catalog people, with the same general rules: input your information and you get searches that are more specific. BigFoot also has surface mail addresses as well as e-mail and telephone information.

Other people search engines to try are as follows:

InfoSpace, *http://www.accumail.com.*

Internet Address Finder, *http://www.iaf.net.*

ValleyNet, *http://www.valleynet.net/~nickh/wede4d2.shtml* (this one is a directory page with links to other search engines).

Virtual Reference Desk, *http://www.refdesk.com/addsrch.html* (another list of links to search engines).

WhoWhere, *http://query1.whowhere.com/jwz/cbspresearch.wsrch.*

WorldPages, *http://www.worldpages.com.*

File Search Sites

To find programs you may hear of, such as new World Wide Web browsers or genealogy programs, you can go to several sites that keep track of software and where the latest versions are. Some of these are as follows.

The Ultimate Collection of Winsock Software, TUCOWS, *http://www .tucows.com*, is a site that tracks more than Windows, despite the name, and has a capsule profile and a rating for each program. There are mirror sites all over the world, so you can choose a site close to you for faster downloads.

Shareware.com, *http://www.shareware.com*, is a premier software search site. Updated weekly, the search engine lets you choose your operating system, choose a keyword, and even choose a date for the newest software, or the oldest! Shareware.com then lets you see where the file can be found and rates the reliability (how easy it is to get in and get a file) of each site.

ZDnet, *http://www.zdnet.com/zdi/software*, has the latest software, usually rated by the staff by a five-star system.

More file search sites are listed at Nerd's Heaven, *http://boole.stanford.edu/ nerdsheaven.html*. This list of links is updated often and sorted by category.

FTP

Browsers can receive files with ftp, but they can't send. For that, you need an ftp client. You probably won't need this until you have a Web page to publish. When you do, ftp is how you'll get your page files to the server that will be on the Internet so people can see your work.

WS_FTP32 for PCs (see Fig. 4.8) and Fetch for Macintosh are good choices, and they are relatively cheap. They both have features that I enjoy: the ability to read text files, saving the addresses of ftp sites you visit, and batch send and receive. Every ftp program is different, so when you get one, poke around its help file or manual to discover its particular tricks. Some let you store the settings for getting to several different ftp sites or let you set a default ftp site. Many that store sites also let you set the initial directory to search, such as /PUB.

To use ftp, you simply give the program an address, probably your address at your Internet Service Provider, and a password. (If you are using ftp to get files from a public site, you log in as anonymous and give your e-mail address as a password. If *anonymous* doesn't work as a login name, try *ftp*.)

Using the command CD to change directories and LIST to look at file names, you can send and receive files, usually by clicking an arrow (as in WS_FTP), but if you have a text-based client, you simply use GET and SEND.

In ftp, case, spelling, and punctuation count. If you try to get to FOOBAR.some.edu by foobar.some.edu, it probably won't work. If you try to get a file called FAMILY.LOCLIST.README.html you must follow that

Figure 4.8

WS_FTP is a good, easy-to-use program for sending and getting files.

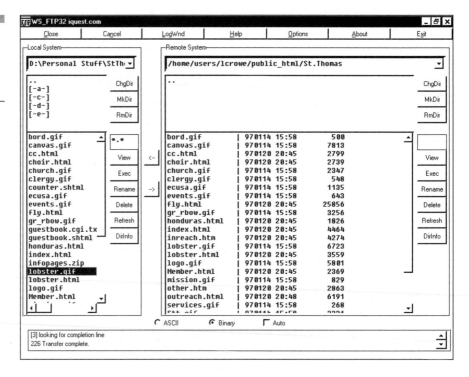

punctuation and capitalization exactly, or you'll get a "file not found" error message.

Many of the remote computers you're ftping to are big machines running UNIX and DOS that have more or less adopted UNIX's subdirectory structure. Therefore, if you know DOS, you can wend your way through a remote computer's subdirectories.

If that server you want to access is always busy, one way to get in is to repeatedly try until you hit that moment when someone has just logged off. Another trick: find out which time zone the remote site is in and access it during local mealtimes or rush hours. A server in the United Kingdom, for instance, will be easier to access at 4 P.M. U.K. time when everyone is at tea. Granted, the Internet is international in nature, but a computer tied to a given university or organization will have peak usage at predictable times—use that to your advantage.

Many Web browsers have an ftp program built in. If you want to jump to an ftp site, just enter the address by prefacing it with FTP://. Be prepared for some unsuccessful attempts to connect to an ftp site. FTP site addresses are always changing. The Internet is dynamic, so expect a few detours along the way.

Any time you are using ftp, you need to know some conventions. Files that end in *.zip, lzh,* .exe, *arj, arc,* and *com* are binary and should be transferred in binary mode. Files that end in anything else are probably text files and should be transferred in ASCII mode. If you are transferring files to a UNIX system, binary mode is generally the best mode to use for all transfers. The programs for uncompressing files are available at many BBSs, as well as at *ftp://ftp.cac.psu.edu/pub/genealogy/INDEX.html.*

Binaries will usually be in zip format with a file extension of *.zip.* A self-extracting copy of PKware's shareware programs is in the DOS file *pkz204g.exe.* Zip files can also be read with the DOS program *unz50p1.exe.*

Some files are also compressed with lharc having the ending *.lzh.* The software to unpack those files can be found in the self-extracting DOS archive *lha213.exe.* Files that end with *.arj* may be uncompressed with *unarj.exe* which is in the zip file *unarj230.zip. .arc* files may be decompressed with a program in *pk361.exe.* There are also several files that end with *.exe.* These are generally either self-extracting DOS archives or DOS programs.

Files ending in *.Z* have been compressed with UNIX *compress.* Files ending in *.gz* have been compressed with *gzip.*

Tips and Tricks

There are ways to use your browser to better surf the World Wide Web. For example, most browsers will input the http:// for you if you type in only the rest. You can type in *www.genhomepage.com,* in other words.

If the type in the browser window appears too small to you, under Options or View you can choose the size of the default body text style. In Microsoft Internet Explorer, in fact, the *A* on the toolbar is for one-click adjustments in type size.

You can choose the first page to appear in your browser each time it launches. In Netscape Navigator, under Options | General Preferences, choose the Appearance tab and type in the complete URL of a page you'd like to start with every time. Many people like to make this a search engine such as *http://www.infoseek.com.* Others like to make their bookmark files (bookmark.htm on your disk) the home page.

You don't have to have the menu bar, the tool button bar, and the location bar all showing at once. With Netscape Navigator, you can have any combination of these turned off. With Microsoft Internet Explorer, you can "collapse" the lowest one into the bar above it.

If you get tired of waiting for graphics to load, turn off the option Auto Load Images under Options in Netscape Navigator, and in Microsoft Internet Explorer, under View | Options | Appearance (see Fig. 4.9).

All browsers save copies of the text, pictures, and other files you see in your Web browser window. They use these stored files the next time you

Figure 4.9
Speed up your Web
session by turning off
graphics.

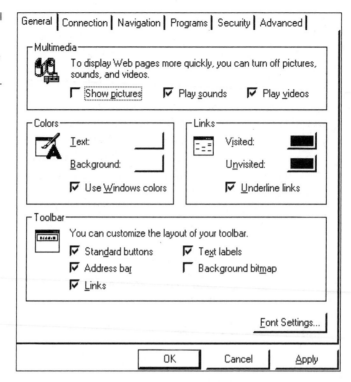

visit the site, loading the ones on your disk if they are the same as the ones at the remote site, for faster display. These are stored in a directory on your disk called the *cache*. You should remember to empty the cache, that is, erase those files, every now and then. In Microsoft Internet Explorer, use View | Options | Advanced tab. In the box, Temporary Internet Files, click the Settings button. Then click Empty Folder. In Netscape Navigator, click on Options | Preferences | Cache and click the button Clear Disk Cache Now. This will save you loads of disk space.

Local BBSs and Their Nets

If your town has a local genealogical organization, chances are you also have at least one electronic bulletin board system with at least some genealogy on it. You might even have access to one devoted to genealogy. And while some BBSs stand alone, sending and receiving messages and files from only local sources, others are connected to networks.

A bulletin board network is based on the same principles as other computer networks, from local area networks (LANs), which can be as small as connecting the two computers in your home, to the Internet, which is so big it's hard to imagine.

In a network, two or more computers share and exchange data and programs through cables, phone wires, and other means. They can do this with interruptions now and then, or constantly, with no interruptions in the connection. Most BBS nets pass mail and files among themselves at a set time each night. They do this by each participant BBS calling the hub BBS, which passes the information on to the next hub, possibly through a *backbone* (a set of connections comprising the main channels of communication across a network, through which the heaviest traffic travels), and finally to all the various local BBSs.

In this way, you can call your local BBS, leave a message for a new-found fourth cousin in Utah, and receive a reply in usually less than two days.

Now this is, of course, costing several people long-distance charges. Most BBS sysops use the highest-speed modems available for the mail runs, and the reason the calls are at night is to get the cheapest rate. Still, the costs do add up. If your local sysop has a subscription or support fee, you really should consider contributing. Most sysops do this because they love it, but if they go broke for the love of their hobby, you've lost your connection.

Be Prepared

There are some dangers out there, as mentioned previously. This is a good time for a cautionary tale.

Every BBS, commercial system, or network requires you to have a password that only you know. One person, who shall remain nameless (because he really did know better than to do this), used exactly the same password on every system he signed on to. From CompuServe to Fred's Pretty Good BBS and everything in between, he used precisely the same series of characters to identify himself as the proper user of that account at that online place.

To be friendly, he also left his ID numbers for some of these other systems he used in messages on BBSs, so folks he met online could meet him in another place, so to speak. It was sort of like saying, "Meet me at the corner pub, and ask for Charlie."

But, unfortunately, some BBSs have users whose morals and discretion are not what they should be. These folks knew that sysops are all-powerful on their own BBSs; they can look up any information deposited on their boards, even passwords. And some people are good at cracking security systems and can pretend to be the sysop.

Well, someone less than ethical decided to try that online ID number left in a message with the password he had hacked from the BBS's secret files, just to see if it worked. It did. Everywhere Charlie had an account. Pretty soon old Charlie found himself paying for other people's joyrides on some of the more expensive online services.

Learn from his costly mistake: your password should be unique on every system. It should never be something easy to guess, such as your maiden name or your birthday. It should not even make much sense to anyone but you. And to make it truly secure, which is the whole point of a password anyway, combine numbers, letters, and punctuation marks. !m51d89y3# cannot be guessed by someone trying every word in a 40,000-word dictionary to break into your account.

Because it's not easy to remember 12 different passwords, some people keep a 3×5 card or a sheet of paper with their various passwords posted by the computer. It works, but it's a big security risk in another way: anyone who can see your computer can use your passworded account.

So, this is where the scripting function of your communications program can come in handy. If you record your first session on a board, you'll have a record of what password you created there. Then, using the scripting language, you can write a script with that system's phone number, your online name, the password for that account, and any other commands you want carried out every time. The thing to be cautious about here is restricting access to your computer communications scripts, in case the kids decide to use your computer.

Finally, once you get the hang of it, look for some navigators to make BBS life easier. For example, RoboComm will automate your access to computer bulletin boards that run PC Board and Wildcat! software. You can set up RoboComm to call a list of BBSs. For each board you call, you create an "agenda of things to do," which it does, and faster than you can type. To do this though, you need to be very familiar with each of the boards in order to write the script for the agenda. Setting up RoboComm is tedious and time-consuming, but once that's done, your BBS chores are a breeze.

There are also offline mail readers with telecom programs in them, such as Speed Read, Off-line Express, and others. Ask the sysops of your favorite BBSs which offline reader works best for their boards. Or, for information, contact:

Parsons Consulting (RoboComm)
5020 S. Lake Shore Dr., Suite 3301
Chicago, IL 60615
BBS: 312-752-1258
Online filename: ROBOxx-A.ZIP, ROBOxx-B.ZIP

J.E. Smith (Speed Read)
344 Observatory Dr.
Birmingham, AL 35206
$25
Online filename: SPEEDxxx.ZIP

Some Examples

Let's look at a few examples of local BBSs, in no particular order:

CatEye BBS

West Virginia
304-592-3390

Sue Moore began her board in 1992, she says, "because we didn't like a lot of the boards we called and thought there was a need for one in the West Virginia area." So, with PCBoard software and two phone lines at 14,400 bps, they were up and running. The opening screen is in Fig. 5.1.

Moore is proud of her caving, genealogy, and other conferences, but she would like to improve the genealogy area. "We are growing bigger all the time," she says. "We try to carry all the genealogy programs we can find. We also are building a good deposit of other people's works for the VA, MD, PA, NC, WV, NJ and KY area."

All callers can call free for 15 minutes a day. The rates are $45.00 for the first year, and $35 a year after that for 1 hour of long-distance or 45 minutes of local per day.

The Files area, reached by the command F from the main menu, has several genealogical files in area 49, as you see in Fig. 5.2. At any prompt,

Figure 5.1
The opening screen of CatEye explains the name.

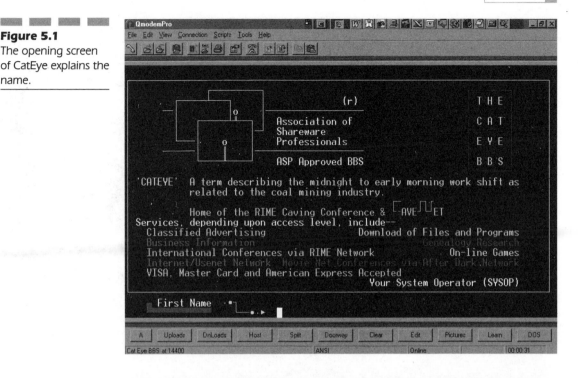

Figure 5.2
Files area 49 has genealogical files, and new ones are added regularly.

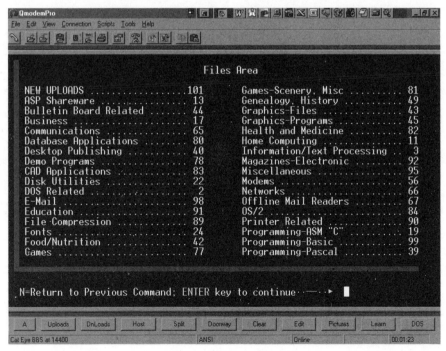

Figure 5.3

Help files are available on CatEye by typing a ? (question mark) at any prompt.

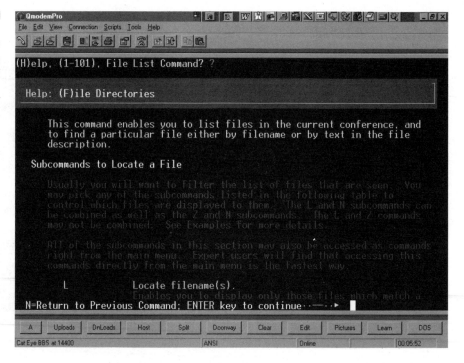

enter a ? (question mark) and you will get a help file as in Fig. 5.3. You can also search the files from the main menu with the z command: Z SPENCER 49, for example.

From the Main Board (main menu) shown in Fig. 5.4, you can choose to read messages while online from the message commands or use the DOOR command to go to the offline mail area. You'll also find reviews of genealogy and history books in the West Virginia message areas. This board has a generic QWK mail and a Rosemail door. Both doors are good choices. On either one, if you try a download without first telling it your preferred protocol, compression technique, and so forth, you'll get an error message. You can also type QWK from the Main menu to download mail, once you have set your parameters. All these are improvements since the first edition of this book.

But Moore didn't stop there. She was instrumental in founding Software Valley Incorporated, a nonprofit organization to help bring technology to rural West Virginia. SV has a bulletin board system, called Software Valley Information Systems, or SVIS, also running PCBoard. Because it is nonprofit, when you call the toll-free numbers, this BBS is

Figure 5.4
CatEye's main board organizes the offerings, which include Internet services such as telnet and file transfer protocol.

severely limited in time: seven minutes per day. So, you pretty much have to download messages and get off when you call in on one of the two 800 numbers:

1-800-SOFTVAL

1-800-SVISWVA (WVA only)

It also has regular dial-in numbers: 304-592-2682 or 304-592-2723 for US Robotics 28.8 modems. These don't have daily time limits. What's really neat is that if you have telnet, you can also use this board that way: telnet 198.77.8.11 or svis.org, type in your user id and password, and you're in. The board looks very similar in a telnet session to a regular session, as you see in Fig. 5.5. This way, members who are travelers and rural users gain access to valuable genealogical information, including Internet mailing lists, Usenet genealogical discussion groups, and genealogical data files available for download from the BBS, a gopher, and an ftp server. Like CatEye, this board carries the RIME message echo, which has a genealogy subject group.

This is a good example of a general board with genealogy on it.

Figure 5.5
A telnet session to
CatEye is all text, but
convenient.

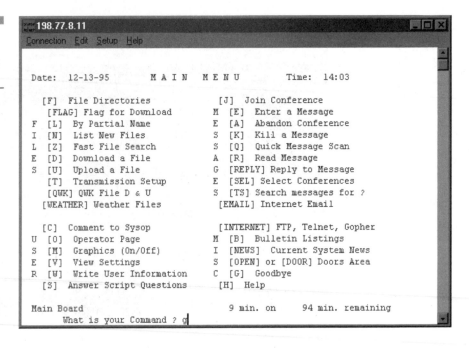

```
198.77.8.11                                                    _ □ ✕
Connection  Edit  Setup  Help

  Date:  12-13-95      M A I N   M E N U       Time:  14:03

    [F]   File Directories         [J]  Join Conference
    [FLAG] Flag for Download     M  [E]  Enter a Message
  F [L]   By Partial Name        E  [A]  Abandon Conference
  I [N]   List New Files         S  [K]  Kill a Message
  L [Z]   Fast File Search       S  [Q]  Quick Message Scan
  E [D]   Download a File        A  [R]  Read Message
  S [U]   Upload a File          G  [REPLY] Reply to Message
    [T]   Transmission Setup     E  [SEL] Select Conferences
    [QWK] QWK File D & U          S  [TS] Search messages for ?
    [WEATHER] Weather Files         [EMAIL] Internet Email


    [C]   Comment to Sysop          [INTERNET] FTP, Telnet, Gopher
  U [O]   Operator Page          M  [B]  Bulletin Listings
  S [M]   Graphics (On/Off)      I  [NEWS]  Current System News
  E [V]   View Settings          S  [OPEN] or [DOOR] Doors Area
  R [W]   Write User Information C  [G]  Goodbye
    [S]   Answer Script Questions   [H]  Help

  Main Board                       9 min. on    94 min. remaining
        What is your Command ? g
```

KC GeneSplicer

Kansas City, Kansas

913-648-6979

The opening screen of KC GeneSplicer (Fig. 5.6) is clear about the mission of this board. This board is by, about, and for genealogists.

Using the Remote Access BBS software with hot keys, this is a colorful, active board. (When a BBS system responds to one-keystroke commands, without an Enter or Return key, that option is called *hot key.* Some BBS software enables it with no option to turn it off; others let you set your user configuration to choose this or not.) This board has the hot keys set on, in an effort to keep things easy.

"I will be changing things from time to time," says sysop Steve Everley (don't forget the last *e!*). "However, the general look will not change much. I have tried to keep it as simple as possible for people. Since I run a Genealogy-only BBS, no games, etc., I find that it is fairly easy to keep it simple. I want the new person in the BBS world to have an easy way to find things."

From the Main Menu (Fig. 5.7), you can choose from many areas. All are open to you, but subscribers get more time per day. You can be a free user or a subscriber on Everley's board; daily time credit is also given for file uploads. It's a complicated formula that allows you to pay for actual

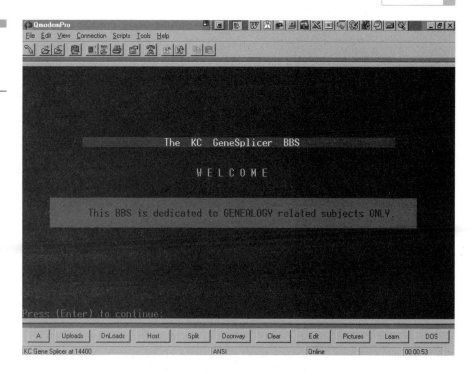

Figure 5.6

The KC GeneSplicer is dedicated to genealogy.

usage, but averages out to about 15 minutes a day for one year or 1 hour a day for three months for about $5.

"I carry echoes from three different networks: FidoNet, IGA_net, and Native Net," Everley says. "This makes about 40 different echoes available to the users with a good range of subjects."

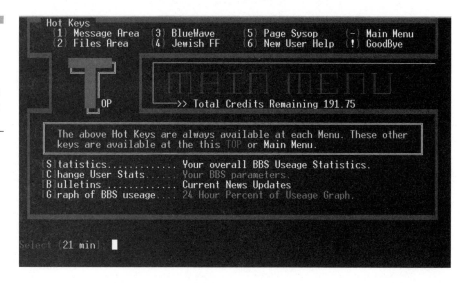

Figure 5.7

The Main Menu of the KC GeneSplicer has hot keys (single-stroke commands) to take you to the most popular functions.

As several of the board's introductory screens explain, not all of the echoes are available to the new user. "I generally don't give access to the BBS without having some contact with the people who call; either voice or my NEWUSER.APP, which is a simple information sheet that can be filled out and sent in. If someone does not feel like contributing to the General Funds account then I feel the amount of time they should have should be limited to 30 minutes. Then if you wish to contribute I will grant more access time. I feel that this is fair since I make three long-distance calls every day to bring in mail and files. People who use the system should share in some of the expenses incurred. It costs me about 50 to 70 dollars a month right now in telephone bills," he says.

An important feature is his emphasis on the more difficult genealogy problems: African-American, Native American, and some across the oceans. The main menu is simple and direct, without a lot of clutter. From any menu, the ! (exclamation point) will log you off, although it asks you twice whether you mean it.

The Blue Wave Mail Reader is a mail door. The mail door must be configured before the first time you use it, or it won't even try to download to you. Of course, you want to choose the echoes first, as shown in Fig. 5.8. You could string together choices, for instance, typing in *12 13 69 109* as your preferred conferences, then go on to the next screenful.

But the nice thing about Blue Wave (and by the way, it's a shareware program that allows you to read the mail on your end and also contains a door for the BBS end) is that you can choose keywords for the selections. If you're interested in Spencers and Ohio, you can set the Keyword function to *on* and have it retrieve only messages with those two keywords. Be aware, however, that in this case it's an OR search, not an AND search, so you could get messages with one but not the other term.

So, after you've selected your conferences (echoes) as in the screen in Fig. 5.8, you can choose *D* to download the package, as in Fig. 5.9. It's quick and easy.

KC GeneSplicer is a good board for the heartland of U.S. genealogy and worth a visit.

TNET BBS

Auburndale, Wisconsin

715-652-2758

Telnet://tznet.com (206.31.5.1)

Sysop John Hrusovskzky started what was the Twilight Zone BBS back in 1984. Today, it runs on a Pentium P166 with 16 megabytes of RAS and 6

Figure 5.8
Choose from the several dozen message topics available, then download a packet of messages to read offline later.

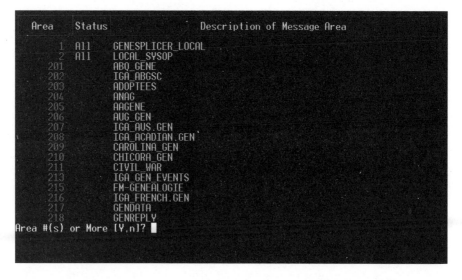

Figure 5.9
Get in the habit of downloading messages from BBSs like KC GeneSplicer; saves time and long-distance charges!

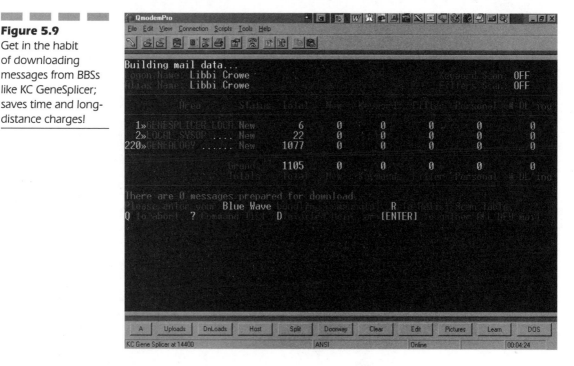

gigabytes of high-speed drives. It has 32 incoming lines and telnet access. It has become the TNET system and even has technical assistance by voice (715-652-3175 from 9:00 A.M. to 9:00 P.M. Central time). The opening screen is shown in Fig. 5.10.

"I started a BBS when I got my first Commodore computer and a 300-baud modem. I signed on to CompuServe and was hooked on the concept. But there was no software to run a BBS on a Commodore. So I learned how to program and wrote my own. We switched to the IBM platform as soon as it came out and it snowballed from there," Hrusovskzky says.

His hobby has turned into a career now, and the fees on this board are $10 a month or $100 a year for local users and telnet access; $20 a month for an Internet shell (text-only) account; and a PPP connection is $5 a month for BBS subscribers in addition to their regular fee.

This site has been carrying the International Genealogy Association Network (IGAnet) for three years now. A network based on FidoNet software, yet totally separate from FidoNet, International Genealogy Association Network has several different subject-related echoes on genealogy (see Fig. 5.11).

"The people are extremely helpful to each other on IGAnet, and that's a big plus. It's the best format on online, international and general genealogy-related discussions I've seen."

Figure 5.10
The TZone is available via telnet as well as dial-up.

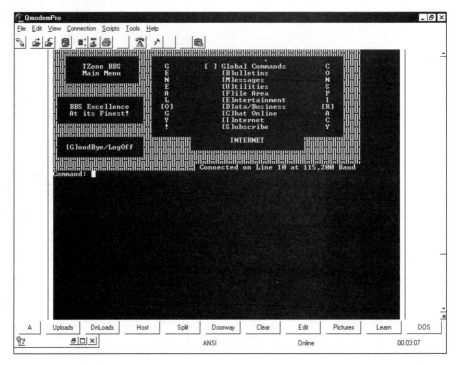

Figure 5.11
TNET features
the International
Genealogy Network.

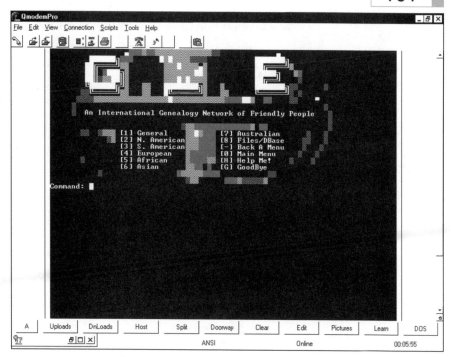

The International Genealogy Association Network has some special rules and guidelines. It is assumed most people on IGAnet are hobbyists, and that some have to make long-distance calls to get the messages. Because of this, you are supposed to keep IGAnet messages short (no more than 75 lines of 65 characters each) and forgo taglines, which just waste space, to the IGAnet's way of thinking. Ditto thank-you notes, and long quotes of answered messages are frowned upon. (See Fig. 5.12.)

Other rules are be polite and friendly. Help others if you can, expect lots of people to jump into conversations you start, and don't flame. All moderating should be left to the moderators.

While IGAnet carries reviews and recommendations on books, software, and so on, advertisement of such is not allowed.

Subject lines should be short but specific: SURNAME—STATE—DATE would be a good format to follow here for query messages. HELP—Family Tree Maker would be another, but never *help* or *genealogy* alone as a subject line. If the gist of a thread wanders from the topic of the message that started it, change the subject line to be clear for latecomers.

Some typographical notes: IGAnet prefers that only surnames you are querying be in all caps, everything else should be punctuated normally. Messages in all caps are frowned upon.

Figure 5.12
IGAnet messages are
short, with no
taglines.

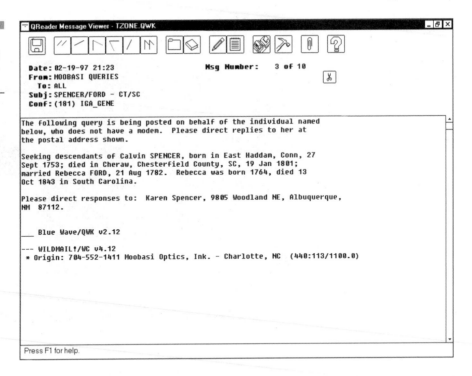

TNET also carries all the FidoNet genealogy echoes. John himself started on his genealogy several years ago, but because of the pressures of running the board, hasn't devoted much time to it recently.

TNET has no doors for genealogy files right now such as TTMS or GSDS searching, but he hopes to add them in the future.

Most of the files he has have to do with research in the United Kingdom. Recently, several databases of surnames have been appearing, too. He feels his best features for the genealogist are the IGAnet echoes and these newer files. The board uses QSO for QWK downloads of e-mail such as IGAnet, so you can do your reading and replying offline.

Genealogy (SF) of San Francisco

San Francisco, California

415-584-0697

Brian Mavrogeorge has put together a simple BBS for genealogy only, and it works quite well. The unadorned opening menu is shown in Fig. 5.13. Your choices are all just a single keystroke away; this board uses hot keys.

Figure 5.13

Genealogy (SF) of San
Francisco isn't big on
fancy graphics, but
has loads of goodies.

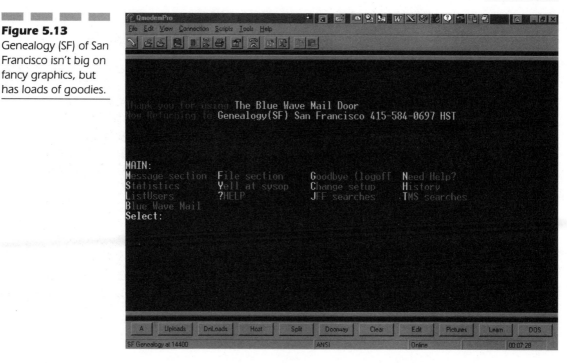

The membership list at the time this was written was small, under 200 people, and mainly from the Bay Area of California, though there were a few from other states. The folks that are there are very active, though.

One of the nice features here: he uses Gary Mokotoff's database Jewish Family Finder Search. Here, you type in the surname, city, country and find the names of other researchers looking for the same lines. A great boon to someone searching this particularly difficult type of genealogy!

He also participates in the Tiny Tafel Matching system: Choose *T* from the main menu, *M* from the TTS menu. If you have a report waiting for you, the menu will change and give you options for scanning, downloading, and deleting your report. If you do not have a report waiting for you, TMs will start to ask you questions as if you had requested another matching report. Simply use *Q* to quit out of the questionnaire; input the name, dates, and how closely to match them (to allow variation in spelling, for example), and you'll be given a list to choose from. Of course, uploading your own TT is the best thing to do; that way you give as well as take.

The files area, shown in Fig. 5.14, has loads of goodies: vital statistics files from the United States and United Kingdom, Mavrogeorge's own excellent articles on genealogical research, GEDCOM files uploaded by members, and software for genealogy and general purposes.

Figure 5.14
Genealogy (SF) of San Francisco's files area has an assortment of useful text and data.

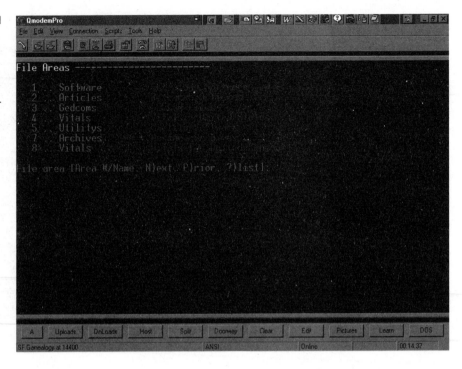

The quick mail package on this board is Blue Wave, shown in Fig. 5.15, a very popular one. With the Blue Wave mail door, you can use filters ("I *don't* want messages with this word") and keywords ("I *do* want messages with this word") as well as select your favorite conferences. And, Mavrogeorge's selection is as good as any local BBS I've found: African-American, several of the European ones, and the National Genealogy echo from FidoNet.

Instant Relatives

Salt Lake City, Utah

801-466-5374

A genealogist, bulletin board enthusiast, and full-time software engineer, Larry Maddocks combined his two favorite hobbies with his work when he started his Instant Relatives board in 1991. His goal is to eventually have the most user-friendly online research help for the genealogist. His board features messaging with popular genealogy echoes, shareware genealogy programs, GEDCOM files (upload and download), and an online search database.

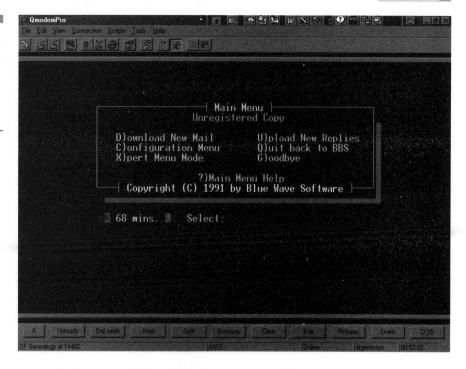

Figure 5.15
Blue Wave, a popular
program for sending
and receiving mes-
sage packets, is
the mail door on
Genealogy (SF).

Some programs Maddocks has as shareware on his board include the following:

InstaRel answers the question, "Who else is researching my ancestors?" by comparing your GEDCOM file with others' GEDCOM files. This has color screens and online help.

GED-Fix will purge errors in your GEDCOM files, relink families, and repair your GEDCOM file so that it will fit into PAF and many other genealogy programs.

GED2Flat will turn your GEDCOM file into a more readable file. Each line shows an individual's parents and spouse. An individual gets a new line for each spouse.

GED-Treasure will teach you how to read GEDCOM files—as you scroll through a GEDCOM file, a screen will show you the family record in plain English. You can also see a report of all the separate family trees in your GEDCOM file and create subsets of your family trees with many options.

These are programs for DOS 3.0 or higher. They require no extended memory. If you buy the whole package of four for $50, you get free pre-ferred access for a full year at the Instant Relatives BBS.

"I hope to someday make it easy for genealogists to share research," he says. "It's not as turnkey as I'd like it to be yet, but I'm still working on it. My goal is to help people, to make my genealogy bulletin board as easy as Prodigy."

Currently running his business out of his home, Maddocks has worked professionally on programs for genealogists at the Church of Jesus Christ of Latter-Day Saints' main office, on GEDFIX, and on other shareware genealogy programs, and is currently working on a genealogy program for Windows. His BBS is how he's tinkering with his grand scheme for online research; he hopes to write a program that will match GEDCOMs throughout a network, letting people know in a matter of minutes who else might be interested in their lines.

"There's a tiny tafel matching system out there, but it took me a long time to figure it out, and I'm a professional programmer," Maddocks says, "so I can imagine how hard it is for a beginning genealogist! What I like best is helping people with their research. I like the messages, really connecting to people. What most people enjoy is the interaction. What bothers most sysops is people who log on, get the latest files, and leave. We're in this to interact with people."

Maddocks is still refining and redefining how his software looks, but let's take a quick tour as it was in early 1994. The main menu gives you several choices in a typical PCBoard setup (see Fig. 5.16). The best feature about this board is the genealogical database program in the DOOR (Fig. 5.17).

One program is his Instant Relatives. This program will allow you to create a genealogy query and find out who may have information on your same line. You can fill out all the fields, entering name, sex, date, and so on, but the search only looks at the soundex code of the surname. If you wonder why you get matches that don't exactly match the name you entered, it is because you are seeing all the names that match the soundex.

There are other programs in the door that allow you to create a query on several different kinds of information, sorted by state: cemeteries, marriage records, and more. When you've tried it out, your comments to the sysop are welcome, as are additional databases.

Once your query is entered, the program searches for surnames in the database that might match.

Another friendly touch on this board is that, as soon as you're a registered user, you'll find several messages waiting for you. They're sent to all users, and have some useful information. Logging off is simple; on all PCBoard systems the command is *G* for *goodbye*.

As of this writing, Maddocks now offers more time to users who donate $25 a year to help defray costs, although he does not require anyone to pay. His files area is extensive, and he encourages uploading GEDCOMs.

Figure 5.16

Instant Relatives has a door at the main menu for genealogy searches.

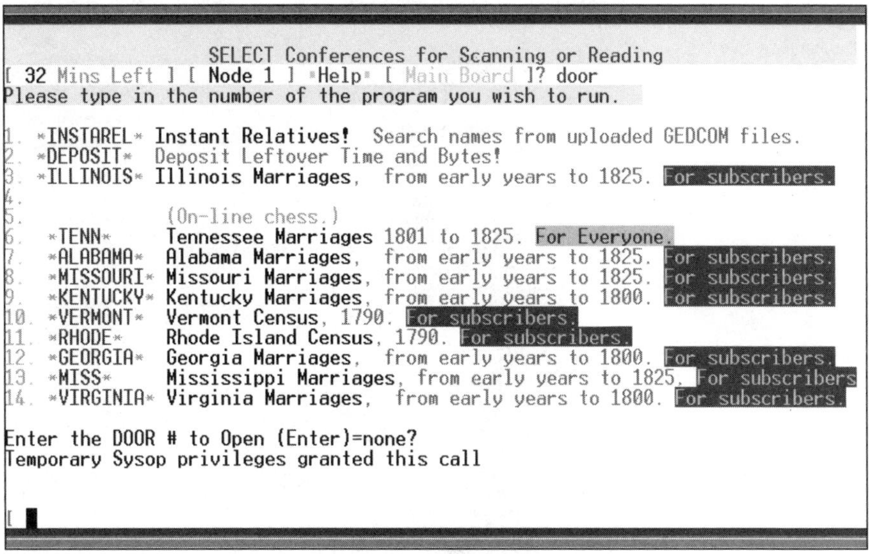

Figure 5.17

The DOOR selection lets you choose from several genealogy programs.

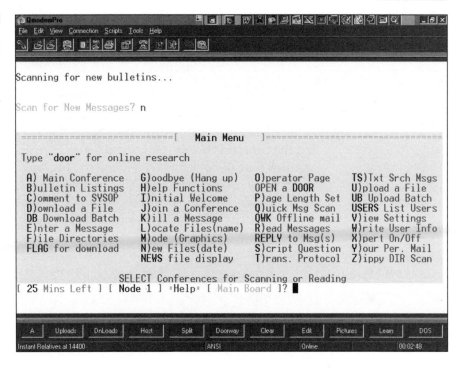

On Your Own

This is just a small sampling of the fine local bulletin board systems that carry genealogy, either in part or as their entire reason for existence. Some that I really liked, but didn't have space to profile completely, follow:

- The Atlanta Genealogy BBS, 770-949-0643 (see Fig. 5.18). All genealogy, all the time; this board is an IGAnet hub, meaning messages get forwarded here to be distributed along the network. The BBS has software to use a front end called PowerAccess that can even automate your first time on the board. There's a Web page describing this board at http://ourworld.compuserve.com/homepages/AtlGenealogy.

- Big Deal BBS, 804-754-0189, centers on adoptee searches. Full of useful resources.

- Ancestors to Descendants, 519-453-9390, also generates a lot of message traffic on the genealogy echoes.

- Three active boards in Texas are the Central Texas Genealogy Connection, 817-753-7970; Family Research, 817-571-1373; and Genealogy

Figure 5.18
The Atlanta Genealogy BBS can be reached with a regular communications program as well as a special front end.

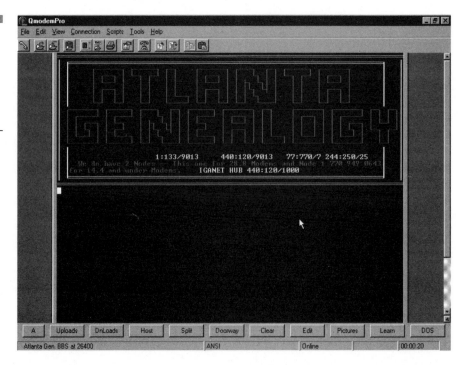

Hotline, 614-855-0955. These three boards generate tons of messages on IGAnet and National Genealogy FidoNet.

More BBS systems are being created all the time. They aren't limited to the United States, either, though I limited myself to the continental United States for this chapter. Because of the variety of BBS nets, you can send mail to and from almost any board in the world, and also sign on to them yourself. You need to search around and find a network or two on a board or two that suits you.

There are several ways to do this. First, ask at your local genealogy meeting or computer users' meeting about what local BBSs are available, especially ones with genealogy on them. Sign on and look at the messages. Almost every message has a tagline with something about the origin of the message, usually the name of the board, and the phone number. Collect enough genealogy messages and you'll soon have quite a list of numbers to try.

For strictly FidoNet genealogy boards, we'll look later at the National Genealogical Society's board, on which Richard Pence keeps a wonderful list of BBSs that carry those echoes. It's updated every month, so I made no attempt to get permission to reproduce it here when you can get a much more current version quite easily.

Finally, look in genealogy magazines and journals. Many BBSs advertise there, as well as in general computer magazines such as *The Computer Shopper*.

CHAPTER

FidoNet

Almost as long as bulletin boards have been around, so has FidoNet. A network system for BBSs, the program was designed to connect the masses at their individual PCs, Macintoshes, and other breeds of computers, allowing free-form communication. This connection is not all the time, as in the Internet, but through modems at scheduled times, usually once a day. The main thing FidoNet does is transfer messages and files among the boards participating in the network.

For the genealogist, FidoNet is useful because of both those activities. There are about a dozen message conferences (called *echoes*) on genealogy, and a file-swapping system to keep you current on the latest shareware and PAF add-ons. The message systems carry anywhere from 10 to 400 messages a day, depending on the subject.

FidoNet has always been a distinct kind of wide area network. The hardware matters somewhat, of course, but the basis for FidoNet is software, which was written because hobbyists and software authors needed utilities to automatically share files, messages, and e-mail among various BBSs.

The first FidoNet software was written by two guys living on opposite coasts: Ken Kaplan and Tom Jennings. The idea was to have a good program for hobbyists who wanted to run a local BBS. These authors required an easy way to swap updates across the continent. The best idea seemed to be to have the computers and modems do it at night, when rates are cheap. So, the programs were set up to fetch the needed data. Legend, in the form of Thom Henderson, has it that this program was concocted from three different programs. The comment was made that "that's a real mongrel," and so the name *Fido* was born. Soon, what was at first a software program to run a BBS became an automated wide area network program as well.

Of course, they weren't the only ones who needed this capability, and it seemed the logical next step was to permit the traffic of private mail messages, called NetMail, between the sysops of various boards along the way. So, the program grew to include routing through hubs, leaving off and picking up messages, either private or public, and then continuing the routine down the line. Thus, we now have EchoMail, or the ability to have a message on a local BBS echoed across several, or even thousands, of other boards.

It got so big that, according to Thom Henderson, the users decided that maybe they needed a framework to manage this system. Thus, the FidoNet Association was born.

"But," says Henderson, who was the last chairman of the last board of directors of this group, "it was shut down. The members had decided they like to be more loose-knit than that." Henderson, author of the ARC programs, says that the organization was just too formal for the sysops on FidoNet. Deep in their hearts, the FidoNet sysops are basically anarchists.

But the advantage of using a FidoNet connection, says sysop Mike Cothran, is "there's more focus on the individual researcher on FidoNet. The Internet still has great resources but the traffic is very dense there."

How FidoNet Works Today

FidoNet is struggling to maintain its identity as a BBS network, not an appendix to the Internet. FidoNet includes about 40,000 bulletin board systems worldwide. The network still exchanges mail and files through modems using a proprietary protocol. The Internet connection with FidoNet, according to the official FidoNet site at http://www.fidonet.org, is now an individual setup, as explained in the following discussion. Most FidoNet sites are not accessible with telnet or ftp, but do carry Internet e-mail and Usenet newsgroups. Despite FidoNet's volunteer history, many sysops now must pay to use this gateway setup, and therefore will sometimes charge those BBS members who use it. This factor, plus the desire of many to access the Internet without being part of it, have led to some tumultuous times on FidoNet recently.

In FidoNet terms, you have nodes and hosts, which are almost synonymous. A *node* is a site made of hosts. Where you're sitting is a *host*. Someone can remotely log on to a host. So, your local BBS can be a host, or a node. The dictionary defines *node* as a point of concentration, a central point. Messages are *echoed* from node to node.

Echo mail is the term on FidoNet for a conference or forum. With echo mail, you're talking to the net at large. With access through a local BBS, you can leave a message to people all over the world. If you leave a message for FidoNet, you assign it to a certain interest group, say Southeast Genealogy. That night, the BBS operator has his or her computer dial a regional hub and upload all messages. The hub knows where the packet came from and will send it to all other BBSs in the region according to which BBS accepts messages on which topics. It also sends it to a national hub, which sends it to every national hub plus every regional hub except the one it received the packet from. The regional hubs also distribute according to what echoes the BBS asks for.

In this processing, echo mail can go anywhere. The backbone knows where it came from and it bundles and sends the messages everywhere except where they came from.

Unless the BBS sysop charges a fee for signing on (some do, some don't, some charge by the message), this looks free to the user. Yet someone, somewhere is paying that long-distance charge. It could be the BBS sysop, who pays the hub sysop, or the university sponsoring a hub. This is why it's so important to stay on the topic of the group to which your message is posted. There are French-only message echoes, and they don't want their time and long-distance calls wasted on messages in German or English. Similarly, echoes specifically for Native American or Jewish genealogy don't need messages about the Civil War unless it's about, for example, a Cherokee or a rabbi involved in that conflict.

The personality of the echo depends on the moderator of the echo. Each echo is required to have at least one moderator, and while this is often a BBS sysop, it is not always. The moderator is required to check that messages are on topic and will often chastise senders who do not adhere to the rule. The moderators do not, however, censor messages.

Be aware that you basically have no privacy on FidoNet, even if a message is sent as private. There's no encoding; the only security is you accepting or not accepting a certain echo's messages.

FidoNet is for the amateur, in the sense of people who do something just for the love of it, whether it pays anything or not. The FidoNet folks love BBSs for their own sake. As with all amateur efforts, it's hard to keep track of it. Some 10,000 BBSs are on the net, and each might claim up to 500 users. But that doesn't really tell you how many people are on the net, Henderson says.

"People who call BBSs call a lot of BBSs," Henderson says. "And some call, register, and disappear. Others are regular users, but of the online files, not the message system. So, on the net, you might have 20,000 people." But that's at any given time. BBSs come and go with dizzying regularity, and members of a defunct BBS have to find another board on the net before they can get back on the EchoMail line.

The sense of community, Henderson says, comes from the message system. It's very big in Europe and Australia, he says, where people love to carry on conversations in written form. FidoNet, while growing, is not doubling every year as it used to, Henderson notes. Still, it's hard to keep up with who's on and who's gone.

Asked what FidoNet's biggest advantage is, Henderson says, "It's free. You pay your phone bill, or a subscription to the local board sometimes to help with his phone bill, and you're in touch with the world, with people on the leading edge. FidoNet people were the first to use protocols, the first to use top-of-the-line modems, the first to figure out how to squeeze every last bit of data into each packet down the line. You know some of these guys go to vendors' shows, and talk about device drivers to support 9,600+ bps. The manufacturer rep says, 'But DOS doesn't do that.' And the sysop is saying, 'Oh, yes it does, if you know how. I do it all the time.' They know how to replace standard UARTS with something that'll go 38,000 bps or better. They'll do what they can to let the users download 1 megabyte in 10 minutes."

Asked what the biggest disadvantage is, Henderson says, "It's free. The sysops can be wonderful, but some can be not nice to deal with for the average user. A lot of them feel their boards are a public service, and try to help the average user. Others feel it's their own baby, and 'I'll do it the way I want to.' To these guys the users are at best unimportant and at worst a nuisance. Remember, these guys are tied into 1,000 other boards, and they sometimes feel they don't need the local user so much."

Many genealogy-only boards have sysops that are thrilled to have new members, though. So shop around your hometown and find a local FidoNet board. One way is to log on to CompuServe at the Roots Forum, download the latest list of bulletin boards, and look for a Fido connection. Another way is to hang out at a local users' group and ask for a local Fido node. Then, after determining which flavor of sysop you have here (the helpful, public-service flavor or the "it's my party and I'll do what I want to" flavor), jump in on the FidoNet EchoMail. You can soon learn how to send a message to the other users of your BBS. And the local area FidoNet. Generally, one keystroke will send your message to everyone who gets that echo on the entire network.

How to Use FidoNet Addresses

To send mail to people using a FidoNet BBS, you need the name they use to log on to that system and its node number. You either have to ask the person you want to mail in person or look at a message from that person, noting the from field and the tagline, which will have the name of the board and a numerical address that looks like this: 1:322/190. The first number tells which of several broad geographic zones the BBS is in (1 represents the United States and Canada, 2 Europe and Israel, 3 Pacific Asia, 4 South America). The second number represents the BBS's network, while the final number is the BBS's FidoNode number in that network. If your electronic pen pal only gives you two numbers (for example, 322/190), it means the system is in zone 1. You can address a personal (as opposed to one that echoes to the whole net) message this way.

The FidoNet/Internet gateway is not as straightforward as it used to be. If you are trying to send messages to and from the Internet and FidoNet, you have to ask your friends for their addresses at their FidoNet boards: instead of a single gateway for all boards, each BBS must now make separate arrangements for Internet news and mail feeds. Therefore, my Internet address at Pot of Gold is now Libbi.Crowe@pog.iquest.com.

Out in Front

FidoNet generally sets the pace for other BBS nets. There are over 1400 FidoNet Echoes, or topic areas, and there are some active and interesting genealogy echoes worth looking for on your local bulletin board systems.

When you first venture into FidoNet, use the BBS's system to subscribe or join the conferences that interest you. Then, using an offline reader, spend a few days just reading messages before you post. If possible, wait for the first of the month to pass, because if the conference has a set of rules, that's usually when it's posted to the network (addressed to ALL). Read the rules and the system bulletins before you begin participating.

The echoes are as amorphous as the number of boards on the net, but the following echoes are popular and fairly stable:

AAGENE African-American Genealogy: This echo focuses on the genealogy of African-Americans in the United States and Canada. The primary moderator and originator of the echo is Mike Wade. It originates from 1:376/140.0 @ fidonet.org and has a message volume of about 100 per month. The moderators are Mike Wade and David Hamiter.

ADOPTEES Adoptees Information Exchange: This is the place to go for help and suggestions for adoptees and birth parents in their search. Discussion of legislation affecting adoptees, birth parents, and adoptive parents. Organizations and agencies offering help with the adoptees and birth parents search are also discussed. This echo gets about 150 messages a week and is moderated by Michael Kirst, Dave Warwick, and Bob Heide.

CAROLINA_GEN Carolina Genealogy: A general conference for genealogy hobbyists who are interested in the specific Southeastern states of North and South Carolina. Those with ancestors from this general area are urged to send queries through this echo to get response from others doing research in the same general area. Moderator approval required for gating into networks other than FidoNet. It has about 30 messages per day and is moderated by Foxy Ferguson.

CHICORA_GEN Genealogy of the Carolinas and Georgia 1650–1865: This echo originates from Carolina Cousin BBS (1:376/140) located in Columbia, South Carolina. The tag name of the echo is CHICORA_GEN. Chicora_Gen focuses on the genealogy of the Carolinas and Georgia from 1650 to 1865. In other words, it focuses on the colonial period to the end of the Civil War. It gets about 500 messages per month. Moderators are David Hamiter, Gene Jeffries, and Van Hoyle.

CIVIL_WAR Civil War History Echo: This is not strictly genealogy, but as the discussion is on historical aspects of the American Civil War, its causes and effects, battles, tactics, the people—military and civilian—and so on, sometimes you can find interesting tidbits to show you where to research next. It's a busy forum, with 350 messages a week and is moderated by Al Thorley and Frank Coleman.

GEN4SALE: This was created to give genealogists a place to buy, sell, or trade any goods or services related to genealogy. It originates from 1:376/140.0, and gets about 100 messages a month. Moderators are David Hamiter and Brent Holcomb.

GENDATA: This is the Tiny Tafel Database: this echo is a method of circulation for one form of genealogy information. These messages consist of a predetermined format and are called *Tiny Tafels*. Discussion of these Tiny Tafels is now permitted within the echo. Anything not related directly to Tiny Tafels is automatically deleted. The TT messages in this echo are archived and distributed via the Genealogy Software Distribution System on a semiregular basis for use on any FidoNet BBS and are intended for use by amateur genealogists doing their own research. The messages sent to this echo are repeated to the BBS networks GTnet, RBBSnet, and Familynet. It gets about 40 messages a week, and the moderators have to approve your message before it goes on. The moderators are John Grove and Michael Kirst.

GENEALOGY National Genealogical Conference: This is the main genealogy message echo. Here, you'll find people exchanging information and data concerning all aspects of genealogy. This conference is primarily oriented toward U.S.–Canadian research and includes queries, requests for help, product/software announcements, and exchange of information between researchers. It gets about 400 messages a day, and is distributed worldwide. The moderators are Don Wilson, Richard Pence, and Frank Williams.

GENEALOGY.CDN The Canadian Genealogy Echo: This one covers topics of discussion including Canadian ancestry, genealogical societies, Canadian genealogical meetings, and announcements and exchanges of data and information. The moderator is Ken Quinn.

GENEALOGY.EUR Genealogy and Family History International: This echo is for discussing anything related to genealogy and family history anywhere in the world, *except* locally within the United States, but immigration to or from the United States is acceptable. It gets 30 messages a day. The moderator is Steve Hayes.

GENEALOGY._WGW Who's Got What: Here you post queries and input to the WGW database. The WGW database is a directory of who possesses what genealogy-related research material. About 50 messages a week pass through here; moderator is Jack Williams.

GENREPLY: The tag for the echo to post a Tiny Tafel Reply. This echo provides a place for users to post reply messages for Tiny Tafels that have been posted in the GENDATA echo. Tiny Tafel generation software may be discussed in this echo. Messages posted here are copied to the WGA_Net. The echo gets about 25 messages a week and is moderated by Michael Kirst and John Grove.

GENSOFT Genealogy Software: This is all about programs to do genealogy, no matter what the platform. Come here to discuss genealogy software, hardware, utilities, how-to, reviews, announcements from suppliers, and help with problems. Distribution is worldwide and the echo gets about 15 messages a day. Moderators are Frank Williams and Richard Pence.

ITALIANO.GEN Italian Genealogy Conference: Here you'll find discussion of the genealogy and family history of Italian-speaking people throughout the world. This list is in English and Italian; it posts about 200 messages a week. Moderators are Rudy Lacchin and Debbi McKay.

JEWISHGEN Jewish Genealogy Conference: This is moderated by Susan King.

SC_GENEALOGY South Carolina Genealogy: This echo focuses on the genealogy in the state of South Carolina; you have to ask moderators Gene Jeffries and David Hamiter to join. It gets about 100 messages a month.

SE_GENEALOGY: This is about genealogy in the southeastern United States: TN, VA, WV, KY, GA, AL, FL, TX, LA, MS, MO, SC, NC, AR, and

MD. A general conference for genealogy. People with ancestors in this general area are urged to send queries through this echo to get prompt response from others who are doing research in the same general area and are more than willing to assist others with the research needed. About 50 messages are posted a day; moderator is Hershel Kreis.

SPANISH.GEN Spanish Genealogy: The place for questions and answers about genealogical research on Spanish surnames. Most of the 50 messages a week are in Spanish, but English and other languages are allowed. Moderators are John Grove, Miny Dittmer, and Fleet Teachout.

TENN_GEN Tennessee Genealogy: This is an open discussion for all individuals interested in researching their family history and tracing their ancestors who lived in or emigrated through the state of Tennessee. It gets about 50 messages a month and is moderated by Foxy Ferguson.

This list is, of course, subject to change, as anarchy sometimes still rules on FidoNet. Some echoes will be added and some may fade away. If you can't find the echo that interests you, you should talk to the sysop about it.

Finding a FidoNet Board

This part is easy; almost any BBS that has networked messages at all has Fido. The trick is finding one with genealogy echoes, all or as many as match your interests.

As mentioned in Chap. 2, first use word of mouth. Ask at the local genealogy meetings and seminars, "Who has a BBS with the genealogy echoes on it?," and give those local ones a try.

If that doesn't work, dial up the National Genealogical Society BBS Genealogy One 703-528-2612 (see Chap. 7) and get the zipped text file GBBSxxxx.zip. (The last four characters will be the month and year as in GBBS1097 for the October 1997 file.)

GBBS is maintained and copyrighted by Richard Cleaveland, with acknowledgment to Richard Pence for his design guidance. Download the latest one, unzip it, and you'll have a text file called GBBSxxxx.TXT, readable by any word processor, of over 1000 worldwide BBS systems carrying at least some of the Fido genealogy echoes. Open it in your favorite word processor, and search for your area code (see Fig. 6.1).

Figure 6.1
The GBBS list is
updated monthly
and can help you
find local BBSs with
the FidoNet geneal-
ogy echoes.

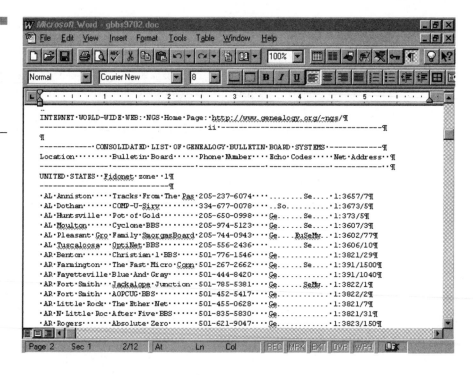

FidoNet Rules

The introduction to this book covered many of the rules you need to remember in FidoNet. Because of the enormous traffic FidoNet carries, it's most important for you to follow these:

- Stay on topic.
- Post to the correct topic echo.
- Quote only what is necessary.
- Include your name in each message and how you can be reached.
- Don't waste time on flames.
- Support your local sysop.

In all, FidoNet is a valuable resource for exchanging information, and usually at a very low cost. There are drawbacks, however.

Sometimes it takes up to four days for a message from one person to another to be relayed around the net, for example, as opposed to the almost instant e-mail of the Internet. Indeed, because of the round-robin way the mail is sent, sometimes the message gets lost completely. This could be due to bad phone lines, power outages, the sysop being sent on travel for his or her real job, and other misadventures that the Internet handles by routing around the problem; FidoNet has no such feature. So, if you don't get an expected answer in a few days, try sending your message again.

Another drawback is the amateur nature of the net: this sometimes means less than professional behavior by some involved. FidoNet flames tend to be intense, but short-lived; learn to take it in stride, and go on with what you need to do.

Finally, because some of the echoes are so very busy, you'll need to use an offline mailer that can filter the messages for you: download only those to *ALL* and those whose subject lines include your surnames, for example. This will save you time, disk space, and eyestrain!

Genealogy One: The National Genealogical Society BBS

Bulletin board systems in general were covered in Chaps. 5 and 6. This chapter is devoted to Genealogy One, the source for many of the messages you find on other systems. Further, it is the place to dial to find the BBS nearest you that carries the NGS's message systems. And, as BBSs go, it is one of the easiest to use, once you set your preferences. Finally, this BBS is a source of information about the NGS itself. For all these reasons, I felt this BBS deserved a chapter all to itself.

The NGS BBS (see Fig. 7.1) is sponsored and provided as one of the services of the National Genealogical Society Computer Interest Group. Use of NGS is free, except for your toll charges if you have to dial long distance. Its sysops are Richard Pence, Frank Williams, and Don Wilson, and the BBS has two telephone numbers. The second line is on a rotary switch, so by calling 703-528-2612, you'll get either line 1 or, if it's busy, line 2. If you call 703-528-2612, you'll receive whichever modem is not busy—therefore it's the best number for most people to call. Both modems should answer on the first ring. If you get more than one ring, then Pence is probably doing maintenance on the BBS and the system is down temporarily. If you get a busy signal calling 703-528-2612, then both lines are busy—not an uncommon occurrence! Here is the BBS's address, phone numbers, and additional information:

Figure 7.1
The opening screen
of the NGS BBS.

4527 17th St. North
Arlington, VA 22207-2399
703-525-0050 (voice)
703-528-2612 (BBS)
109/302 (FidoNet)

Both modems are capable of speeds up to and including 28.8 Kbps and support MNP 4 error-correcting protocol and MNP 5 file compression.

The BBS is only available through direct dial; however, it has some Internet services: Internet e-mail in and out is available to registered users. Your Internet address at NGS is

<firstname>.<lastname>@ngs.blkcat.com

The major Internet Usenet genealogy newsgroups are here, too, treated just like any other e-mail echo.

During the sign-up process, choose and record your password carefully; this BBS software is case-sensitive when it comes to passwords! Once you have registered, you can do a fast sign-on: at the first name prompt type

<first name>;<last name>;;<password><CR>

Don't use any spaces and separate the fields by semicolons. Put only one carriage return at the end of the line. Don't put < and > symbols in your string, just the correct name and password as you registered.

How It Began

"It started in my basement," Richard Pence says. He had seen a BBS with some genealogy on it and thought it was a great idea. A friend said he had a computer to donate if someone would set it up. Pence did and ran it out of his home for a while until it really took off.

"We had come from a conference in 1982, right before we had this meeting [that started the BBS]. Paul Anderek had had an early experience, and kids had messed up his system, so we learned from that quickly," says Pence. There's nothing on the board of interest to game-playing, security-cracking adolescents.

The board was one of the first to log on to the FidoNet genealogy echo; now it's sort of home base for that set of messages on FidoNet.

Pence is famous throughout the online genealogy world for starting the monthly updates on boards carrying FidoNet genealogy echoes. The list of genealogy BBSs, now compiled by Richard Cleaveland, is in File Area 2 in GBBSyymm.ZIP and GBBSyymm.TXT, where *yymm* is the year and month of the file. You can download the text file and read it in any text or word processor.

As a new user on the NGS BBS, your first step should be to read the bulletins and the system information files available from the main menu. These will help you learn to use the system more effectively. Capture them to your buffer file to refer to later.

This information about the National Genealogical Society is also in File Area 2. You can download the file NGS.ZIP to get all of the information in the 10 or so separate files. All the files on this BBS available for download are in File Area 2 in the file NGS-BBS.ZIP.

Messages

An abundance of messages on any genealogical topic you can imagine is the primary feature of this BBS. You can leave public or private messages on NGS to seek assistance with your research or respond to others seeking help. The only places you can leave private messages on this system are to the sysop, the Local Message Area, and the NetMail Area. Even then, you're reminded by the sysops that they can read the private messages. All messages entered into the FidoNet National and International Conferences are public messages and can be read by all callers. The NGS BBS has national/international message areas for the following subjects:

General Genealogy: All these are public messages and are for general questions and discussion.

NGC: The National Genealogical Conference deals mostly with U.S. genealogy (see Fig. 7.2). This is the most widely read genealogy echo and your messages will receive the greatest distribution here.

Genealogy Software: Information about *all* genealogy software programs.

European Genealogy: The International Genealogical Conference. This echo area is for messages pertaining to international genealogy only— please do not use this area for U.S. only genealogy messages.

Jewish Genealogy: For special Jewish-related problems.

Southeast U.S. Genealogy: Use this area *only* for messages concerning the Dixie states.

Figure 7.2

The NGS FidoNet echo is the most widely read of the message bases.

Genealogy Data: Use this area *only* to circulate a Tiny Tafel—replies to messages you see here should be sent by U.S. mail, NetMail, or be placed in the NGC Message Area.

The local message areas cover the following:

Messages to the SYSOP: Private questions about using the BBS.

Local messages: Public or private messages to callers of this BBS. These messages are not transmitted to any other BBS. Private messages can be read by the sysops and the addressee only.

The BBS is set to delete messages over 30 days old. It will keep about 15,000 messages available in the message areas. Messages are renumbered each Tuesday morning, once a week.

The messages are available through the QSO mail reader. QSO allows you to use any offline reader that supports the QWK packet format to interact with TBBS, the bulletin board software. When used in conjunction with a QWK-compatible offline reader, QSO allows you to do the following:

- Download mail from selected conferences (either all mail or only mail that's addressed to you) for reading offline.

- Reply offline using any reader that supports the QWK format, and use QSO to bulk upload your replies and have them integrated into the message base as though you had made those replies online. All reply linkages, private/public flags, and so forth, are maintained as if you had entered the message(s) online.

■ Customize its operation so that only desired actions take place.

■ Reduce connect time. Instead of staying online to read and reply to messages, you can do this offline. If you're calling long distance, this can result in a drastically reduced phone bill.

■ Read and reply to messages at your leisure. Once you download a bundle of mail, you can read messages in that bundle any time you want. Upload the replies back to the system whenever you want.

■ You need to obtain a QWK-compatible offline mail-reader package before you can use QSO. Since most are released as shareware, they're usually available from BBSs supporting the QWK offline readers. On NGS BBS, they can be found in File Area 1 with other General Utilities. Remember, if your reader is shareware, you should register your copy with its author.

■ When you first select the TBBS menu item that enters QSO, you'll see an opening screen with the following options:

—Configure User Parameters
—Download Messages
—Upload Messages
—Keyword File Upload
—Goodbye (Hangup)
—Go back to the Main Menu (Quit)

If you've never used QSO before, you must first press *C* to select the Configure User Parameters menu. There, you'll select the message conferences you want QSO to get for you, and you'll also be able to configure several options, following. You must at least select some message areas before QSO will do anything else useful.

Download Messages. This is one of the two QSO commands you'll use most often. By pressing D to select this option, you cause QSO to scan all the conferences you've selected for new messages and package them into a QWK packet for transmission to your offline reader. QSO will also add to this packet any other files you've selected. After the packet has been assembled, it's then downloaded to you. You download a QWK packet just as you would any other file.

Upload Messages. This is the other most frequently used QSO main menu command. When you select this command, QSO will prompt you to upload the NGS-BBS.REP file that your offline reader produced when you entered replies to messages you previously obtained with the Download Messages command. After you've uploaded this file to QSO, it will unzip it and enter your replies into the message base.

Keyword File Upload. This command will prompt you to upload an ASCII file that contains keywords to qualify the message download command's actions for this session with QSO. You can use up to 25 keywords in this file. The format of a keyword file is discussed later in this chapter.

Goodbye (hangup). This command will cause an immediate log off from the system.

Quit to TBBS. This command exits QSO and returns to the TBBS menu from which you entered QSO (main menu).

User configuration. The first time you use QSO, you must do two things: select the Configure User Parameters option and select one or more message conferences.

Many QWK interfaces allow you to select which archive format is used. QSO uses only the PKZip 1.x implode archiving format, so this can't be selected. You must set up your offline reader to use PKZip with QSO. Other archivers cannot be used! (PKZ110.EXE is available for download in File Area 1.) The options you can choose to set are as follows:

Option Change. Selecting this command allows you to enter the number of one of the options listed on the status portion of the screen to toggle it from No to Yes (and vice versa). You can also enter just the number directly and QSO will assume the O selection automatically. These options configure the operation of QSO for you in several detailed ways. Let's examine what each one does.

Include Enclosed Files. If this option is set to Yes, QSO will include any files that are enclosed in messages you retrieve in your QWK packet automatically. Note that if there's more than one enclosed file with the same name, you might have trouble retrieving the files from the QWK packet. If this option is set to No, then only the message text will be in your QWK packet.

Download Your Replies. If you set this option to Yes, your QWK packet will include any messages you've previously posted (either online or by uploading them as replies using QSO). If this option is set to No, the messages you've originated won't be enclosed in your QWK packet.

Send Welcome Screen. If this option is set to Yes, then QSO will include the initial welcome file you see when you log on to this BBS in your QWK packet.

Send News Screen.   If this option is set to Yes, then QSO will include the system news file for NGS BBS in your QWK packet. Note that this option has been set to include the news file only when the file has changed.

Send Logoff Screen.   If this option is set to Yes, QSO will include the goodbye file you see when you log off this BBS in your QWK packet.

BBS Time Stamp on Replies.   If this option is set to No, QSO will post your replies with the time and date your offline reader put in them. If you set this option to Yes, then QSO will post your replies with the time and date it enters them into the BBS message base.

Logoff after U/L Replies.   Normally, QSO will return to its main menu after you upload your reply packet and QSO processes it. If this option is set to Yes, then QSO will automatically log you off after your uploaded packet is processed. Note that if set to Yes, you should do your upload as the last part of your QSO session, or you'll have to dial back into the system to carry on with your session!

Logoff after D/L Msgs.   Normally, QSO will return to its main menu after you download your QWK packet. If this option is set to Yes, then QSO will automatically log you off after your QWK packet is successfully downloaded. Note that this means you should do your download last!

Suppress NDX File Creation.   This option should normally be set to No. For some offline reader programs, however, the NDX files aren't necessary. If you have such a program, then you can set this option to Yes and no NDX files will be included in your QWK packets, saving disk space.

Scan for New Bulletins.   If this option is set to Yes, then QSO will send you any of the bulletin files from this BBS that have been updated since your last call. If this option is set to No, then no bulletin files will be included in your QWK packet.

D/L Packet w/o Messages.   Sometimes you'll scan for new messages and find that none have been found since your last QSO session. If this option is set to No, then no packet will be downloaded until messages are available. If you set this option to Yes, however, then QSO will still package any new bulletins, service files, and other nonmessage data and transmit it to you in a QWK packet that has no messages.

D/L New Files Listing.   If this option is set to Yes, then QSO will include a listing of any new files that have been posted since your last call. This option is very time-consuming! Do not select it on a regular basis unless you're willing to wait the time (and pay the toll) it takes to scan all file areas for new files.

Only selected confs in DAT. If this option is set to No, then QSO will include the names and numbers of all conferences this BBS provides to you in your QWK packet's CONTROL.DAT file. This allows you to use the remote configuration Add and Drop options. However, when a system provides many conferences, it can be annoying to see all the conferences listed on your offline reader screen. You can set this option to Yes to limit the list to only those conferences you've selected to download.

Send Session Log. If this option is set to Yes, then QSO will include the file SESSION.TXT in your QWK packet. This file is a transcript of your online session and includes all QSO screens and your input as it occurred. If this option is set to No, then SESSION.TXT isn't included in your QWK packet.

Omit Download Verify Prompt. If this option is set to No, then QSO will prompt you after the message scan to begin the download. If you set the option to Yes, then QSO will immediately begin the download process when the message scan completes. I keep this set to No, so I can abort more easily.

Conference Selection. This command will display all the message conferences available to you through QSO. Some conference numbers might be missing, either because the BBS doesn't use them or because you haven't been given access to a particular message conference. You'll see one or more screens of conference names that look much like this (a leading asterisk indicates the conference is selected):

Available Conferences
3	LOCAL
4	GENEALOGY
5	JEWISHGEN
9	GENEEUR
11	GENDATA
15	TECHNET109
16	SEGENEALOGY
17	GENSOFT

Select Conference, (HELP or QUIT)? At this prompt you can use the commands Select, Deselect, or Reset to select conferences and/or reset the high message pointers. You can also simply enter conference numbers to toggle the selected status. Conference numbers can be listed individually, as a range (specified by lowest number and highest number), like this: 4-17. You can also select all conferences with the keyword *All.*

The high message pointer indicates which messages will be scanned and placed in your QWK packet. You can set the high message pointer explicitly using the Reset command, or include a pointer reset command as part of a Select command. The syntax of the Select command is:

```
SELECT conf [conf] [conf] ... [pointersetting]
```

where *conf* specifies one or more conferences (#, the number sign, is a single conference number in decimal, *l–h* is a range specifying all conferences from *l* to *h* inclusive, and *ALL* specifies all conferences).

The variable pointer setting specifies the new value of the high message (# is an explicit message number, *LOW+n* specifies *n* above the lowest message in the conference, and *HIGHn* specifies *n* below the highest message in the conference). For example:

```
SELECT ALL HIGH-50
```

would select all listed conferences and reset all high pointers to 50 below the highest message in the conference, and:

```
SELECT 1
```

would select conference 1, which doesn't affect the high message pointer. High message pointers default to the high message pointer you had on the conference before entering QSO. The following:

```
SELECT 10-15 HIGH-10
```

would select conferences 10, 11, 12, 13, 14, and 15 and set the high message pointer to 10 below the last message in each conference. The Deselect command has the same syntax as the Select command except that it doesn't allow resetting of the high message pointer. For example:

```
DESELECT 5-11
```

would deselect any selected conferences in the range 5 through 11. The Reset command has the same syntax as the Select command, but it won't select any deselected message conferences. It allows you to reset high message pointers without affecting the select status. For example:

```
RESET 10-15 HIGH-10
```

would set the high message pointers of any selected conferences between 10 and 15 to 10 less than the highest message in the conference.

Protocol Selection.   This command allows you to select your preferred filetransfer protocol for use when uploading and downloading QWK packets to and from QSO. You can either be asked each time for your protocol selection or pick a default that will be used automatically.

Limits Configuration.   This command allows you to set your own limits for QWK packet creation. When selected, you will be prompted for the maximum number of messages QSO is allowed to place in one packet, as well as the maximum number of messages allowed per conference. Some offline mail readers have internal limits on the number of messages they can handle per packet and per conference. If your reader has such limits, you should configure QSO not to exceed those limits.

Downloading a Packet

Once you've configured QSO, you're ready to download a QWK packet. Do this by selecting the Download Messages command from the main QSO menu.

If you have many messages to scan, this process can take a good while. If you want to abort the scan, press either *S* to stop, or Ctrl+C or Esc to abort. The scanning will abort immediately, and you'll return to the main QSO menu. All pointers will be reset to their status prior to the scan (i.e., there will be no effects from the partial scan you aborted).

Begin the download process by answering *Y* to the prompt at the end of the message scan. QSO will next prepare the message portion of the QWK packet and then add in any nonmessage files (bulletins, services, etc.) that your configuration demands. All these files are combined into a file named id.QWK (where *id* is the identifier the sysop has established for this system) as a PkZip format archive.

Note that if you've already downloaded a packet earlier in the day, QSO will change the last letter of the packet name to prevent overwriting your previous packet. The change creates files named .QW1, .QW2, and so forth, then .QWA through .QWJ for a total of 21 unique packet names in a 24-hour period. Not all mail packagers do this!

Uploading a Key File for a Selective Retrieve

You can condition a message scan to select only certain messages by uploading a key file prior to doing the Download Messages command. To upload a keyword file, you must select the Keyword File Upload command from the main QSO menu. You'll be prompted to upload the file and QSO will receive it. This file is stored in your temporary directory for use during the next Download Messages command.

A keyword file is an ASCII file that allows you to select which messages you want to receive. Each line of the file is a one-key selection filter, and you can have a maximum of 20 keys in a single key file. The keys are not case sensitive, that is, they will match either upper- or lowercase strings in the message. The format of a key line is as follows:

[/] [+|–] [(conf)] keytext

If the line begins with the / (slash) character, then this key applies only to the From: and To: name fields in the message. If there's no leading / character, then the key applies to the message Subject: field and the body of the message text. The + (plus sign) or – (minus sign) characters are used to indicate if you want only messages that contain this key (+) or only messages that don't contain this key (–). If neither + nor – is specified, then + is assumed. This is how you can filter out messages from a certain person, often called the twit filter.

If a conference number in parentheses precedes the key, then this key applies to only the specified conference. If there's no conference number given, then the key applies to all conferences. The remainder of the line (beginning with the first nonblank character) is the key text to use for selection. A keyword file is deleted after a scan is done, so you can do multiple scans with different keyword files by uploading a new keyword file between each scan.

Uploading Responses

As you read messages offline (using your QWK-compatible offline reader program), you can reply to messages. If so, your reader program will generate a file named NGS-BBS.REP, which contains those replies. To post those messages on this BBS, you need to select the Upload Messages command from the main QSO menu.

You'll be prompted to select a protocol (if you haven't set a default) and then you can upload the .REP file. Once the file is uploaded, QSO will decompress it and post your reply messages into the TBBS message base. After this process completes, you'll return to the main QSO menu (unless you've set your configuration to log off after uploading replies).

A final word about messages: be sure to leave a message to the sysop as you sign off if you have questions or encounter problems. That person will do his or her best to answer as quickly as possible, usually within a week.

CHAPTER 8

Everton Publisher's BBS

This chapter will show you a typical for-fee genealogy BBS system. There are several of these around, some direct dial, available through the Internet or the World Wide Web. Everton's is available in both ways, and so is a good example.

The respected genealogical publishing house, Everton's, has for years been in the vanguard of American genealogists, so it's no surprise that it has a helpful, usable, and online service. It's not as cozy as some of the homegrown ones, and of course there are fees, but it's very good. You can get there by dialing up just as you can any bulletin board, or you can use telnet. Furthermore, the services are now available via a Web interface. I'll deal just a little bit with the BBS interface (for those of you who use or like older machines and operating systems) as well as tour the Web site.

The Old-Fashioned Way

You can dial up the BBS at the following phone number or sign onto your local Internet Service Provider and telnet to bbs.everton.com. Figure 8.1 shows the welcome screen to On-Line Search, Everton Publisher's

Figure 8.1
The welcome screen to On-Line Search, Everton Publisher's for-fee bulletin board.

genealogical bulletin board. Figure 8.2 shows the main menu. The following are Everton's address and access numbers:

P.O. Box 368
Logan, Utah 84323-0368
Attn: Online Search
800-443-6325 (voice)
801-752-6095 (data)
801-752-0425 (fax)
ale@cc.us.edu (e-mail)

Everton's BBS rates for subscribers to *Genealogical Helper* are $59.50 for 6 months and $89.50 for 12 months. For nonsubscribers to *Genealogical Helper,* you can use the services for one month for $15.00, $29.50 for 6 months, and $49.50 for 12 months. You can also subscribe to the online service plus its magazine *Genealogical Helper,* one year of both $66.50 and six months $46.50. You can register online by credit card or send a check.

Besides several FidoNet echoes, the outstanding feature of this board is a set of searchable databases, which we'll look at later (see Fig. 8.3). On-Line Search began in September 1992, with two computers and two phone lines. Today it has a unique searchable database of about 2 million names

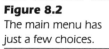

Figure 8.2
The main menu has just a few choices.

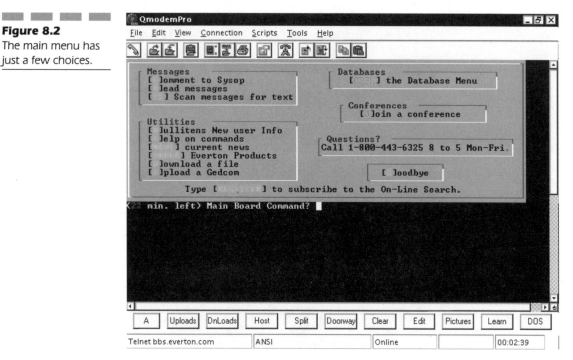

Figure 8.3
The Everton BBS has
16 databases, but
only 2 are open to
the public.

Figure 8.3
The Everton BBS has
16 databases, but
only 2 are open to
the public.

and Internet access. It's not information you'll find anywhere else, and it's cross-referenced with the names and addresses of over 150,000 submitters.

The BBS software here is PCBoard which has a built-in QWK mail function. The first time you log on and thereafter as a nonsubscriber, you get about 30 minutes a day.

The first time you log on, you receive the standard warnings about using real names, not misbehaving, and so on. Then you're led through a registration questionnaire. Be sure to select the protocol for downloads you want to use; it will save time later. At the main menu, type *register* to become a subscriber. When you subscribe to On-Line Search, you'll be able to

- Access the BBS for 30 minutes each day
- Access all the databases
- Leave messages for other users
- Reply to messages
- Access future databases or conferences when available

Each time you log on, you're told whether there are new items in News and Bulletins. A sample News is shown in Fig. 8.4.

Figure 8.4
Current news for the system is presented at logon. By typing *N*, you can avoid the automatic display and read it from the News menu instead.

Searching the Databases

As mentioned before, an outstanding feature of this board is the databases. The following example will perform a search in the Roots Cellar, Volume 1. This one is available to you the first time you call; most of the other databases are open only to subscribers. All the databases have a similar design and use the same commands for the searches. This example will take you through the search process, narrowing the search, and adding the information to a download list.

First, enter the ROOT1 database. To do this, type *Open* and then press Enter at the Main Board Command line. As a nonsubscriber, you can use the ROOT-1 database, so choose *1*.

To search for SPENCER, press *A*. This will take you to the surname field. Type *Spencer* in the surname field and then press Enter. To start the search, type *S*. To search the entire ROOT1 database will take approximately 35 seconds and will yield several records. (If you want to stop the search at any time, press any key.)

You now have the results of the search for SPENCER. With the results on the screen, you can move to the next page (type *N*), the previous page (type *P*), or go to a certain page (type *O* and then enter the number of the page you want to go to).

If you want to narrow the search by adding a first name, type *B*. The cursor will be in the first name field. Type *Abraham* for the first name and press Enter. (Whenever the cursor returns to the top of the screen after you enter a search criterion, you can press *S* to search again or add more criteria for the search.)

If you want to add a date and event for the example, type *C* and the cursor will move to the event field. Events used are: B (birth), D (death), M (marriage), and R (resided). Type the event you want to search (*B, D, M,* or *R*) and press Enter. Then type *D*. The cursor will move to the date field. You can enter dates in two ways. First, if you know the exact year you can type the entire year, for example, *1878*. Second, If you want to have the entire decade searched you can type *187*. The second option would give you any of the SPENCERs in the 1870s.

A useful command is Cross-Reference to the Submitter. Once you have some results, type *X*. You'll be asked:

Cross-reference which number? [ ]

For this example, the submitter number (in the far right-hand column) was 12290, so type this number and press Enter. You'll be shown the person who submitted the information. When you get the submitter's address, you'll be asked if you want to add the information to a download list:

Do you want to add this information to the download list? [ ]

If you choose *Y,* the name will be added to a list in preparation for downloading. If you'd like to add the ancestor names to a list to download, press *L*. You'll be asked:

From which page? [

Type in the starting page number.

To which page? [

Type the ending page number. The download limit for each database is 90 individuals per database per day—about eight pages. The computer will then ask:

Are you sure?

At this point, you're ready to download the information that you've searched to your computer with the D command. As this board is accessible up to 14.4K, you can get a lot of information in a short visit!

The Web Connection

As fun as the BBS is via dial-up or telnet, it's even nicer via the World Wide Web. You have to have a forms-capable browser in order to use it though, something such as Microsoft Internet Explorer or Netscape Navigator. In your browser's address window, type the following:

http://rro.everton.com/index.html

to access the nonsubscriber's page, just to test the system. The opening page is shown in Fig. 8.5.

"The Website is an extremely different interface from the old, BBS System," notes Darrin Hobbs, "but all of the same information are contained on both systems. The purpose of the BBS now is to maintain a way into our information for those who do not have internet access. They are tied together, because they use the same databases and message bases, but are just a different interface."

Scroll down the opening page until you see the Free Trial Databases link, and click on it. As with the BBS, you'll first be asked to give some information about yourself, and once you enter the information, you have

Figure 8.5
You can get the same information via the Web.

a choice of four databases you can search for free: Roots Cellar, GEDSRCH, Photofind, and Vietnam Casualty. The first two are the same ones on the dial-up BBS, but the latter two are only available via the Web. For this example, let's look at the Vietnam Casualty database. The database is a list of known U.S. military casualties from the Vietnam Conflict. The form is in Fig. 8.6; fill in what information you have and the results can be displayed in your browser or put in a file you download and read later.

Messages

On both the BBS and the Web site, you can access messages. You can click on the link Messages on the main free area page, shown in Fig. 8.7. The advantage to the Web site is that the queries are archived and can be searched by date or text string. In the Web version, you see four links:

- Surname Queries, as you'd guess, are for specific family name messages.
- Research Queries are for questions and answers about genealogical techniques.

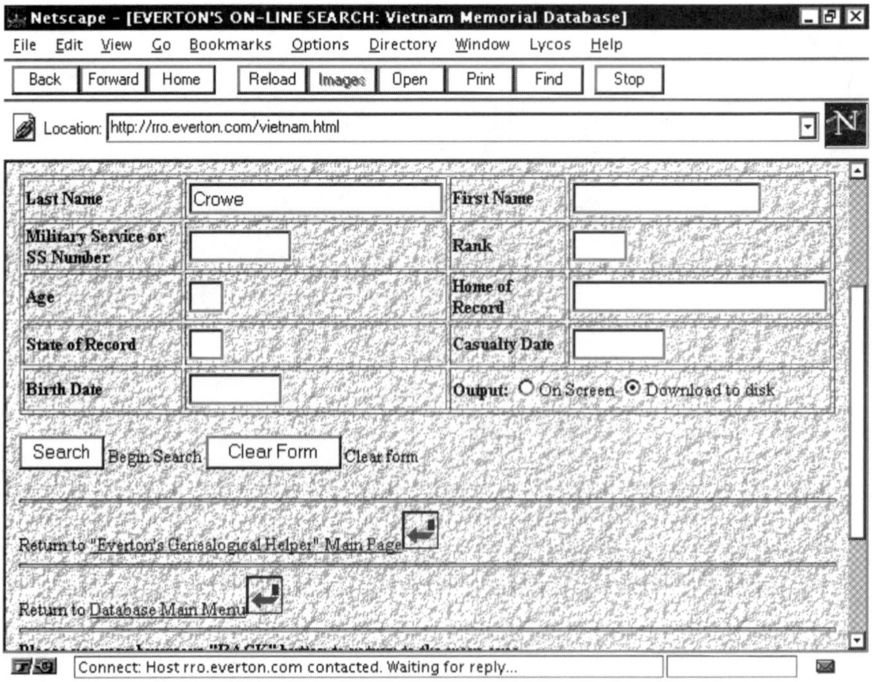

Figure 8.6
Fill in what information you have, and the Web page will search the database.

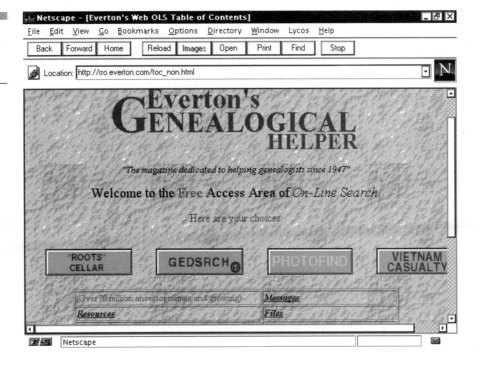

- General Questions about the Web site itself.
- The ubiquitous Frequently Asked Questions file.

Another link, Internet Conferences, leads you to the more popular Usenet genealogy groups. Your browser must be set up to find your Internet Service Provider's news server in order for you to follow these links.

There are also other message bases in the subscribers-only area.

Another good link off the main Web page is the Genealogical Resources page. Here you'll find an online example of *Genealogical Helper* magazine, links to pages, and resources and information for the beginning genealogist.

Finally, you can click on the Files link from the page shown in Fig. 8.7. This leads you to a page with an essay on the types of genealogical files you'll find on the Internet and links to some of the better sites that hold them. As of this writing, however, the page is over a year old, and so not as current as it could be.

This is a very quick overview of Everton's online services. You can access a tutorial at http://rro.everton.com/tutorial.html for more detailed explanations.

Family Sites

This is a new project at Everton Publishers which will allow your family from around the world to easily correspond online. A sample is shown in Fig. 8.8.

You may consider this your own Family Home Page. Members of your family who have Internet access can read and post messages to the entire family 24 hours a day. This service is offered for $30 a year to paying subscribers of the online service, $60 a year to nonsubscribers.

To do it, you can send in up to three pages of information, a total of four photographs. Then a secure Web site is set up for you: only those who know your family username and password will be able to view them, aside from the system administrators at Everton's, of course.

Your site will have a private message area where you can post, read, and browse your family messages. If some family members are not online yet, you can easily download a week of messages to your own computer, print them out and mail them to the unconnected in your family. And there's an archive service, where every six months, the staff will save all of your family messages and send them on disks (for a nom-

Figure 8.8
One service Everton's offers is a newsletter/message/communication site for a whole family, password-protected.

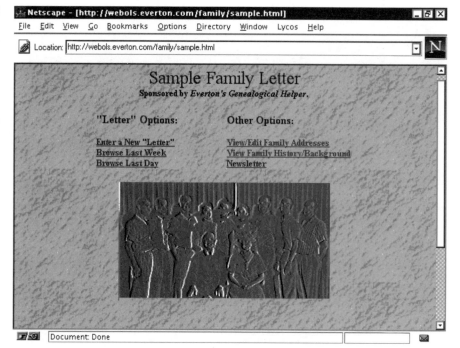

inal fee) to your family host. This disk will come with its own search engine.

The package also includes a family data page you and your family can create and edit online with e-mail links to each individual, home addresses, phone, birthday, and miscellaneous information all viewable only by your family.

There will also be a newsletter page where you can put upcoming events like reunions for all family members to see.

Other Services

Everton's also offers subscribers online chat, almost every day and sometimes on special subjects, and online genealogy courses.

Everton's is an example of how genealogy services for profit can be offered online in a very usable form.

Online Library
Card Catalogs

One of the most wonderful things about the online world is the plethora of libraries going to electronic card catalogs. This speeds up the search when you're physically present in the library, of course. With an online card catalog and many terminals scattered throughout the building, you don't have to look up your subject, author, or title on one floor and then go to another to actually find the reference source. If your local library hasn't computerized its card catalog, it probably will soon.

But oh, the joy of looking in the card catalog before you actually visit the library. You know immediately whether that library owns the title. You can find out with a few more keystrokes whether that title is on the shelf, on reserve, on loan to someone else, or lost without a trace. If the title in question isn't at that library or branch, you can find out if it's available on interlibrary loan. Some more advanced systems will even let you enter your library card number, in effect checking the book out to yourself before you get there. All before you leave home.

Card Catalogs with Telnet

Currently, the most common connection to card catalogs is via telnet. Don't forget Hytelnet, which I mentioned in Chap. 1; the latest edition will have hundreds of libraries available via telnet. A typical one is the South Carolina State Library card catalog. You need a program that can telnet: either a telnet client such as Yawtel, or a communications program like Procomm, Qmodem, HyperACCESS, or the like. Tell your browser under Options (or Preferences) your telnet application's location on your disk, the program name, and command to launch it in telnet mode. Then when you tell the browser the address telnet://leo.scsl.state.sc.us, the telnet application is automatically launched. In Figs. 9.1 and 9.2, I'm using HyperACCESS, but any program that can emulate telnet will do.

The LION system at the South Carolina Library is very typical of an online card catalog. Incidentally, you may often dial these up directly, instead of using telnet, and the interface looks much the same.

The Main Menu of LION is as shown in Fig. 9.1. Choosing the first item, I'm presented the opening menu, which lists the commands I can use: S= to search for subject, A= to search for author, and so on. Typically, I go for the subject search first. I have ancestors in Edgefield County, South Carolina, so first I enter

    S=Edgefield.

Figure 9.1
Telnetting to a card catalog looks just like dialing it up with a regular communications program.

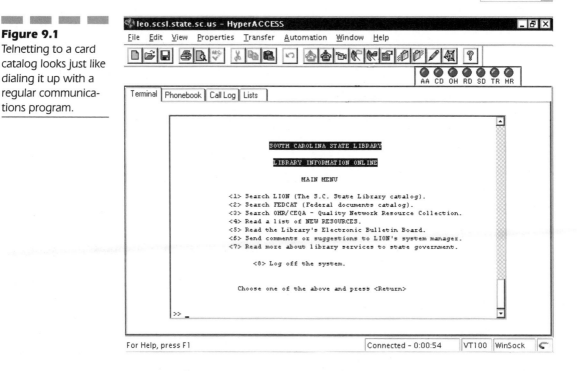

Figure 9.2
You'll typically be given a command list, which includes subject. Here, I've searched for Edgefield County, SC genealogy and got three hits in the holdings.

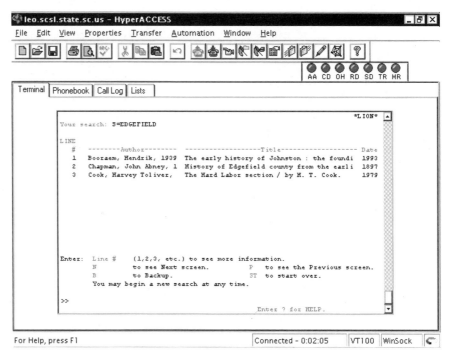

The results had two screens of categories, and one of them was Edge-field—Genealogy. Selecting that one from the menu, I get the listing in Fig. 9.2. From here, I can look at the complete card on any of these, including how many copies the library has and which ones are available for check out at this moment, as in Fig. 9.3. Many card catalogs are set up with this particular program.

Card Catalogs with TN3270

Telnet is fairly straightforward in a plain vanilla setup such as the South Carolina State Library. Occasionally, you'll be asked for a terminal type in which case, stick with VT100. It's the most common. But sometimes you'll find an oddball site that uses an odd interface called TN3270.

One example is the Books Division of the South Carolina Library (http://www.sc.edu/library/socar/books.html): if you want to access its card catalog via the World Wide Web, you have to get and tell your browser about a TN3270 helper application. Many browsers are set up for telnet, but this one requires a TN3270 program. How sad to see such a valuable resource hidden behind a curtain of old, clunky interface!

Figure 9.3
The catalog card for one of the books shows an available copy.

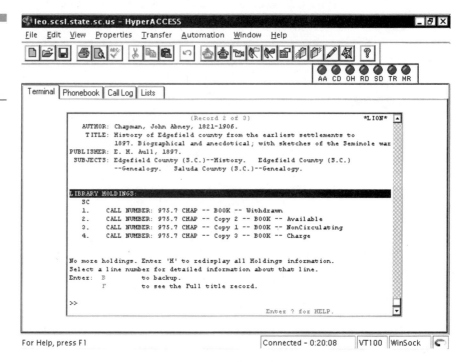

But there are solutions. A freeware TN3270 client can be found at http://helpdesk.uvic.ca/how-to/support/windows/qws3270/qws3270.exe. Other versions, some free, some cheap, at ftp://snoopy.tblc.lib.fl.us/pub/users/cpl/qws.exe. Other TN3270 clients can be found at the following sites:

ftp.cdrom.com q3270v26.zip (153K)

ftp.digital.com q3270v26.zip (153K)

http://tucows.iwebstudio.com/files/q3270v25.zip (145K, 117K)

ftp://ftp.ccs.queensu.ca/pub/msdos/tcpip/qws3270.zip (71K)

Again, you have to tell your browser under Preferences (or Options) and the Applications what the location and name of your TN3270 program is. Then when you click on or enter the link for USCAN (tn3270://univscvs.csd.sc.edu/), the program is launched. This one works much like telnet, except you have several buttons at the bottom. Often what they do is decided by the server you've connected: Clear, for example, sometimes takes you back a page or just clears the screen in others.

The first two screens of this catalog system let you choose which collection, the university's or the medical library, and then you can begin your search. This system allows not only subject, author, and title, but also keyword searches (see Fig. 9.4). This means that *genealogy Edgefield* will have meaning to the system. And sure enough, as in Fig. 9.5, I got 35 hits of

Figure 9.4
Some older systems still use a format called TN3270. You need a special client for such systems.

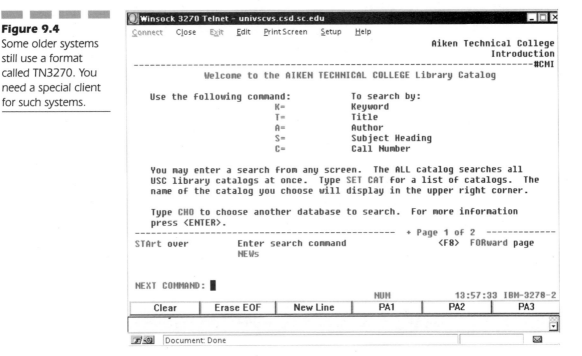

Figure 9.5
Your *F* keys work
with a TN3270 sys-
tem: F8 goes forward
a page, F6 forward a
record, and so on.

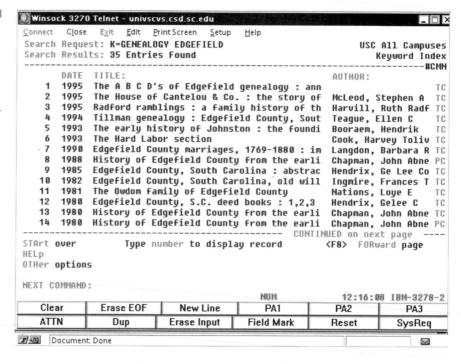

Figure 9.5
Your *F* keys work
with a TN3270 sys-
tem: F8 goes forward
a page, F6 forward a
record, and so on.

books that might help. In this format, seeing the complete card means first selecting the record number and then using the F7 and F8 keys to page back and forth in the record; the F5 and F6 keys will take you back and forward one record each.

Card Catalogs on the Web

An exciting addition to this mode of research is that many card catalogs are now reachable via the World Wide Web.

Most commonly these are connected to a telnet server as previously described, but many have taken away the tedious text interface and added a World Wide Web page that submits the commands for you.

A wonderful example is the UTNETCAT at the University of Texas at Austin (http://dpweb1.dp.utexas.edu/lib/utnetcat/). You can use the Web page's form to search by author, title, subject, or any combination, as in Fig. 9.6. The results link you to the catalog card.

Another, slightly more complicated one is at the University of Alabama in Huntsville's site. By going directly to the card catalog at http://libsirsi

Figure 9.6
UTNETCAT is one
Web-based card
catalog.

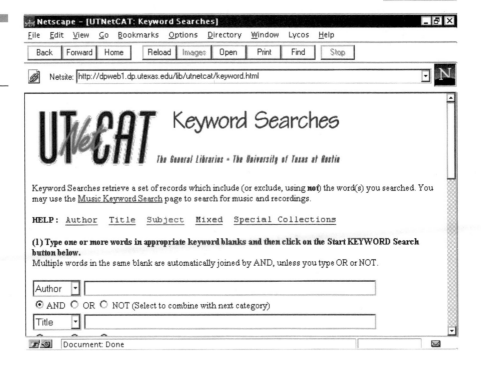

.uah.edu/uhtbin/cgisirsi/22/1/1 (see Fig. 9.7), you can choose one of several ways to search. You can find items which contain certain words or phrases in any field. Using the combination option, you can specify that words, author names, title words, or subject terms must have a specific relationship to each other. If you would rather find an item written by a particular person, an author search is for you. If you know most or all words of a title, find out if the library has it and where it is. Even if you don't know an author or title, you can find items in the library by subject. You can find more specific items if you can enter an author with title. You can check on recent issues of magazines with the periodical title option.

For this search, I chose Combination, and looked for *genealogy* in any field, and *Alabama* in the subject field. The results, shown in Fig. 9.8, came up with seven Alabama genealogy books. By clicking on the icon by a result, I can see the author, publication date, and so forth, and several items in the card catalog will be links to cross-referenced entries. You can print the results or have them e-mailed to your account. Designed by SIRSI, this system is becoming more common among libraries.

Another nice card catalog on the Web is the Library of Virginia's system. What's wonderful about this one: the library's collection of Bible

Figure 9.7
UAH's catalog search
is complicated but
powerful.

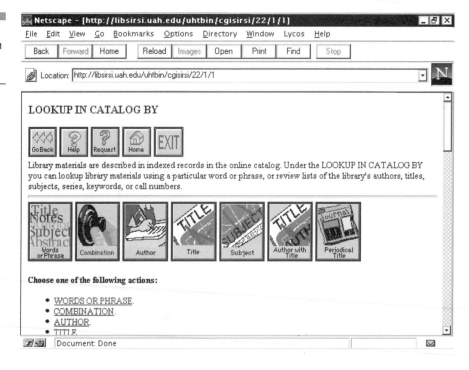

Figure 9.7
UAH's catalog search
is complicated but
powerful.

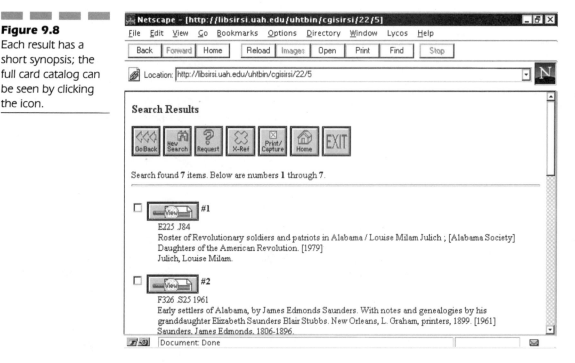

Figure 9.8
Each result has a
short synopsis; the
full card catalog can
be seen by clicking
the icon.

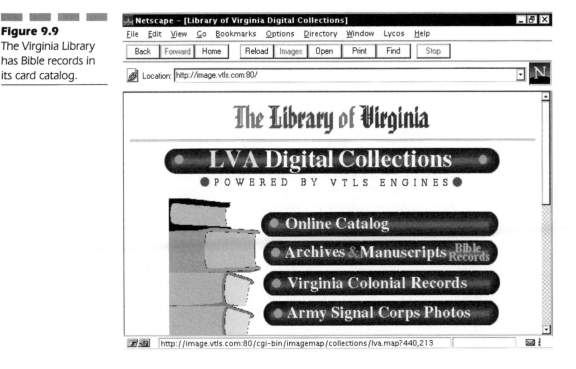

Figure 9.9
The Virginia Library has Bible records in its card catalog.

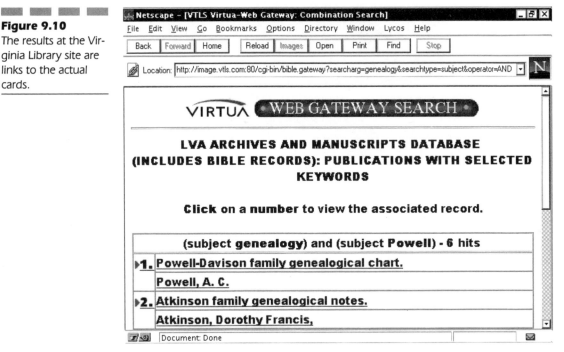

Figure 9.10
The results at the Virginia Library site are links to the actual cards.

records is included in the database. Choose Archives and Manuscripts from the home page, http://image.vtls.com:80/, as in Fig. 9.9. Choosing the Combination search, I asked for the general keyword *Genealogy* and the subject keyword *Powell,* and got the results shown in Fig. 9.10. You can also use boolean searches (NOT, AND, OR, WITH) in this card catalog. This card catalog presentation is very easy to understand and read, a real delight to use.

For even more libraries on the internet, keep a close watch on Chris Gaunt's page, Genealogy Resources on the Internet, at http://www-personal.umich.edu/~cgaunt/gen_int1.html, and look at the telnet and WWW sites. A list of online libraries is also at http://utstdpwww.state.ut .us/~archives/referenc/!cats.htm, but it's not updated very often.

Learn to use these systems, and you may find a gem!

10

The Library of Congress Online

The Library of Congress has extraordinary amounts of information for the genealogist, but until very recently you had to go to Washington D.C. and rummage in dusty confusion and frustration to find the treasures. But now, several research aids and services are available, some in print and some online.

Over 26 million Library of Congress records in 35 different files became available to the general public on the Internet in 1992. Previously, such access had been available only to researchers at the Library, Library staff, congressional offices, and selected institutions and agencies involved in cooperative programs with the Library of Congress. The Library of Congress requires no fee to search its files, but many Internet access providers do charge fees to connect to the Internet.

The host address for telnet access to the Library of Congress Information System (LOCIS) is locis.loc.gov (140.147.254.3). You can also connect via the World Wide Web at this URL: http://lcweb.loc.gov/.

LOCIS includes more than 15 million catalog records for books, microforms, music, audiovisuals, manuscripts, microcomputer software, serials, maps, name and subject references, and in-process items. LOCIS also contains citations to federal legislation (1973_), copyright registrations and legal documents (1978_), braille and recorded materials for those unable to read print, selected foreign legislation (1976_) and foreign legal references (1989_), and a listing of 13,000 organizations that provide information arranged by subject.

Except for national holidays, LOCIS is available for searching at the following (Eastern) times: Monday through Friday 6:30 A.M. to 9:30 P.M., Saturday 8 A.M. to 5 P.M., and Sunday 1 P.M. to 5 P.M.

Complete instructions for searching LOCIS and obtaining the LOCIS Quick Search Guide and LOCIS Reference Manual is available on the initial screens presented to users upon connecting to LOCIS. That manual, in searchable form, is at gopher://lcweb.loc.gov/11/locis/guides.

The availability of selected Library of Congress computer files over the Internet is a major step toward the creation of an electronic "library without walls" as outlined in the Library's strategic plan for the year 2000, which was delivered to Congress last year.

Although documentation for searching Library of Congress files is available for free downloading over the Internet, you can also purchase it in a packaged, easy-to-use format (described in the following sections). Use this documentation to understand the content of the databases available for searching and learn how to formulate search queries. Instructions for signing onto the Library of Congress Information System (LOCIS) over the Internet are also available.

LOCIS Reference Manual, 1993 ($30.00, including postage). This printed reference manual describes how to gain access to the Library of Congress Information System (LOCIS), which includes more than 26 million Library of Congress records in 35 different files. File descriptions include LC's MARC (machine-readable cataloging) files; copyright files, 1978 to present; and federal bill status files. Commands for searching both the Library of Congress technical processing/cataloging system (MUMS) and the reference/retrieval system (SCORPIO) are also described. The manual includes instructions for signing onto the system over the Internet and for conducting searches. Approximately 200 pages long and measuring 8.5 by 11, the manual is spiral-bound for easy reference. A handy index to the files, commands, and search points is also included.

LOCIS Quick Search Guide, 1993 ($15.00, including postage). A handy, quick-reference guide for searching the Library of Congress Information System (LOCIS) over the Internet. Spiral-bound for easy use at your workstation, the guide features approximately 30 pages of brief, clearly formatted instructions for searching Library of Congress files. For each file, a brief description of the content is followed by concise instructions for formulating search queries and selecting and displaying records. User tips, examples, and instructions for limiting searches are also included. The guide is 8.5 by 11. To order, use your Visa or MasterCard and call: 800-255-3666 (toll-free, United States only), or 202-707-6100, or send a fax to 202-707-1334.

Web Access

Let's look at a Web session with LOCIS. In Fig. 10.1, you see the Web page. The opening page tells you about the offerings here:

General Information and Publications. Find out about the Library and its mission, information for visitors, publications (including *Library Associates* and *Civilization* magazine), employment opportunities, and other general information.

Government, Congress, and Law. Search THOMAS (legislative information), access services of the Law Library of Congress (including the Global Legal Information Network), or locate government information.

Research and Collections Services. Browse historical collections for the National Digital Library (American Memory), visit Library Reading

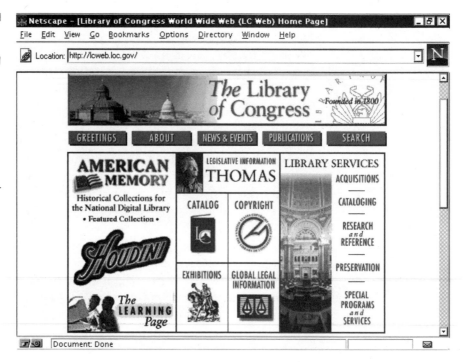

Rooms, access special services for persons with disabilities, and read about Library of Congress cataloging, acquisitions, and preservation operations and policy.

Copyright.   Learn about the U.S. Copyright Office and the registration process, access copyright information circulars and form letters, and read about many other copyright-related topics.

Library of Congress Online Services.   Search Library of Congress databases and online catalogs (including LOCIS) or connect to the Library's Gopher (LC MARVEL).

Events and Exhibits.   Read about Library events, conferences, and seminars or view electronic versions of major exhibits.

Explore the Internet.   Search the Internet, browse topical collections of Internet resources organized by Library of Congress subject specialists, and learn more about the Internet and the World Wide Web.

At the top of the page, you'll notice the link to *search*. This is a text search based on topics (not a full-text search) of the offerings at LOCIS. If you click on the word *search,* you'll get to the page shown in Fig. 10.2. You

Figure 10.2
You can search the
entire site for *geneal-
ogy* or any surname,
or state, or combina-
tions of these.

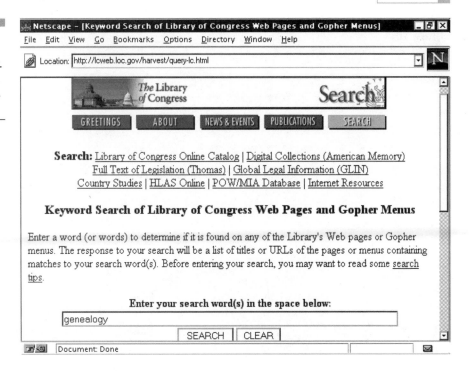

Figure 10.2
You can search the
entire site for *geneal-
ogy* or any surname,
or state, or combina-
tions of these.

can put in just one very general word, such as *genealogy* and get very general results. But you can add words to get more specific results.

One of the few full-text offerings you can search at the LOC is the collection of the WPA Life Histories. Go to the URL http://lcweb2.loc.gov:8081/ammem/wpaquery.html and enter a surname, place, or even date, and you can search the entire collection of life histories. Figure 10.3 shows just some of the results of searching this collection for *Spencer.*

Gopher Access

Also worth a visit is Marvel, the gopher of the Library of Congress. Its URL is gopher://marvel.loc.gov and you can get there with a browser or with a gopher client. From the first menu (or page in a browser), the last option is *Search MARVEL menus.* Searching Marvel for *genealogy,* you get the results shown in Fig. 10.4. Just one file you can go to is the Index of the U.S. 1790 census (gopher://gopher.nara.gov:70/00/genealog/holdings/

Figure 10.3
You can search the
WPA Life Histories for
surnames; here are
some results on
Spencer.

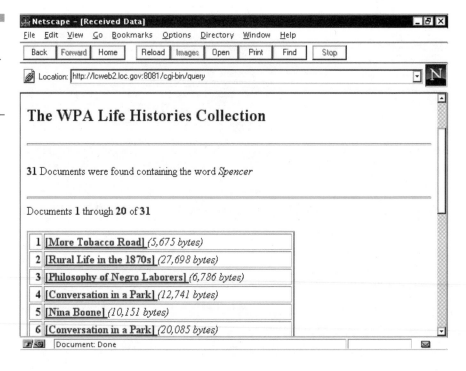

Figure 10.4
MARVEL is a Gopher
of text information
files. There are several
on genealogy.

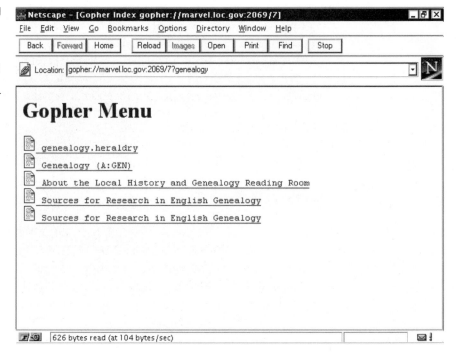

catalogs/census/1790/1790pt1.txt) or to information about Interlibrary Loans or dozens of other text, picture, and even sound files.

Text-Only Access

If you prefer text-only access to the LOC oferings, you can use telnet. To use LOCIS from a telnet program, tell your browser the location of your telnet. (For example, if you use QmodemPro for your telnet, and Netscape Navigator for your browser, click on Options | General | Apps and tell Netscape your telnet program is D:\QmodemPro\qmwin.EXE telnet.) Click on the telnet link on the Web page http://lcweb.loc.gov/ homepage/online.html, and you'll get something like Fig. 10.5, although your telnet may look a little different. To find out if there are books in the Library of Congress that interest you, choose 1 from the opening menu. Choose 1 again, at the next menu, to search books. From here you use the *browse* command. You could type in *browse genealogy ohio spencer* and see whether any books on that subject come up. The information you get there can help you place an interlibrary loan request.

Figure 10.5
LOCIS via telnet, this happens to be QmodemPro's telnet function. Simply input 1 to search for books you might want via interlibrary loan.

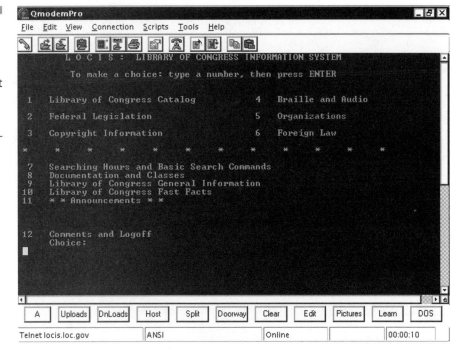

You will also want to visit the Library of Congress's ftp site. Here you will find:

/pub/american.memory.   This directory contains various reports and papers written about the American Memory Project at the Library of Congress.

pub/exhibit.images.   This directory contains images and text from various Library of Congress exhibitions, with a separate directory for each one.

/pub/folklife.   This directory contains the text of Folkline, a weekly co-operative information service of the American Folklife Center of the Library of Congress and the American Folklore Society. Folkline information is subdivided into three categories: professional opportunities; training opportunities; and conferences, calls for papers.

/pub/reference.guides.   This directory contains the full text of various reference guides, finding aids, and bibliographies produced by Library of Congress reference staff. Large and/or binary files are found in this directory while smaller text files are available through LC MARVEL.

Explore the Library of Congress online often, as the offerings are large and changing.

CHAPTER 1

LDS: The Church of Jesus Christ of Latter-Day Saints

As I've noted before in this book, one of the most frequently asked questions online is, "Can I connect to Mormon genealogy information with my modem?" The answer is "No." So, why include this chapter?

First, because The Church of Jesus Christ of Latter-Day Saints (often abbreviated as LDS) has many computerized resources and although most of them are not available in network form, they willingly share them as a public service through their Family History Centers. Second, because those sources are slowly becoming available to libraries, archives, societies, and the general public, it's only a matter of time before this information is available by modem somewhere. And finally, because you simply cannot talk about modern genealogical research and leave out the Mormons, it seems natural to include their publicly available resources.

Some Background

Without trying to explain the theology involved, I'll simply say that Mormons consider it a religious duty to research their family history. A detailed explanation can be found at the LDS home site, http://www.lds.org/ (Fig. 11.1).

The results are archived at the church's headquarters in Salt Lake City and are distributed in microfilm, microfiche, and CD-ROM to their many Family History Centers throughout the world. The data is in several forms, but the most important to the online genealogist are the Ancestral File and the International Genealogical Index. Both of these were updated in early 1997: new data were inserted in the databases, but new compression techniques kept the set to 7 CD-ROMs.

One of the LDS's objectives is to build their copyrighted databases known as the Ancestral File (AF) and the International Genealogical Index (IGI) and continually improve their accuracy and the software used to search them. The IGI is a record of the temple work; the AF offers pedigrees that the IGI doesn't. The IGI and the AF are really unrelated, as data entered in one file doesn't necessarily show up in the other file. Each has a value of its own, and both files are worth searching. The advantage of the AF is that you can get pedigrees from it; the advantage of the IGI is that there's more detailed information.

Most non-LDS genealogists see the IGI as the more valuable of the two. While errors turn up in both, the IGI is closer to the original records (data is normally entered into the IGI first) and it has excellent bits and pieces of information, especially its references as to where the information came

Figure 11.1
The LDS home site
has tips on family
history.

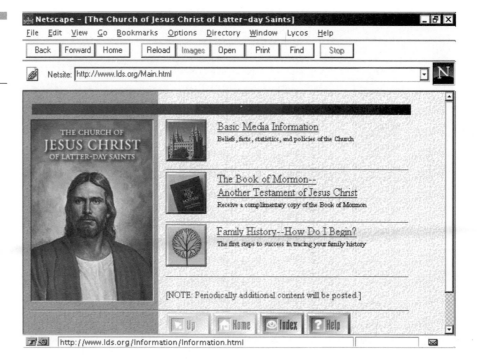

from. Many non-LDS genealogists will always go to the IGI first, but the Ancestral File with the new 5.5 GEDCOM format allows you to find out what documentation supports the entry. Considering you can get the submitter's name and address, as well as pedigree or descendancy charts, the Ancestral File is a very valuable resource, too.

While errors do exist, the percentage seems low; plenty of genealogy books printed in the past 100 years have more errors than these databases. The fact that the data is computerized and compiled by a religious organization is irrelevant.

Treat the AF and IGI the same way as you treat a printed book about a surname—with great caution. Use it as an excellent source of clues but always cross-check it with primary records. While the computer increases the amount of data you can scan and makes things much easier, it doesn't necessarily improve accuracy. Human beings are still the source of the data.

The LDS apparently wants to make the AF and IGI available to more people. Originally, you had to visit the Family History Library in Salt Lake City, Utah to use these databases. Today, that library has these CD-ROMs on a LAN that's connected to the Joseph Smith Memorial Building next door and about 200 access terminals scattered about the buildings. But there's still no remote access.

About 15 years ago, the church set up local Family History Centers around the world. In 1988, they started selling the databases on microfiche. In 1991, the church released them on CD-ROM to its local centers, and later to societies and libraries. The New England Historic Genealogical Society has a copy at its library in Boston, as does the California State Sutro Library in San Francisco. More are certain to follow suit. In 1994, the LDS began testing in-home use of the CD-ROMs, but as of yet they are still not available to individuals. Discussion continues about future online access.

The pattern here is more and more access via more and more means. However, the Mormons are very cautious and they take very small steps, one at a time. The church has not worked out all the legalities of online access and is very concerned about presenting a useful, viable program and database for its members and the rest of the world. Its main concern is in not turning out a bad product.

Right now, there are no plans to sell the Ancestral File.

For information about obtaining the IGI CD-ROMs, write to:

FamilySearch Support Unit
50 East North Temple
Salt Lake City, UT 84150

A Visit to an FHC

Terry Morgan, genealogy forum staff member on America Online (terryann2@aol.com), is also a volunteer at the two Family History Centers in Huntsville, Alabama. The setups there are very typical, she says, and she gave me a personal tour of the one closest to our homes.

"The best way to find one near you is to look in the white pages of the phone book for the nearest LDS church," Morgan says. "Call them and find out where the nearest FHC is, and the hours. Honestly, since the hours vary so much from place to place, the best time to call is Sunday morning around 10; everyone's at church then!" If you call any other time, she says, give the staffers lots of rings to answer the phones, which might be on the other side of the church from the FHC. Or, she says, you could write to the LDS main library at the address listed in the last section and ask for the latest list of FHCs. There's also an excellent list of FHCs maintained by Cyndi Howells at http://www.oz.net/~cyndihow/lds.htm and a list of the larger FHCs at the LDS home site at http://www.lds.org/Family_History/Where_is.html.

All Family History Centers are branches of the main LDS Family History Library in Salt Lake City. The typical FHC is a couple of rooms at the local Mormon church, with anywhere from one to ten computers; a similar number of microfilm and microfiche readers; and a collection of books (usually atlases), manuals, and how-to genealogy books.

The FHC I was visiting had two IBM-compatibles that shared a printer in a room with a small library of about 25 reference books. A room away there were two film readers and two fiche readers. Users are asked to sign in and out, and a cork bulletin board holds the latest genealogical technique brochures from the Salt Lake City Family History Library.

In some FHCs, Terry told me, the computers are networked so that patrons can use the CD-ROMs in a shared environment. In the future, perhaps before the year 2000, FHCs might have a direct satellite hookup to the main FHL and the latest version of the CD-ROMs there, cutting distribution time of the member data. However, this is still in the development stage. Meanwhile, FamilySearch and IGI are available at most FHCs, and usually only one person at a time can use them.

"Some centers offer training on the programs, some insist they train you before you start using the computers, and some just help if you ask," she says. "We offer help if you ask. We've not had much trouble installing ours here. The only tricks were it has to have expanded memory, and you can have some TSRs [terminate-and-stay-resident programs, which sometimes cause conflicts] running, but few enough to have low memory and expanded memory as well." The programs as of this writing won't run under Windows, but Morgan said that could be different in the future.

In the typical FHC setup, you must reserve a computer and you get a certain block of time to use it. Printouts to paper of what you find are usually a nickel a page. Some centers allow you to bring your own disk to record the information, but others insist you buy certified virus-free disks from the FHC at a nominal fee.

The Databases

The computers are set up to run FamilySearch, a set of programs that search five CD-ROM databases. When you begin, you have an opening screen with these eight choices:

- Tutorial
- Ancestral File

■ International Genealogical Index

■ United States Social Security Index

■ Military Index

■ Family History Library Catalog

■ Scottish Church Records Index

■ TempleReady

■ Personal Ancestral File

The first ones are the ones you'll use most often, and in a moment we'll examine them. First, however, let's look briefly at the last two.

TempleReady is a program of interest only to church members; it helps you prepare genealogical records for Mormon religious rites. Personal Ancestral File is the popular LDS program for personal genealogical data. GEDCOMs and family groups are its greatest strengths. If you've ever considered buying this venerable program for yourself, you can come to an FHC to test-drive it. The FamilySearch tutorial has helpful text files about using this program.

The other programs are arranged in the order most people want to use them. They are as follows.

Tutorial. The tutorial takes you step-by-step through the database programs, showing you how they work. It's worth 15 minutes of your time to explore this. When you're through, you're ready to investigate the other programs.

Ancestral File. This is a good place to begin your search. This database has pedigree charts of family groups sheets, donated by people from all over the world, usually in GEDCOM format. "It's important to remember," says Terry Morgan, "that this information is not verified. It's best to consider it an opinion file. The Salt Lake City FHL can't check out each of the millions of submissions, but they will try to find and merge duplicate pedigree lines and they accept corrections that you choose to submit." All are invited to donate their data, and so you're likely to get good clues on where to start looking from this database.

The Ancestral File searches are slightly different from those on the IGI. In the Ancestral File, a *place* reference is not required when you do a search; IGI allows that variable. The AF search is conducted on the basis of a name (required) and an event date (not required, but narrows the results).

You select a record from a menu of *hits.* In the IGI, the documentation for that record is shown; for the AF, the submitter's name and address at the time of submission is shown. (This will be changing in the future, as they plan to release an upgrade with more documentation for AF entries from donators.)

The IGI record screen will show you what documentation was entered for that person: an original document, a book, a microfilm of a courthouse record, or whatever. To the left is a set of numbers—the call number. If it's microfilm, you can rent the source material. For $3.00 you can examine the material at your local FHC for up to three weeks. It takes about three weeks, on average, for the material to arrive after you fill out the request form. Books cannot be circulated this way unless they've been microfilmed, Morgan says.

The results of an AF search can be printed out (F2) or saved to a diskette. You can also use this program to produce family group sheets. The IGI results can also be printed or saved to disk.

Morgan also points out that if you find an error or omission, you're invited to submit your data to the library in Salt Lake City. Expect to see your data reflected in the CD-ROMs in a year or two, she says.

IGI. Separate from the Ancestral File is the IGI. You need to check both, but the IGI is mainly submitted by church members. It isn't in pedigree format, but there are more names overall in the IGI. You can search by name, event, and location, and print or save the results to disk. Call numbers of documentation will also come from the IGI.

The CD-ROMs of the IGI cover the entire world; remember, Morgan says, that if you order a microfilm of a record that came from France, it will be in French!

United States Social Security Index. The United States government made these records public domain; the LDS put them on CD-ROM, indexed them, and wrote a search program for the data. It contains very good death records for 1962 through 1994 and some records back to 1937. But for any record to be on this disk, the death had to have been reported to the Social Security office.

The data includes birth and death dates, the last place of residence, where the death payment was sent; the state of residence when the Social Security number was issued, and the Social Security number itself. It's searchable by name.

Military Index. Another set of public-domain records that the Mormons made into a usable database, this CD-ROM covers U.S. citizens who died in the wars in Korea and Vietnam. It has birth and death dates, rank and serial numbers, and vital statistics as far as the military knew them: marriage status, state of residence, and so on.

Family History Library Catalog. This is a CD-ROM with the entire contents of the main Family History Library in Salt Lake City, updated yearly. It's also available in every FHC as a microfiche. The search choices are as follows:

Search Locality.   You can put in a country, state, county, city, or township, and get a list of everything the library has that mentions that locality. The record will show the author, date, format of the item, and call number. To search on a subject (say Mayflower or Land Grant), type the term in the Search Locality field.

Browse Locality.   This is more open and will result in more hits. "I do recommend using the microfiche only to 'browse' through a subject," says Morgan, "if you just want to see what was filmed from a particular state or country, you could pull out the 'Nebraska' fiche and read it all in perhaps an easier way than using the computer, but only in that one instance do I think the fiche are easier to use than the computer."

Surname Search.   This allows you to not only search for surnames, but also to add keywords. After the initial results, you can hit F6 to add a locality, related family name, and so on. You can also search by author and title under this function.

Film/Fiche Number.   If you have the call number of a microfilm or fiche and want to know what else is included on that microfilm roll, this search will tell you. Sometimes widely diverse items are included in one roll; sometimes very closely related items are.

Computer Number Search.   If you know the computer index number to a certain record, you can retrieve the rest of the information with this search.

Tutorial.   This is a guided tour of the catalog search system.

Scottish Church Records.   This index consists of nearly 10 million names from parish registers and similar records of the Church of Scotland (Presbyterian) and a few other denominations. The index contains entry dates from the late 1500s through 1854.

Other Resources

Other valuable resources are available at FHCs. "A very good resource is the Research Outlines," Morgan says. "Each Family History Center has a full set, like this one we keep in a three-ring binder here. They are also available for sale by writing to the main library in Salt Lake City."

The outlines, for every state, Canadian province, and dozens of other countries, are guides with ideas for how to research in those localities. It includes addresses of genealogical societies, government addresses such as courthouses and archives, maps, and short histories—in short, any resource that particular location might have. It also points out tips and techniques for research in that particular place that might be different. "When you're stuck and don't know what to do next," Morgan says, "these research outlines are just wonderful."

Another resource is the word lists. As mentioned before, if you find that a microfilm you ordered is in French, these short booklets have the translations of the terms genealogists care about most: birth, death, baptism, marriage, wills, deeds, land transfers, and so on, for several dozen languages. They're available for sale, and every FHC has a set for reference.

In fact, most FHCs can help you order microfiches, books, and other materials the LDS sells. Some also offer regular courses on genealogical research.

The Connection

Right now, you have to go to your nearest FHC to access these resources. If your local FHC has a staff of knowledgeable volunteers like Terry Morgan, it's well worth your time to leave the modem behind for a while to investigate these resources. Another reason to try out your local FHC is that someday, if time, money, and security issues permit, you might be able to dial into the FHCs. If that happens, you'll want to be familiar with the programs and ready to go!

CHAPTER 12

AOL

Introduction

You probably got a free trial membership from America Online in the mail or with your modem. But just in case you didn't, here's how to contact the company:

8619 Westwood Center Drive
Vienna VA 22182-2285
cs@aol.com
1-800-227-6364

The history of America Online is nothing short of amazing. Just five years ago, AOL wanted to be as big as CompuServe and Prodigy. Now it's as big as those two services combined, in both number of users and depth of content. And the genealogy forum is one of the best offerings on all of AOL.

AOL is open 24 hours a day and seven days a week. Its basic rate is unlimited use for $29.95 a month; that includes AOL's own content as well as surfing the Internet with its browser, Usenet reader, and ftp programs.

A warning though: AOL sends out software with a free month's membership about three times a year. Whenever it does, getting connected to AOL and staying connected are problematic because AOL's hardware gets overloaded. And, even if you get on and stay on, the response from the system can sometimes slow to a frustrating crawl. This has caused some people to deride the service as "Almost Online."

In such a case, your best bet is to sign off the system and log back on at a time when things are less busy. Mornings are usually good, the earlier the better, as well as late afternoons. And the offerings in the AOL genealogy forum are worth trying at those times of day.

Like most commercial online services, AOL is available only through its proprietary front-end software. AOL's network has local access numbers throughout the world, but not necessarily in rural areas. The software package will find the phone number closest to you during the setup procedure, but every now and then go to the list of local access numbers (keyword: phones) to see whether you are using the best and closest connection.

During the sign-up process, you choose a main screen name for your account. Choose this carefully; you cannot change it without closing the old account and starting a new one. However, you may have up to five screen names assigned to the main account, so each family member can have a mailbox, a set of favorites, and a place to file messages and downloads. To add and delete additional screen names, use the keyword Names.

Your screen name can be close to your real name (as mine is, see Fig. 12.1) or something totally whimsical. Your address at AOL is your_screen _name@aol.com.

A quick note about AOL e-mail: the most cost-efficient way to use it is to click on the menu item Mail, then Set Up FlashSessions. You simply answer the questions in the check boxes and then you can retrieve your mail to be read offline and answered offline. To activate your FlashSession, click on Mail, then activate FlashSession Now, or make sure AOL is running at the time you have set for automatic sessions. Given how slow AOL is sometimes, this is a real frustration saver.

Keyword: Genealogy

To move around AOL, you use keywords. You can click on the menu item GoTo or the toolbar button KEYWORD or just use Ctrl-K and type in the keyword you need. Capitalization doesn't matter in typing in keywords, but spelling does. You must be exact. There's a keyword to find out about the whole list of the keywords: Keyword.

As you click on pictures and words to see new things on AOL, new windows open. The old ones don't close themselves, so try to be aware of how many you have open at a time. Unclutter the screen by closing a few now and then.

Figure 12.1
Your screen name is shown in the Welcome box when you load the AOL software. You can have several names assigned to one account, for family members to use.

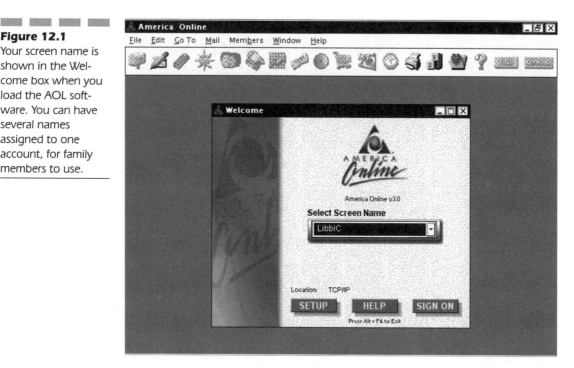

To get to the genealogy area, use the keyword *Genealogy.* (Keyword *Roots* also works.) Before you sign on, you can set yourself up to get to the genealogy area quickly. Click on GoTo in the menu and choose GoTo Menu Editor. You'll get the dialog box in Fig. 12.2.

You can put in either *Roots* or *Genealogy* in the column Keyword; I put mine as the first entry. Be sure to click on the Save button. Now, whenever I am online at AOL, Ctrl-1 will take me to the Genealogy Forum. These shortcuts only work when you are online.

Just click the Sign on button, and AOL will dial. You can input your screen name and password manually or set it up for automatic sign-on under keyword MY AOL. Be aware that if you use the automatic option, anyone who can sit at your keyboard can use your account.

Once you are signed on, you can go to the Genealogy Forum. Within the main screen (see Fig. 12.3), you'll find links to all genealogy offerings, to the Web, Usenet genealogy newsgroups, and chat rooms.

By far, most people find the best thing about AOL's Genealogy Forum is the people.

One of the sysops, GFS Judy, told me: "The genealogy forum provides a sense of family. Not only the 'real' relatives you are searching for, but the sense of family you get entering a chat room and being recognized, the information that total strangers go out of their way to type up and e-mail you, the forwarding of problems to others so that everyone can offer a

Figure 12.2
Make life easy on yourself: put the Genealogy Forum in the GoTo Menu. Now two keystrokes will take you to the Genealogy Forum from anywhere on AOL.

Key	Menu Entry	Keyword
1	Genealogy	Roots
2	Usenet	Usenet
3	WWW	WWW
4	Top News	top news
5	Stock Quotes	stocks
6	Center Stage	center stage
7	Internet Connection	internet
8	Press Releases	Press
9	Web Review	Web Review
10		

Favorite Places

Save Changes   Cancel

suggestion or just encouragement to keep on going. I am constantly amazed that people who have spent 20 years of their lives and countless dollars researching their family lines, will freely give you information just to help another researcher and perhaps get a tidbit in return. The materials people upload into the genealogy libraries save me hours of time traveling around the country as does the Internet access. Computers truly make genealogy a realistic, global project that anyone can join in on regardless of age or income."

The genealogy area is full of wonderful resources for the beginning, intermediate, and advanced genealogist. One of the best features about this genealogy forum is the excellent staff of experienced genealogists to help you.

Personnel

GFL George is the forum leader. GFA Robin, GFA Terry, GFA Beth, and GFA Drew are some of the sysops. There are over 100 staff members in the forum; anyone with GFS at the beginning of their screen name is a

Genealogy Forum staff member. A list of the staff, with short bios, can be found in the Welcome Center folder called Volunteers.

GFA Terry is one example. Director of a Mormon Family History center (FHC), she's the AOL Genealogy Forum expert on FHCs and the Family History Library in Salt Lake City.

"I have been working in the Genealogy Club for years," GFA Terry says. "It started in about 1986 when I joined Q-Link (the first network from the owners of AOL for Commodore computers). I worked in the genealogy area of Q-Link as a staff member. When AOL came about and when my husband and I upgraded to an IBM, we joined this network. I was already a staff member on Q-Link (owned by the same company), so it was possible to become one here, too.

"My duties cover many things—I greet the new members, answer some of the questions on the message boards, do some librarian duties as I help make files go live, archive message boards, host meetings, and well, there's a lot to do, but I enjoy it very much."

The network has helped her with her genealogy as well, and she says:

"I have made contact with several folks by posting the surnames I was looking for. I even found a distant cousin! This all works on a volunteer principle—folks helping other folks. One of them lived in Connecticut where I had ancestors and looked up some information for me. In turn I looked up some information for her from Georgia. There are helpful text files in the genealogy libraries, too."

Another person you should know here is GFL George, the forum leader. A professional genealogist, George Ferguson has over a decade's experience with online genealogy and is willing to share, help, and inform.

"The Genealogy Forum on AOL has been my love and my passion since its inception in 1988," George said. "With the help of many wonderful and dedicated volunteers we have guided it to the place it is today. My Great Aunt Gertrude Durham started me on my genealogy work when I was a boy and she presented me with a ten-generation pedigree chart that was partially filled. I knew right then my life's work was to fill in the spaces." George started teleresearching genealogy the day after he got his first modem.

George told me:

> The best feature of the America Online Genealogy Forum would have to be the ability to get 48 people from all over the country together in one online room and talk about genealogy. It's great because you don't have to leave the comfort of your own home but you can get all kinds of questions

answered. We also have an outstanding collection of downloadable files. We have programs and utilities for IBM-compatible systems, Macintosh systems, as well as Apple II systems. We have hundreds of lineage files, GEDCOM database files, genealogical records files, tiny tafel files, alphabetic surname files, as well as logs of past meetings. We have a surnames area where anyone can post a message about someone they are looking for. We also have message boards that are designed to exchange information about computer- and non-computer-related genealogical subjects.

We have started several special-interest groups (SIGs), which are becoming quite popular. On different nights we have beginners' classes, an African-American genealogy SIG, a Southern SIG, and a Scot-Irish SIG. In the near future we hope to expand these offerings with expanded beginner services, a New England research SIG, and a reunion software users group.

He points out that the online real-time conversations are a valuable resource. There have been many meetings where somebody finds a cousin or a possible link. It is also an opportunity to chat with people who have a similar interest as you and you don't have to go out at night or drive into a big city to do it. Also, unlike the big genealogy groups that get together only once every month or so, AOL members can get out and talk almost any night of the week.

"We expect people to come and share the passion for genealogy," George said. "We expect nothing but hope that everyone will share what they have with the rest of us and have fun doing it. What we find is that people freely give of themselves and that we can have a good time while learning different ways of investigating the past."

Another Forum host, GFH Ranch, says:

Long before I assisted with a chat or had any formal involvement with AOL, I was a regular. For me, personally, the chats and message boards have been very instrumental in meeting cousins, which in turn leads to more sources, more information, and more options for research.

I had used the genealogy newsgroups but prefer working the break down of topics that AOL offers. Message boards are broken into portions of the alphabet and geographic locations which dramatically reduces amount you have to look through to find a possible connection. Chat sessions are narrowed to geographic areas (as well as offering general and beginner chats) and historical time periods.

Like many others on AOL, she has had good luck finding real information there. "It is especially fun the first time you find a cousin. One time I helped a lady find a missing link because I had an editor's note in a book. And another contact sent me an ancestor's photograph giving me a rare opportunity to share it with my family. I now have trouble remembering all the cousins I've met. Chats focus on families and heritage with a strong sense of 'helping our brother out.' We have folks in Tennessee offering to assist someone in Texas by calling the courthouse or photographing a tombstone."

The Forum's Features

Beginner's Center

On your first visit, spend some time in the Beginner's Center (see Fig. 12.4). Read the profiles of the online staff, the how-to files, and especially any announcements and news. Other important sites are as follows:

FAQ. The Frequently Asked Questions folder is a set of small text files with the most common beginner's questions. From "What is a ZIP file?" to common abbreviations, you'll find many of your questions

Figure 12.4
The Beginner's Center should be your first stop.

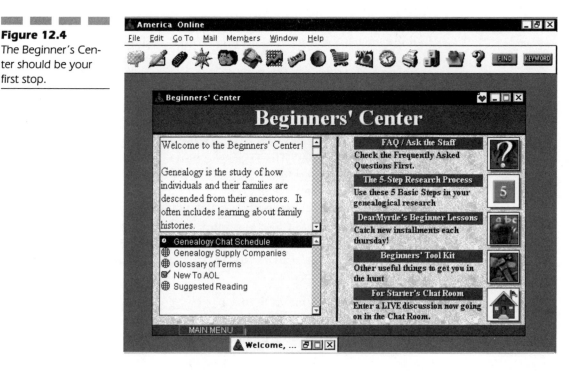

answered here. If you don't, at the bottom is a link to ask the sysops your specific questions.

5-Step Research Process.   This is an excellent tutorial on how to get started in genealogy. Family history research is asking yourself the same questions, in order, in cycles:

1. What do I already know?
2. What specific question needs to be answered?
3. What records might answer my question?
4. What do the records actually tell me?
5. What conclusions can I reach now?

Click each of the buttons at the right to learn about each step in this research cycle.

DearMyrtle Beginner Lessons.   Begun in January 1997, these are weekly text files on aspects of genealogical research for the beginner. Worth saving to disk.

Beginner's Tool Kit.   This is a grab bag of files of information, from how to get addresses to what different forms you can use to display your research.

Beginner's Chat Room.   This is an ongoing chat where beginners can come to pose and answer questions.

Main Menu

After you're familiar with the beginner's area, you'll spend a lot of time in the Main Menu. The first stop will usually be the messages.

MESSAGE BOARDS.   The message boards operate on a volunteer basis; you're invited to post any questions you might have and are encouraged to post a reply in answer to anybody else's question that you have information about. Also, don't forget to post the family names you're looking for in the message board under the Surname category.

If you need help downloading or learning how to use the front-end software, you can go to the customer service Members Helping Members area and post questions. I recommend this area because it's free (it won't cost you any online charges) and is geared for beginners as they learn their way around America Online.

AOL has made major improvements in its message boards since the second edition of this book. You can now download and read messages offline, even alphabetize the subject lines. However, not all message boards were upgraded at the same time. As you enter a message board area, check if the window has textured, multicolored background and buttons for you to set your preferences, as in Fig. 12.5. (If you open a message board which has not yet been converted, it will *not* have the Preference button, and the background is an ordinary white color.)

You can choose to have the list of messages formatted in a list that is alphabetized, or from newest to oldest, or from oldest to newest. You can also choose to see only those that are new since you were last on.

You can also design a signature phrase for yourself when you post—such as a list of surnames or your contact information. It is best to enable the More option. The MORE button, will make the program automatically open the rest of the collection of messages without your having to click the MORE button at the bottom of the message board screen.

You can choose a default number for the earliest date on messages you show, but it really isn't necessary to change these numbers if you plan to use the List Unread or Since Last Visit options and come to the boards often, anyway. *List Unread* works like Usenet readers, but to do a true Find New search of messages, you need to click on Find Since:. If you always want to read *every* message in a topic, use List Unread. *SINCE LAST* is different from List Unread. If you just want to see what was newly posted, skim over many and read only a few of those messages each time you

Figure 12.5
The message boards have options to set your preferences.

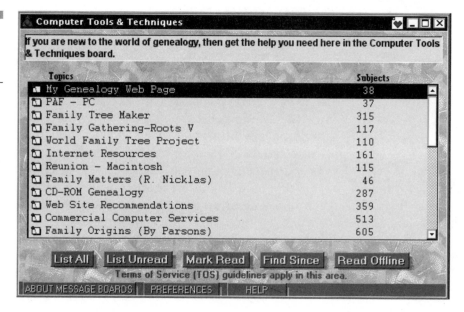

come to the boards, use the Find Since followed by the Since Last Visit option.

FIND SINCE (a certain date) Messages is more thorough and encompasses Find New—you can set how many days back or specify a date range or even do a Since Last Visit. Click the Help button here to see how to write in a date range.

MARK READ works just like the Internet newsgroups. This will be most useful to those who opt to use List Unread instead of Since Last Visit. The messages you have marked as read will not appear on the list for the message board when you go in to view it again.

LIST ALL is limited by the number of days you set in your PREFER-ENCES to make messages available.

READ OFFLINE is the most useful option in my opinion. Using the other preferences you set, it will load the proper messages to your filing cabinet during a FlashSession, to be read and replied to offline just like e-mail. When you set it to on, it stays that way until you come back to change it. The messages will be downloaded to your NEWSGROUPS folder (this may change). If you reply to messages offline, you will need to do a FlashSession to get them posted back online.

The message boards are divided into several different categories, from surname searches to specific ethnic and geographic areas. Poke around and find the ones you need, then set them for reading offline for the most efficient use of AOL.

DEAR MYRTLE DAILY COLUMN. A daily column on genealogy topics, this option is always helpful and informative. Save it to disk with File|Save As and read it offline.

LATEST NEWS. Here you find announcements, the monthly forum newsletter, schedules for chats and classes, and all the other fast-changing information in the forum.

FILE LIBRARIES. If you choose to upload a file to the Genealogy Forum, put the file in a plain ASCII text format. That way, more people can read it. Most people can read an ASCII text file, but only a few might have the same word processor that you used.

You'll find files here ranging from trial versions of popular genealogy software to GEDCOMs and other genealogy information from members. Use the Search Genealogy Forum from the forum's main menu to find whether there are files that mention your surnames or geographical regions of interest.

SEARCH GENEALOGY FORUM. When you enter a search term in this window, the program will search the file library articles in the Forum, but not the messages. You'll get a list like the one shown in Fig. 12.6.

Resource Center

The resource center, in Fig. 12.7, is chock-full of information to save you lots of trial and error. This area has articles, help, and tips in the subjects of Regions of the World, Ethnic Resources, Vital and other records, and additional resources. Here you'll find guides and tips to making your research more productive.

Chat Rooms

The genealogy chat areas are where you go to type online, real-time conversations with other genealogists. There are genealogy chat rooms for many different topics. Some are going on all the time, some are there at specific times; schedules and the line up are to the left of chat main window.

There are five rooms that have someone in them almost all the time: For Starters, Golden Gates, Family Tree House, Ancestral Digs, and Fam-

Figure 12.6
Search Genealogy
will show you all the
files and articles that
mention your topics
of interest.

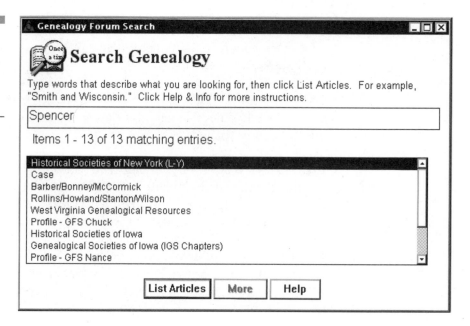

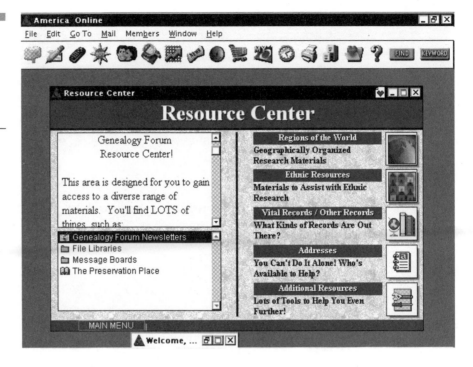

Figure 12.7

Next to the Beginner's Section, the Resource Center is the most useful area of AOL's Genealogy Forum.

ily Reunion. Other scheduled chats on specific topics occur almost every weeknight. Check the chat schedule for the latest dates and times.

One very popular one is the U.S. Civil War History SIG, which holds regular meetings in the chat rooms, led by SIG hosts GFS Jim and GSD KathyD. Be sure to check it out!

Internet Center

The Internet Center in the Genealogy Forum is where you'll find Web sites, ftp and gopher sites, newsgroups, and mailing lists that specifically have to do with genealogy. This saves you a lot of time as opposed to floundering around the general AOL Internet area looking for those specific genealogy items. However, if you want to go farther afield, be sure to check out Net Help—the Answer Man, where tips, tricks, and FAQs about the Internet in general and AOL's connection in particular are stored. You can subscribe to newsgroups here or at the keyword window Usenet. Click on Expert Add and type in the soc.genealogy newsgroups you want.

A tip as far as newsgroups: in your FlashSession Settings window, check the box "Retrieve unread NewsGroup messages" and the box "Send outgoing NewsGroup messages." Then, when online, go to keyword USENET. Click on the Read offline button. Your subscribed newsgroups will be listed on the left. Any you add to the box on the right will be put in your filing cabinet during FlashSessions. This will increase the time of your FlashSessions with very busy newsgroups, but your online time will still be greatly reduced. You'll just have to remember to erase the old messages regularly to save disk space.

Other Areas

AOL's Genealogy Forum also has areas where you can find chat schedules, genealogy supply companies, an Internet and genealogy glossary, AOL tips, and suggested reading.

Classes

Another AOL feature worth noting: the online genealogy courses. Go keyword Classes for the AOL online campus; genealogy is among the topics there. You'll find courses for new and experienced users who want to learn more about the resources available and LDS family history centers. You don't have to be an advanced genealogist to take these classes; beginners will find useful information, too.

Online interaction with the instructor can help you solve specific research problems and acquaint you in detail with resources available from the Salt Lake Family History Library. To join the class, sign on at the appointed time and go to the assigned chat room. The instructor presents material and the students ask questions. Each session lasts about two hours.

Tips and Tricks

Like all services, some things are obvious about the best way to get around AOL, and some aren't.

AOL's latest software will support 28.8 Kbps. Check to see if there is an AOL Net number in your area for even higher connect rates. This can save you money in download time. Remember that connect charges are suspended when you *upload* a file to the system, so don't hesitate to contribute your research!

One way to get faster access: if you have a TCP/IP dial-up account, the new AOL software will connect via PPP. So, you could dial your local ISP as fast as your modem can go and connect via TCP/IP. Choose SETUP | Edit Location and in the Network: drop-down box, choose TCP/IP. After that, you'd dial the ISP first, then launch AOL, then connect.

The AOL message system won't tell you that a message you left previously on the genealogy message board has been answered, nor that you have a message in the Genealogy Club. All messages are to everyone (all). You have to remember which category and topic you employed to leave the message, search for new messages under that topic, and read them all to see whether one of them answers your previous post. If you want a particular person's attention, send private e-mail to that person's AOL mailbox.

The F3 key will log you off AOL from anywhere in the system, although it always asks first. Ctrl-F4 closes the topmost window, which is usually faster than clicking on the upper left corner. You can also switch from one window to another with a mouse click on the new window.

Once you read a mail message, it goes into your old mail file. While online, click on the Mail menu and choose Mail You've Read to refer to it again. If you want to save it to your computer, use the File function to write it to a text file.

13

CompuServe Interactive (CSI)

CompuServe's basic rate is under constant review and revision. It almost always has a "try the first month free" offer going; call the toll-free number that follows. Access is usually a local call to its PPP connection allowing you full Internet access with your membership.

As a CSI member, your Internet address is ####.######@compuserve .com, where the number signs are replaced by your member number, with a dot where the comma usually goes. As of 1996, you can also now choose a name in addition to the number, such as EPCROWE@compuserve.com.

The service is accessible 24 hours a day, but cheapest between 6 P.M. and 6 A.M. your time. The address and phone number are

5000 Arlington Centre Boulevard
P.O. Box 20212
Columbus, Ohio 43220
800-848-8199 (phone)

CompuServe, the granddaddy of online services, has over 2 million subscribers; of those, over 10,000 a week visit the Roots Forum, according to Sysop Dick Eastman. However, true to form for most CSI forums, only about 5 percent of those who visit actually leave messages. That's a lot of lurkers! Yet the forum sees plenty of action, and the files and messages are valuable and worthwhile.

CompuServe's online genealogy resources have much to offer:

- Social Security Death Records online (CompuTrace).
- Online telephone directories, both residential and commercial (Phone*File and Biz*File).
- Nearly 2000 genealogy book reviews available online in the Roots forum.
- Tables of contents of hundreds of genealogy magazines. This allows you to quickly find the articles that you want.
- More than 8000 genealogy-related files available online, including shareware and free genealogy programs for Windows, MS-DOS, Macintosh, Amiga, UNIX, and even older computers.

The members of the forum are varied. There are online assistant sysops and some recognized professional genealogists who drop in; other members are rank beginners. Many are in between. The members are just as cooperative, outgoing, and friendly as anywhere online; in my opinion, this is one of the best online hangouts for the online genealogist.

The year 1997 promises to be a banner year for CompuServe Interactive. More and more of the service is moving to the Internet; the content that stays internal is all being transformed into HTML files. Soon, using CSi won't be much different from using the World Wide Web.

The newest software, CompuServe 3.0.1 as of this writing, will allow multitasking: you can download a file while continuing to read messages in a forum, for example. You can look for more efficient e-mail services, and a way to block unwanted junk electronic mail, too. The year 1997 will also see some enhanced features for handicapped users. This software incorporates Microsoft Internet Explorer (see Chap. 1) for internal and external navigation.

The downside of all this: gradually the text-only access to CSi is going to fade away. Those of us who remember the service from the early 1980s will be sad to see the day when you can no longer just dial into Compu-Serve and type CIS: GO ROOTS. This also means, as of this writing, that the only alternative you have to CompuServe's own front-end software will be TAPCIS, which I'll explain later. But first CSi's own software.

First and foremost, getting to CompuServe via the Internet and getting to the Internet via CompuServe is wonderfully easy with CSi 3.0.1, and the software's interface hardly changes a whit when you do. You can either have a local ISP account and use that TCP/IP connection to get to CompuServe, or you can use the CompuServe Dial-Up Network connection, and surf from CSi. Microsoft Internet Explorer is so masterfully integrated into the software, that you don't realize that's what you're using should you want to jump from the Working From Home forum straight to the Small Business Administration's Web site. The only way you can tell the difference: the page: box in the top of the screen simply has the page title if you're still in the service and http:// if you're on the Web. On Installation in Windows 95, CompuServe 3.0 does a good job of installing the proper dial-up connection, complete with logon script. It worked the first time I used it.

The new interface gives you loads of information. The menu bar will change according to where you are: on the service or on the World Wide Web. What used to be called *Special* in the menu bar is now *Access:* this is where you change your preferences on everything from connecting to the toolbar. The page: box tells you exactly where you are. The toolbar, which you can change to suit yourself, includes a GO button, which works just like the GO command always has. The difference here is that the GO words have been changed to more simple terms: *Working from Home* instead of *WAH,* for example. The old GO words still work, though.

The Favorite Places list, as always, is sortable by name, last visit, or the priority you assign to it. Just as nice is the Recent Places list, just under the page: box, for that place you visited yesterday but can't remember the name of right now.

Wherever you are, there's a color associated with that function. Forums are brown, Chat is purple, and so on; this is another good clue to where you are at any given moment. The available functions are shown as buttons and tabs in the screen. Across the bottom, the status bar tells you when the program is busy working, how long you've been online, and whether you have mail.

The help files are greatly improved, and the Search now can search either CompuServe's online index or the Web itself, your choice of search engines.

The Main Menu (Home Desktop) is the usual launching place for a CSi session. Under the Main Menu, you can navigate throughout CSi and call up the Web browser to go to the Internet. Under GO, you will find a history of your most recently visited places (you can set how many under Preferences). Find and Mail Center are as they always have been. My Information is what has become of the Filing Cabinet. You can not only file, switch, and sort your saved messages and files, but also search them by subject line, text, and many other ways. The Learn About button is the improved Help files I talked about. You can explore these offline and really learn your way around. Much of the information is also under the menu item Help.

Some areas, such as chat (GO CB) are revamped now, too. Chat especially is easier to understand and use than ever before. Files, pictures, and so on can be shared in Chat now, too.

A nice feature is the To Do List. Throughout your CompuServe session you can create an ongoing to-do list of tasks you want to carry out, such as save forum message topics to your disk or send e-mail messages you have written. You can then process the tasks on your to-do list all at once (or individually) whenever you want. You add tasks to your to-do list by clicking buttons such as Retrieve Later (rather than Retrieve), Send Later (rather than Send), and so forth, as you go along. You can look at your to-do list by clicking the My Information side button (on the Home Desktop) and then click the to-do list top tab.

However, you can't build your To Do List offline. This limits its ability to save you time and money.

Access

Many modems come packed with a $15 to $25 credit on CompuServe, complete with a trial membership number and password. Or, you can call the 800 number and talk to customer service. The membership kits contain detailed instructions for how to set your modem, how to sign on, and the basic commands you need to know.

In the beginning, your only choice for accessing CSi is its own program, and for learning the ropes, it's very good. But when you are sure of what you want to do, you should investigate TAPCIS (GO TAPCIS).

As it's a business, CompuServe charges for connect time but strives to be competitive in its pricing. You, on the other hand, have to strive to be frugal in your online time. Once you're in the habit of getting messages on certain topics, looking for files that interest you, and keeping up with the online community, there's no reason to do this by hand, so to speak, unless you're going online for a conference (chat). This is where TAPCIS comes in.

You can set TAPCIS to go to any forum. You can tell it to get all the messages there, or get only messages that match your keywords (or don't have certain keywords), or simply retrieve headers and let you choose to get messages on another pass. You can choose to get catalogs of the files, too, and make a list of the ones you want TAPCIS to retrieve.

The program will carry out your agenda in DOS, leaving you free to work in Windows or go get a cup of coffee, while your messages and files download. Then you can read them at your leisure, while the phone is back on the hook.

TAPCIS will do all the same things for your CompuServe electronic mailbox, too. Since it does this much faster than you can type or read, it can soon save you the $39.95 price tag. As soon as your CSi bill goes over $50 a month, give TAPCIS a try; there's a free 21-day version in the TAPCIS forum (GO TAPCIS).

The Forums

As mentioned previously, research and business services abound on CompuServe, but many members belong for the forums and use little else. Forums on CompuServe are divided into three parts: messages, libraries, and conferences.

Messages have up to 17 different categories of topics. The libraries, which contain programs, text files, and pictures (graphics files), are often designed to match the message structure. All messages and files are searchable by subject (or title), date, and sender. The Roots Forum has a searchable member database with information contributed by members on their surnames of interest. Conference areas are for live, online chats and the Roots Forum has several scheduled and unscheduled ones each week.

All forums are arranged the same way; once you learn the forum software in one place on CompuServe, you can easily use it in another. The best way to do that is to try the Practice Forum (GO PRACTICE). This special forum is free of connect charges. It has message areas for you to discuss specific problems with sysops and has libraries of helpful files you can download and read later.

Find (the flashlight on the toolbar, or on the menu under Access | Find) is the command to discover what CompuServe areas cover your interests. Genealogy, for instance, will uncover the Roots Forum, the Genealogy Software Support Forum, and many other topics such as INFORMA-TION USA and Phone*File (an extra-charge service).

There are more than 200 forums on various topics, and the choices will seem overwhelming at first. But with Find and Go, you'll be able to navigate. GO, with a keyword, takes you to the forum you want. GO ROOTS, in this case, will take you to the Genealogy Forum.

A Visit to Roots

Membership in the Genealogy Forum is free and open to everyone interested. When you first come to Roots, you're asked to join, which is simple to do. You're asked to use your full name, both first and last—"handles" are not permitted. Since this is a forum dealing with tracing surnames, it's assumed you're proud of yours! Then you can input any interests you have.

With CompuServe's software, each forum has a similar basic layout, with different logos. The Roots Forum looks like Fig. 13.1.

One of the first things to do is choose to search the membership directory. There you should enter your name, how you prefer to be contacted, and the surnames you're searching. This database is searchable, but it's one of the largest member directories of any forum on CIS, so your search should be a little different here.

First, search for interests, not names, to find people looking for the same surnames you are. Second, if you're using CompuServe Information Manager (CIM), you must change your interface.

To begin the session, use the Services menu to GO ASCII. You'll be put in terminal mode. You might also want to hit F5 to capture the session to a log. When online, type GO ROOTS. At the Forum menu, enter 6 (the members directory). From the next menu, choose 6, Interest, and enter the search

Figure 13.1
Forums have buttons
on the left for the dif-
ferent areas and tabs
in the right window
for different functions
of that area.

string, for example, SPENCER. Be patient; there are more than 20,000 entries for the system to search. The system will list Roots Forum members, their member numbers, and the surnames they listed when they signed up.

Other front-end programs have different ways to access this feature. Check out ROOTS.MAP in Library 1 for details.

Messages: The Heart of the Forum

The Messages Board is divided into two dozen different topics from alphabetized surname searches to specific geographical and ethnic searches, as shown in Fig. 13.2. This area, like most of CompuServe, will be changed and improved periodically. But there's always a section called Ask the Sysop, where you can pose any question on using CompuServe, doing genealogy, or making your computer behave.

If you have any questions as to which subject area is applicable, leave a message to *SYSOP and ask. The Wandering messages section is for all nongenealogy messages. It's the place for chit-chat, like the Hot Tub conference, following. Each section on the menu is followed by two numbers,

Figure 13.2
When you click the
Message button, the
tabs become Read,
Create, and Search.

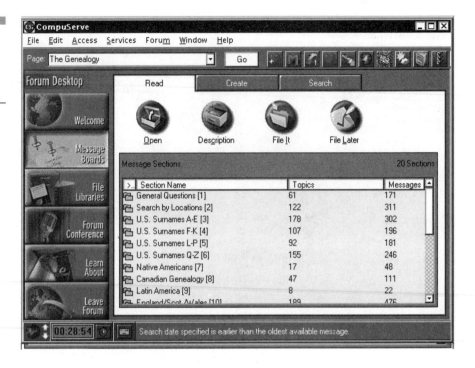

which stand for the current number of topics and messages under that category. These numbers change constantly. The Hot Topic changes from time to time and is usually whatever has genealogists stirred up at the moment: new software or a census release, for example. Keep an eye on the Software/Computers area concerning the latest genealogy programs just becoming available.

If you choose Read from the message menu, you'll be presented with the latest messages to read and answer if you want. To reply, click on the Reply button at the bottom of the window. It's nice that the system flags you when someone has posted a message to you: in WIMCIM the Waiting Messages button on the toolbar will be selectable, and when you click it, the messages addressed to you will be listed in a window for you to read, reply to, and save as you choose. The system keeps track of what you read last and presents only the new ones; the highest number read can be changed under Options in the main forum menu.

Another very nice thing about CompuServe's system is that it gives you the ability to search both messages and files by keyword, submitter, and date.

You don't have to read all the messages and reply to them online, though, even with CIM. You can use the F5 key to mark those that catch your eye and then download those messages. You can read and answer them offline, when the meter isn't running (and all these actions can also be applied to files in the library, which is discussed in a later section).

By double-clicking on a topic, you'll get a list of the messages in that topic. You can use your mouse to put a check mark in each message you think you'd like to read. Then, clicking on Messages | Retrieve marked, all the messages you marked are downloaded. Uploading replies and files of your own is just as simple.

When CIM has logged you off, you can select Mail, open the Filing Cabinet, and read new messages in Genealogy+. Your replies will be stored on disk until you sign on again and tell CIM to deliver them. Manage the files as you ordinarily would—uncompressing and so on, if necessary.

With front ends such as OZCIS, the message and file process is even easier, as the message and file menus are stored in OZCIS's software. Simply choose which forums to visit, and for each forum you'll have a catalog of the forum's message categories and all the libraries and files to select from. Before you sign on, simply tell OZCIS what you want and it takes care of the entire online session.

And those are just two examples of front-end software programs and their potential to save you money online with CompuServe. Others are around, and I urge you to read AUTO.CIS and sample those that fit your platform.

Conferences

As mentioned previously, online conferences (often called *CO* online) are when members type messages to each other in conference rooms while logged online.

Obviously, front-end programs such as OZCIS, NAVCIS, and TAPCIS, won't help you here, as this is an interactive function that's different each time. Also, remember that the faster your modem speed at logon, the higher your charges for connect time to CompuServe. Since you probably can't type or read at 14.4 Kbps, it's best to log on at lower speeds for conferences.

Often, special online conferences are announced in the Forum's Announcements section. Recent topics have included the following:

- Tracing Your Roots in Eastern Europe, Elizabeth Rohaly, moderator.
- Southern U.S. Roots, every 2d Saturday, 7 P.M. Eastern, Karen Bosze, moderator.

- Newcomers' Evening.
- Welcome to the Genealogy, History & Adoption Forum Conference Area.
- Daily Informal "Anything (almost) goes" online conferences are held every evening beginning at 10 P.M. EST, 7 P.M. PST. Drop by and discuss whatever topics you want.
- Regular conferences are held each Tuesday evening at 10 P.M. EST in the Main Room.
- Adoption Searches Conference Room (Room 4), Sundays at 12 noon EST (9 A.M. PST, 17:00 GMT), Wednesdays at 10 P.M. EST (7 P.M. PST), 03:00 GMT (Thursday mornings).
- Irregular conferences at the drop of a hat—anytime, anywhere.
- Jim Claunch 74563,1543 hosts Military Records Conferences, first Monday of the month except for Labor Day and one other holiday at 10 P.M. Eastern.

The "open topic" online conferences are held every Tuesday evening. They start at 10 P.M. Eastern time (7 P.M. Pacific) and are open to all for anything you want to discuss. Often, the more productive conferences are saved and edited, then uploaded into the libraries for future reference.

When a conference you wish to attend is scheduled, you sign on with CIM and then GO ROOTS (which should be in your Favorite Places list by now. If it isn't, click on the green light, type in *ROOTS*. When you have the forum's opening screen, click on Favorite Places, and click ADD. The genealogy forum's address will appear, then click OK).

In the forum toolbar, click on the door icon. You will get a small window that lists the current rooms where people are typing messages to each other (see Fig. 13.3).

Entering the room, you will have a small window split into two panes: the top pane shows you the conversation as people type lines of messages and press Enter. The bottom pane is where your own messages appear until you press Enter; you can back up and correct typos here before your message appears to others. The sender's name appears next to the message he or she typed.

Libraries

The Libraries are where files are stored in CompuServe forums. These may be sample versions of the latest programs; text files on how to do

Figure 13.3
Getting into a conference with CIM: the door icon (Enter Room) will give you a list of conference rooms. Clicking Enter gets you into the conversation.

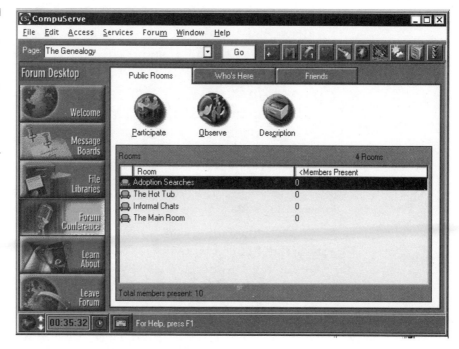

Figure 13.3
Getting into a conference with CIM: the door icon (Enter Room) will give you a list of conference rooms. Clicking Enter gets you into the conversation.

genealogy; GEDCOMs of members' families, or anything else the Roots communities thought was worth sharing.

A notable feature of CompuServe's Roots Forum is the 1400 genealogy book reviews written by professional reviewers, under Book Reviews. Hundreds of other files are available on this forum, covering basic techniques and historical background, GEDCOM files of famous people PAF utilities, lists of genealogical societies and libraries, the Family History Library newsletter, and files from the Internet. Newcomers should find these files interesting:

SEARCH.TXT—An excellent tutorial for the beginner and old-timer alike.

QUICK.TIP—Sandy Clunies's excellent list of tips and advice.

ROOTS.MAP—A frequently updated file about the forum, including how to search the membership directory.

HOW2.MSG—A file on effective forum messages, effective answers, and so on.

GENBOOK.TXT—A collection of messages discussing the best books for a beginning genealogist. (Such a discussion is called a *thread.*)

BOOKS.SIX—Another thread resulting from Bill Ewing's post: "If you could own a maximum of six books to generally aid your genealogical research, which six books would they be, and why would you pick them?" Enlightening.

WHATIS.TT—A file defining tiny tafels and ahentafels.

COUSIN.TXT—How to calculate relationships.

MASTER.ZIP—A list of all the files in the forum. This is a compressed file and must be unzipped to be read.

SUMMRY.ZIP—Also a list of all the files in the forum, but the descriptions are abbreviated, compressed, and much smaller than MASTER.ZIP.

AUTO.CIS—A list of front-end programs for CompuServe for all platforms.

Browse is the button with a hand over the books: it allows you to look at the list of categories and to look at the list of files within each category. This is OK for a while, but usually you just want something on a particular subject. For that, you use *Search*, the button with a magnifying glass over the books.

You click the box next to the library or libraries, type in the keyword(s) and the age (in days) to search. You'll get a list of what matched your criteria. You can read the descriptions and download files with a click of the mouse.

Who's Who

You'll find professional genealogists, software authors, and even genealogy publishers here. But, in keeping with CompuServe's policies, advertising is not allowed. Messages that contain advertising or solicitations for commercial services will be removed from public view by the sysops. The Genealogy Forum sysops and staff are as follows:

Dick Eastman, Forum Manager; 76701,263.   Dick is the author of *Your Roots: Total Genealogy Planning on Your Computer,* published by Ziff-Davis Press. He also lectures frequently on computer genealogy topics and will be featured in the upcoming "Ancestry" TV show on public television.

Gay Spencer, Associate Forum Manager; 76702,1353.   Gay is a doctoral candidate and an expert at genealogy research, photography, and the use of electronic photo enhancements. She owns her own specialty photoprocessing business. She lives in Ohio.

Michael MacCannell, Associate Forum Manager; 76702,445. Michael retired as a captain in naval aviation and has been a long-time user of home computers. Michael resides in California.

Phil DeSilva, Associate Forum Manager; 76702,1032. Phil is a long-time member of the National Genealogical Society and has been very active in promoting the use of home computers in genealogy work. Phil lives in Virginia.

Elizabeth Rohaly, Associate Forum Manager; 76710,100. Elizabeth lives in North Yorkshire, England. She is an expert primarily in European research (particularly Ireland, Switzerland, Hungary, Slovakia) and records pertaining to post–Civil War immigration to the United States.

Jacques Tucker; 76710,105. Jacq' has a good knowledge of New England genealogy as well as French, German, and Swedish sources. He's been involved in computing since tab card equipment. Jacq' lives in Kansas City, Missouri.

Martha Reamy, Book Review Editor; 71271,2042. Martha is past editor of the *Maryland Genealogical Quarterly* and has written a number of genealogy books. She lives in Hawaii and works as a volunteer at local Family History Centers.

You may address messages to any of the preceding people via their user ids. You may also leave a message addressed to SYSOP (to make it a private message, address it *To: *SYSOP.* The asterisk in front makes it private).

Dick Eastman, Genealogy Sysop

"It's lots of fun, but no money," Dick Eastman says of being a sysop. Along with several other Roots Forum members, he was at the 1994 GENTECH conference in Texas to help promote the forum. That's just one of his many functions as sysop. He also manages the files, checks for viruses, keeps the messages where they should be, and offers advice to new genealogists. Eastman recruits assistant sysops as well. He's the buffer between the technical people at CompuServe headquarters and the CIS user. The goal is to keep problems to a minimum, both in using the service and in doing genealogy.

"We're very much a referral service," Eastman says. "Like a football coach, we won't play the game for you, but we'll help you learn the best game plans." He likes to do that on the forums, but, amazing as it is to him, he says that many people are too shy to post a public message; they send him private e-mail with their questions instead. He'd prefer to answer questions where all can benefit from the answers, though.

"We're a social group," he says, "and we have a lot of fun. We get together at conferences like this [GENTECH] and meet face to face when we can. But I love the online environment. I'm a die-hard techie, and I think it's so much fun!"

Over and over, he says, people have found relatives on the Roots Forum, or because of it. One of the most affecting, he says, was once when he was demonstrating Roots and the Phone*File system at a National Genealogical Society meeting. A woman found a name and number she thought might be her long-lost father, though she didn't dare hope. Still, she went to the pay phone, and sure enough, was on the phone to him in minutes, arranging a reunion after 30 years. "She had tears running down her cheeks, because she was flying to Philadelphia to see her father that next week. I could hardly talk the rest of the day, I was so choked up," he says.

Gay Spencer, one of the sysops, had a mysterious Amirilla Eastman in her lineage, whose parents she just couldn't place. That is, until one day a long message was posted on the Roots Forum about an Eastman family of the right period and all the siblings of that family, and there was Amirilla!

Dick Eastman himself found a relative he was able to help online. His French-Canadian Dubay line was hard to find, partly because of variant spellings. But he knew of a history professor of that name, and using Phone*File, Eastman discovered that the fellow lived within 25 miles of where Eastman knew his ancestors to be from.

Calling the gentleman, he found out that the professor had just self-published 1200 copies of a genealogy of the family and was having trouble selling them. Eastman sent the professor gummed labels with every Dubay (and variant spelling) he could find on Phone*File. The professor mailed each one a notice of the book, and the results were a wonderful Dubay reunion and a sold-out printing of the genealogy!

Eastman's Online Genealogy Newsletter

Dick Eastman has another service available: a weekly electronic newsletter on genealogy. Software, services, research resources, anything newsworthy is available in this free newsletter. To subscribe to the newsletter, send an e-mail to subscribe@rootscomputing.com. This automatically adds you to the list of subscribers. The text of the message and the message title are both unimportant, as no humans ever read those messages. To cancel a subscription, send an e-mail to unsubscribe@rootscomputing.com.

In addition, the latest copy of this newsletter and an archive of all previous editions will be kept in the New to Genealogy Library on the Genealogy Forum on CompuServe (GO ROOTS). Many people prefer to have newsletters arrive by e-mail, but you can always obtain the latest ones online on the Genealogy Forum.

Genealogy Vendors' Forum

For help and information on books, magazines, software, and other genealogy products, visit the Genealogy Vendors' Forum (GO CIS:GENSUP). Here you'll find representatives from the New England Historic Genealogical Society; Wholly Genes Software, producers of The Master Genealogist; Leister Productions, producers of Reunion for Macintosh and for Windows; Jim Steed, the author of *Brothers Keeper*; CommSoft, producers of Roots IV and Visual Roots; The Family Edge; Everton Publishers; the National Genealogical Society; and Schroeder & Fuelling, a genealogy research firm in Germany, to name a few. Message, Forum, Conference, and other functions are just as in the Genealogy Forum.

Other CompuServe Resources

CompuTrace (GO TRACE) and Phone*FILE

CompuTrace is a surcharged area ($15 a hour) but many people use it because it's basically the Social Security death records in a searchable form. This database has information on over 100 million living and dead United States citizens. Available every day between 2 A.M. and midnight, CompuTrace verifies name, partial social security number, and year of birth; for living people, the data is much more limited. For this reason, CompuTrace is more useful as a genealogical tool.

To get there, click on the GO button in CIM and type *TRACE*. Select the menu option with the dollar sign, and when the text menu comes up, type 2, Begin search. Then you have to select a database. For this exercise, let's choose 3, the Deceased file. You choose a state or states from the list and input the first and last names. If you know the date of birth, enter it, as it will speed the search. Use the File | Capture in CIM to save the results to disk; you don't want to waste time studying the list online at $15 per hour!

CompuTrace searches match individual's information from either of two separate databases: the Deceased File includes over 40 million people who died after 1928. All individuals contained in this file were United States citizens residing anywhere in the United States or in one of 14 countries at the time the death was reported. The Living File includes over 90 million individuals whose names appear in public record filings throughout 27 states.

But if you want to find living people who share surnames you are searching, try Phone*File (GO PHONEFILE), also for $15 per hour.

The setup is much the same as with CompuTrace: you type in a name, city, and any other information you know. You'll get back names, addresses, and phone numbers. The more you know, the faster the search, but if you put in a zip code, say, and the person no longer lives there, you'll get no match. Usually, the problem is the opposite: dozens of matches. Again, capture the results to a file and let them fly by as fast as possible at $15 an hour.

CompuServe and the Internet

CompuServe membership now includes full Internet access, including Usenet newsgroups, WWW access, and everything else covered in Chaps. 4, 5, and 6. The software for this all comes with CIM 2.0.1 and is quite simple to use.

Usenet on CompuServe

You can use the browser that comes with CIM, but it's really not the best way to read Usenet on CompuServe. Click on GO and type in *USENET.* (Again, once you're there, click on the Favorite Places icon and add it, so you don't have to type it every time.) Click on the Newsreader (CIM).

The first thing to do is select Subscribe to Newsgroups. From there, type in the keyword *Genealogy* and click on Search. A list of genealogy newsgroups (19 at last count) will appear, as in Fig. 13.4, and you can click on the ones you'd like to read regularly. You can preview a few messages if you like, before you subscribe, to see if alt.culture.cajun is close enough for you, but it's not necessary.

Once you have subscribed to all the Usenet newsgroups you'd like, you can return to the first window (by clicking Cancel until you get back

Figure 13.4
Usenet on Compu-
Serve is really easy; it
will search out the
newsgroups you
want and even let
you download them
for reading later.

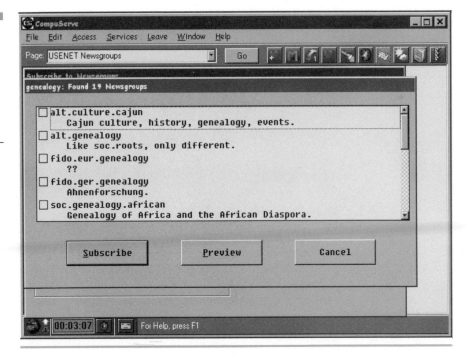

there) and choose Access Your Newsgroups. You can search newsgroups for specific text strings. This is a wonderful feature: you don't have to read soc.genealogy.surnames article by article, simply search for SPENCER or POWELL and the matching ones will appear. If there are none today, you can simply mark them all read, but if there are, you can mark them for retrieval to disk later. If any of them are *encoded* (pictures or programs changed to ASCII for transmission), CIS will decode them for you, if you click on the Decoded button. *Clear* marks them all as read, even if you didn't bother to read them.

Reading Usenet on CIS isn't really fast, but it's less hassle than on several other commercial online systems.

CompuServe WWW Pages

Roots Forum Home Page

CompuServe's new set of programs means that you can dial up CIS's PPP network, fire up a Web browser, and get to CompuServe services via the

Web. If you'd like to read more about the ROOTS Forum or check out what's new in the world of genealogy, go to http://ourworld.compuserve .com/homepages/roots (see Fig. 13.5).

Here you'll find some tidbits and information and a link that will call up CIM from the browser and take you to the Roots Forum. It also has more information on links to other genealogy pages on the Web; it's updated frequently, so check it often for new sites.

Linkstar

Another place worth visiting on CompuServe's genealogy Web site is http://www.linkstar.com/home/partners/genealogy-forum-on-compuserve, Linkstar (see Fig. 13.6). A Web search engine, Linkstar can help you find Web pages, genealogy-related businesses, and even e-mail addresses. Type in *Genealogy* as the keyword and any surname you are searching as the name, to see if anyone out there has put up a page with your lines on it!

Figure 13.5

CompuServe's Roots Web page has news, links to other genealogy sites, and more. You can get there by typing the URL in the Go box in Compu-Serve's CIM.

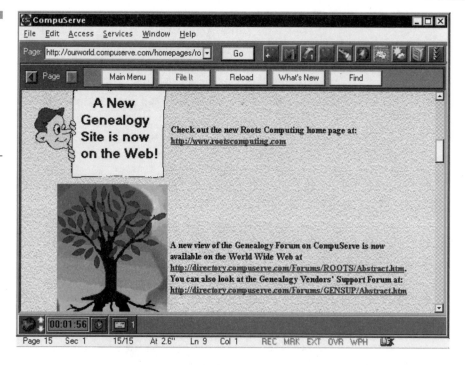

Figure 13.6
LinkStar, a search engine on the Web, has a special CompuServe Internet Search.

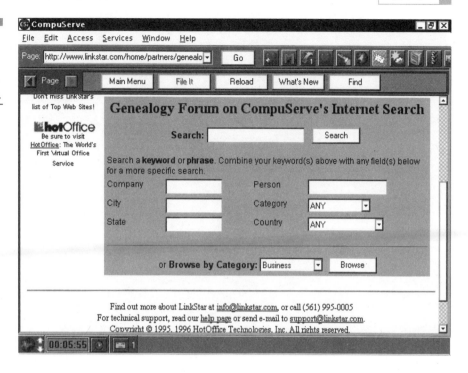

Summing Up

The CompuServe Roots Forum is one of the oldest and most respected online genealogy communities. Great for neophytes and helpful to accomplished genealogists, it offers a lot. If you get and learn to use a program such as NAVCIS, TAPCIS, or OZCIS, you can do most of your reading and replying offline and save money; if you do a lot of chatting and browsing, CompuServe can get expensive.

14

MSN: The Microsoft Network's Genealogy Forum

In what was probably the most ballyhooed launch in computing history, Microsoft gave us Windows 95 in September of that year, and with it, its very own attempt at an online service. Though the software is slow and sometimes crash-prone, as far as content, MSN is settling down into a nice service. As with all online services these days, you get an Internet connection as well as the service's proprietary content.

The basic service costs $6.95 a month, which includes 5 hours of usage per month, with each additional hour at $2.50. If you intend to be a frequent MSN user, you can sign up for a plan that's $19.95 for all the Internet you can surf, plus MSN services. If you already have an ISP and just want to try out MSN's content, you can get a $69.50-per-year deal.

You get the MSN software free with your Windows 95; it won't run without it. And you'd best have at least 16 megabytes of RAM in your computer before you try it, or you'll spend hours and hours to get very little information.

Setting Up MSN

You can get Windows 95 anywhere IBM-compatible PCs are sold; if you bought an IBM-compatible computer in the last year, you probably already have the software for MSN on your machine, like it or not.

A tip: if you are installing MSN, first uninstall any Norton programs, especially Norton Anti-Virus. MSN makes changes to the operating system, which makes NAV think MSN is a virus. This can make things get hairy! Simply uninstall all Norton products, then install MSN. Insert the CD-ROM and be prepared to spend the next 20 to 30 minutes at the computer, and at least two reboots during the process. But once it's done, it will take you right to the service. Expect a short download of software updates the first time, and perhaps another reboot. After you have finished this first sign on, then you can re-install Norton Anti-Virus, Utilities, and any other programs you had, and everything should run just fine.

Getting On

The MSN software released in early 1997 has a metaphor of a show or broadcast (see Fig. 14.1). With a great deal of sound and moving pictures,

Figure 14.1

The opening menu of MSN has buttons for featured areas (channels) and a menu bar. Click on Communicate in the menu bar to get to forums.

you are launched into the mostly black, hard-to-read desktop of the service. This part is so lugubrious you might be very discouraged from trying to go any further. Take heart, it gets better.

In this chapter, I'll cover the genealogy areas mainly, but do explore the service. Features such as the Encarta Atlas, the History and Archaeology Forum, and the computer support areas can be a real help to supplement the genealogy area.

As you move around MSN, remember you can have many windows open on the service at once; you can download a Tiny Tafel in one window as you read messages in another. It's very easy to use once you get the hang of Windows 95. Still, if you want some detailed help, I highly recommend *Surfing the Microsoft Network* by Wallace Wang (Prentice Hall, ISBN 0-13-241944-0) as a guide to getting the most out of the service.

Navigating

MSN includes access to the Internet. The MSN software includes a TCP/IP connection, and the software itself is based on Microsoft Internet Explorer. In fact, it will sometimes be hard to tell when you are in MSN proprietary areas and when you are on the Internet. The best way to tell: click on the down arrow by the MSN logo in the toolbar. This shows you the Internet toolbar, which is the browser's toolbar. If the Address: box shows msn.com in the URL, then you are still on the service.

Signing on is as simple as clicking the MSN icon on your Windows desktop. You can input your screen name and password each time or check the box for automatic login. As Microsoft Internet Explorer is the basis of the software, getting around MSN involves menus. When at the main window, click on Communicate; choose Forums from the menu and you will be shown the Forum Choices. (See Fig. 14.2.)

A box on this page holds up to five areas as favorites. Click on Customize to change one of these to Genealogy. Then you can click the link from this page to go to the forum.

As of this writing, the Genealogy forum uses older MSN software, and doesn't use the MSN browser. So, when you click on Genealogy, you get a new window that looks like Fig. 14.3.

As you move through the windows in this MSN window, you must use FILE | UP ONE LEVEL, not close window, which is hard to get used to if you've been using Windows a while. If you close the window, you'll close the connection to the forum, but don't despair. Simply reconnect using the Communicate page.

Figure 14.2
The forum portion of the Communicate page shows a list of favorites. Click on Customize to add Genealogy to the list.

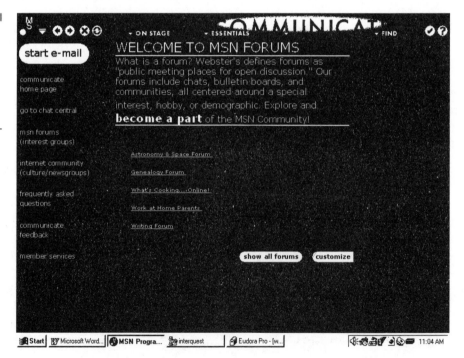

Figure 14.3
Genealogy Forum
offers message
boards, file down-
loads, and Internet
links.

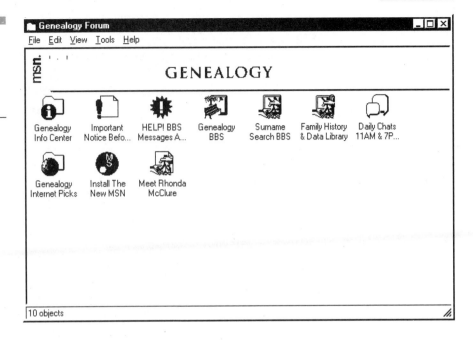

Another time-saver is to click on File |Create Shortcut from this win-
dow. Then you will have a desktop icon that launches MSN, dials, and
takes you to the Genealogy area.

Let's take a quick look at what's here.

Genealogy Info Center

This describes the Genealogy forum's offerings, has tips for using the
board, and a suggestion box for your comments on how to make the area
more useful.

Help

You'll find several files of advice here. First and most important is the
notice on messages that seem to disappear. The messages you have read
become invisible the next time you log on. This is so that your next logon
will go more quickly. If you would like to see every message, or just go

back to reread one, click on Tools in the message menu bar. Select Show All Messages, so that a check mark appears. Now you will see the headers of all the messages. You can turn it back off the same way.

Another tip the forum leader feels was worth posting several places: your subject line should have the surname first, a given name if you wish, and a date. Most people sort the messages alphabetically, so using this convention will get your message more attention than any other format.

Meet Rhonda McClure

Rhonda McClure is the forum leader. A professional genealogist specializing in New England research and computerized genealogy, she has been involved in online genealogy for almost 10 years. Her activities include sysop of Palladium Interactive's Family Gathering Web site and data manager of the Genealogy RoundTable on GEnie. She has written articles in Everton's *Genealogical Helper* and *Heritage Quest Magazine* and is a contributing editor for *American Genealogy Magazine* and *Heritage Quest Magazine* with general genealogy columns. She is also a contributing editor for the two most prestigious genealogical computing publications, the National Genealogical Society Computer Interest Group's *Digest* and Ancestry, Incorporated's *Genealogical Computing.* Rhonda lives in Florida with her husband of 15 years and their four children. Her e-mail address on MSN is rhondam_msn.

The Genealogy Forum

But let's go now to the heart of the matter. The main window of the Genealogy forum has several choices for you. The Genealogy Info Center describes what you'll find there and has the forum's news flashes. In the Genealogy Forum folder you'll find the following:

Genealogy BBS. A message board that contains general genealogy discussions. Ask beginner questions in this folder or share your research expertise with others. Topics include adoptions searches, genealogy software, general help, hints, and tools, getting started, introduce yourself, resources, and reunion announcements.

In the message boards, you click on a yellow file folder to get the messages in a general topic. By default, they are sorted by date line, oldest first. If you click on Author, Size, or Subject, though, the sort will switch to that column. Messages you have not read appear bold; messages you have read appear in regular type. You can mark them all as read under the Tools menu of the message window.

While reading a message (see Fig. 14.4), you can go to the next one or the previous one with the blue up and down arrows. You'll notice, too, that with MSN messages you can use bold, colors, and different typefaces in your messages; all of these are found under the Edit menu.

Surname Search BBS.   A message area to exchange information on a specific surname. Post both your research requests and information in the appropriate alphabetical subfolder. Subfolders are arranged both in alphabetical and country order; simply click on the column header to change the sort order. *Tip:* The Surname Research BBS and the Family History Library are arranged in alphabetical order. To obtain the messages within the subfolders in alphabetical order, simply open the folder and click on the subject toolbar.

Family History Library.   Here you will find the latest genealogy and shareware programs. Members upload research data to this library in text, GED, PAF, and TT format.

Figure 14.4

Messages in e-mail and the MSN BBS can have different typefaces, fonts, and even colors.

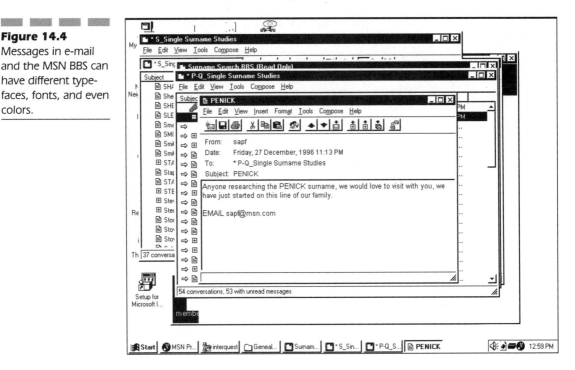

Genealogy Chat Room. Twice a day, unmoderated chats are held on the MSN Genealogy forum at 11 A.M. and 7 P.M. Pacific time. (See Fig. 14.5.)

The Chat window has three panes: the upper-left one shows the messages being typed by the people in Chat. The lower-right one is where you type your messages and edit them before you send them by pressing Enter or clicking the SEND button. The pane on the right lists who's here. With the tools at the top, you can make each person's type appear in a different color or make some conversations disappear entirely so you can concentrate on just one conversation. Chat is a wonderful place to exchange information, according to MSN member Wanda Cowart.

"I got my first home computer just about a month ago. I signed up for MSN not knowing what I was getting myself into. It was unreal! Now every night I am on the chat line for genealogy doing what I love best...making friends while searching my family tree," she says.

Wanda admitted she did a lot of searching the hard way before finding MSN: microfilm, microfiche, census searches, and so on were not nearly so much fun as she has had online. "It has become addictive and something I do not dread doing or spending a lot of time with," she says.

Figure 14.5
Forum chats are informal.

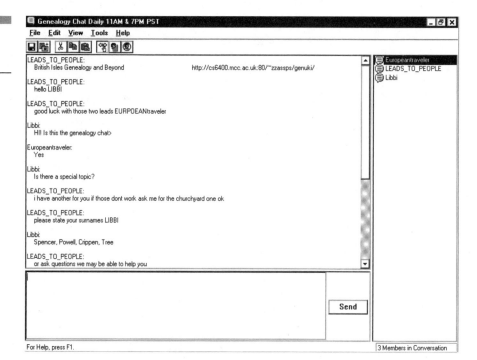

In less than a month she found some people searching the same surnames, although she had yet to find a perfect match with her lines. But the fun was in trying, she says.

"I like MSN a whole bunch," Wanda says. "They have great customer service and I am very satisfied. I get immediate responses for immediate questions. They are so kind. I only wish they would have the Chat sessions earlier. Mine starts at 10 P.M. and we last until midnight sometimes. That is hard for me being that I am enrolled in college full-time and I am a mother of three. I also wish they had a chat for Southerners [Dixie]."

Wanda was instrumental in helping to find three people for other members, people who are living but lost relatives (at this time genealogy shares the chat room with adoption searchers).

The people I searched for and found were called on the telephone.... Thank God for MA BELLE!!!! Later, they would come online and tell me what the info I had given them produced and we would talk for hours...about how much more relieved they felt. One man had never met his father. So, now he knows how to contact him.... I am sure that they will meet someday. As they have already talked on the phone. These are wonderful stories to me because I am also searching for lost loved ones who were put up for adoption.

We all laugh about going on *Oprah* so that we can meet each other in person!

I love the "Newbies" as we call them. They remind me of so much that I had to learn when I came online. I only wish they would come online and state their surnames instead of being shy and quiet. MSN chat is no place for people who don't talk.... It would be a big waste of money for those people. I welcome each one with a glass of lemonade \-/ and ask them to pull up a comfy chair and stay awhile. Part of my Southern upbringing I guess.

Wanda Cowart is very typical of the people you'll meet on MSN.

Genealogy Web Links. An area that, at this writing, is mighty sparse. As of this writing, the CLIO server of the National Archives was the only entry, but if you use FIND as previously described, you'll find links to Helm's Genealogy Tool Box, Everton's Genealogy on the WWW, the Jewish Genealogy site, and more.

Electronic Mail on MSN

Microsoft Network uses Windows 95's Exchange for e-mail. If you click on E-Mail from the MSN Communicate page or the Inbox icon on the desktop, Exchange launches. You set up a profile that includes the MSN service, and you're in business.

MSN e-mail is connected to the Internet. Your Internet address is username@msn.com. All mail lists and other Internet e-mail services can reach you at MSN.

The e-mail works almost exactly the same as the reading BBS messages, with two exceptions: (1) you can retrieve your mail, sign off, answer the mail, and send the answers later, and, (2) you can sort the e-mail into folders to suit you for later reference.

Reading Usenet

MSN has full Usenet newsfeed, but you don't want to search through them all. Instead from the Genealogy Internet Picks, choose Genealogy Internet Newsgroups, and the soc.genealogy.* and you'll get the list in Fig. 14.6. Reading the newsgroups on MSN is exactly like reading the BBS messages, minus the fancy fonts and colors you can do with the BBS messages. Again, all reading and answering must be done online while the meter is ticking.

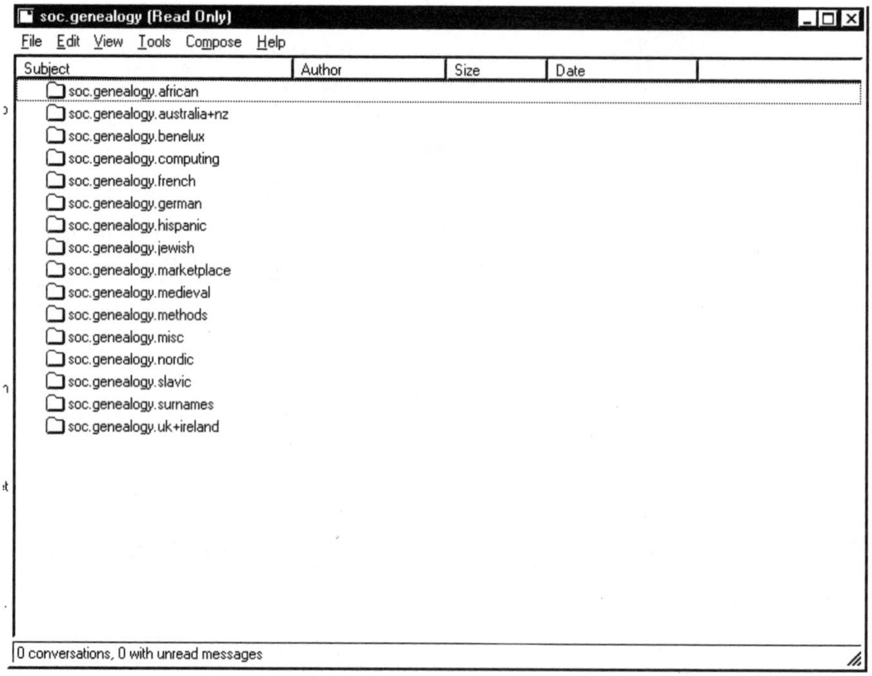

Figure 14.6
Reading Usenet with MSN must be done online.

```
 soc.genealogy (Read Only)                                          _ □ ×
 File  Edit  View  Tools  Compose  Help
 Subject                          Author      Size      Date
    soc.genealogy.african
    soc.genealogy.australia+nz
    soc.genealogy.benelux
    soc.genealogy.computing
    soc.genealogy.french
    soc.genealogy.german
    soc.genealogy.hispanic
    soc.genealogy.jewish
    soc.genealogy.marketplace
    soc.genealogy.medieval
    soc.genealogy.methods
    soc.genealogy.misc
    soc.genealogy.nordic
    soc.genealogy.slavic
    soc.genealogy.surnames
    soc.genealogy.uk+ireland



 0 conversations, 0 with unread messages
```

The Verdict

All in all, MSN's genealogy offerings have come a good way since the launch in September 1995. It's still building, but the members are all helping each other learn genealogy, MSN, and the Internet at the same time. My problem with MSN is not content, but the software. It's slow, it asks too much of the hardware, and the animation and sound don't add that much to your enjoyment of genealogy research, for my taste. But you may feel differently. If a free-month offer is still going on when you read this, try MSN for a month and see if it's what you want in an online service.

15

Prodigy: Prodigy's Genealogy Bulletin Boards and Column

The basic rate for Prodigy Classic is $9.95 a month for five hours of core services and bulletin board and genealogy column use, which are in the *plus* services. It's $2.95 an hour for connection after that, or you can get 30 hours for $30. Prodigy also has an all-Internet service for $19.95 a month that's slowly being integrated into the content of Prodigy Classic. Prodigy's address, phone number, and e-mail access are as follows:

945 Hamilton Avenue
White Plains, New York 10601
800-776-3449 (voice)
userid@prodigy.com (e-mail)

Good News, Bad News

A few years back, Prodigy was good news and bad news for the online genealogist. The good news was weekly columns on genealogy by Myra Vanderpool Gormley, several other helpful professional and amateur genealogists on the bulletin board, messages sorted alphabetically by surname, a real feeling of community and camaraderie, all for a flat monthly fee no matter how lengthy the logon. In fact, it was one of the best online bargains five years ago.

The bad news back then was that Prodigy had no Internet connection at all, screens that looked crayonish, advertisements that took up more than half the screen, and s-s-s-l-l-l-o-o-o-w-w-w front-end software. You spent a lot of time online because there was no download and upload function for mail or messages.

Today, Prodigy is mostly good news and only a little bad news. The good news is that the columns and bulletin board are still there, still sorted in that easy-to-use way, and folks from Family History Centers and the New England Historical and Genealogical Society are online willing to help you. More good news is that Prodigy now has complete Internet access, although the software isn't the best in the world. Still, if you just want to test out the World Wide Web, Prodigy is not a bad place to start.

More good news: the mail-reading and Web-browsing software have improved considerably. So have the genealogy offerings, with new file download areas, an online newsletter, and more.

On Prodigy, bulletin boards (or BBSs) are where you leave messages on a certain subject for others to read and respond to. *Core* services are those included with the basic membership fee, including news, weather, shopping, and other information. *Plus* services are the bulletin boards, some online games, and so on.

Prodigy now has file libraries with GEDCOMs, ahentafels, chat records, sound files, photographs, software, and more. Use the jump word FILE LIBRARIES and scroll down to GENEALOGY. You can download files in batches on Prodigy Classic.

The messages on Prodigy are divided into surname searches and geographical topics, with several specialized topics such as ahentafels and a beginner's corner. Reading while connected, you can search the message base somewhat by choosing a topic and typing in the beginning of the subject line you would like to see. Remember if you decide to use this method, however, that Prodigy is still the slowest software around for an online service. It's also aggressive in getting computer resources, so it's very hard to have any other program running with Prodigy open, even in multitasking systems.

Still, Prodigy has several features that make it worthwhile. Among them are the weekly syndicated column and questions and answer message area with Myra Vanderpool Gormley, a recognized certified genealogist. The atmosphere at Prodigy is helpful and friendly, so much so that my mother still swears its the online place where she gets the most done, including the Internet.

Prodigy users have access to 28,800 bps connections, at no more hourly cost than the slower speeds. Nowadays, the screens are crisper, neater, and the area for your use has a bigger share of the screen than the advertisements at the bottom than previously. The software is improving month by month: you can download messages, read and answer them offline, and upload your replies almost as easily as you can on Delphi or CompuServe with a program called Bulletin Board Manager. With the new Internet mail program you can get Internet mail lists, set mail lists to index, look at headers, and decide whether to spend your nickel to get them. In short, almost all that was good is still there and many improvements have been made.

The bad news is that it's not the bargain it was. To use the Mail Manager (required to send and receive Internet mail) or Bulletin Board Manager, you'll have to pay extra to download the programs to use with the front-end software. And, at this writing, they're available only for Windows and DOS. You'll also pay from 10 to 25 cents for receiving an Internet e-mail message.

Unfortunately, the price hikes chased off many people who made Prodigy (*P to the online diehards) such a friendly place. And sometimes those pretty screens still take a bit of time to generate (although never near the glacierlike pace of years gone by). There is hope, however, offered by third-party programs (see the following) to make the chores easier, and Prodigy is still *P, an online place like nowhere else.

The Difference

Prodigy has always been a different kind of online community. For one thing, it's been a leader in the front-end software area for online services. Some think the popularity of *P's easy-to-understand screens, as opposed to hard-to-remember commands, forced the established, stuffier places like CompuServe to follow its lead with graphic interface front ends.

At the bottom of each Prodigy screen, you'll find a command bar with buttons that execute commands for you. Not all the buttons are there all the time. On the far left of this command bar is an icon that zips you to the main menu of *P, from which you can choose the latest news (updated hourly) or any category of Prodigy service. If a triangle appears in the command bar, then the current screen has more text; clicking the > triangle takes you forward and clicking the < triangle takes you back in that text file.

Menu allows you to go to the last set of choices you had before getting to the current screen. Jump and Path are the buttons you'll use most often. Jump allows you to type in a word, or even part of a word, to go somewhere right away. Path will take you through a set of services you choose for yourself. Web calls up Prodigy's Web browser, for Internet access. You also can connect to the Usenet from Web.

A—Z and XRef are for finding services and functions according to subject. Copy allows you to save what you see right now, either to a file or to the printer. Tools allows you to set up Prodigy the way you want it (this is where you choose File or Printer for the Copy button). The selection ? (question mark) gets help screens, Exit gets you logged off, and at the bottom right of the screen is a word to tell you whether you're in a free, core, or plus service.

Prodigy allows on-screen advertising (but, please note, not by the members in their messages to each other). Almost every screen has a commercial at the bottom for some product or service. You click on a button called Look to get the details and order the product or service online if you want. (If you go off into a Look and then want to return to where you were, click on Tools, click on Change Path, and find the previous location.)

Another important difference is terminology. On Prodigy, *bulletin boards* (which it refers to as *BBs*, instead of the more common *BBSs*, for bulletin board system) are where you leave messages on a certain subject for others to read and respond to. However, files associated with that topic are available only under ZiffNet for Prodigy, a custom choice that adds an extra per-minute charge when you use it. Core services are those included with the basic membership fee, including news, weather, shopping, and other information. Plus services are the bulletin boards, some online games, and so on. Most *P plans allow about two hours of Plus and unlimited Core use per month. After that, it's 6 cents per minute for Plus and Custom Choice services. A little box in the lower right-hand corner of the screen shows you where you are at any given moment.

But the most important difference about Prodigy to its users has been the atmosphere. As one user put it, it's the place for "the rest of us," meaning those who want to use an online service without understanding its every esoteric technical detail. Or any of them, for that matter. The "punch-and-go crowd," so to speak. It's still a very friendly place and very popular.

A Prodigy Visit

Let's visit *P on a typical day. One nice thing about Prodigy is its flexibility. When you install the software, it has you set up the port, speed, and phone numbers to dial to access Prodigy from your computer. These can all be changed by clicking on setup.

Using the tab key or your mouse, get the cursor in the ID and Password boxes to type these in. Or, you can automate this by clicking on the button called Tools and choosing AutoLogon while online. A warning will appear to tell you that completely automating your logon is lowering the security of your account. Then you can choose to automate both password and ID, only your ID, or turn off AutoLogon. You'll be told to choose a nickname, which is another password to start the automatic logon. From then on, you need to type only *prodigy*<nickname> to start the session. For example, if your nickname is *cathy*, the command to start an autologon session would be *prodigy cathy*. Every time you use this option, your first screen online will be the Highlights screen.

In a standard logon, you get the highlights page, as shown in Fig. 15.1. But you can use the logon screen to jump straight to the genealogy area by typing *genealogy* in the Jump box.

But, *P has many different areas for genealogists. You should take a look at the A—Z Index and then type in *gene*. To do this, you can click on GoTo

Figure 15.1

The Highlights page of Prodigy has headlines and featured items. From here, you can Jump genealogy to the BULLETIN BOARDs area or go to the A–Z Index and search for *genealogy*.

in the menu and then choose A–Z Index. Once there, type in *gene* in the little box at the top, and you'll get the screen in Fig. 15.2.

The MENU selection is a page with the choices below it: the Bulletin Board (messages), the weekly column by Myra Vanderpool Gormley, and a Web page of genealogy links.

You can click and go to those choices from here. But if you're going to use *P's genealogy services often, you can make future sessions easier. From this screen, click on GoTo and click on Add to Hot List. This menu item will add any current page to your *hot list,* or the list of places you like to visit often. If you want to rearrange the hot list, click on GoTo | Hot List. You'll get the screen in Fig. 15.3. In this screen, I've added all the genealogy items from the A–Z Index and used Move Up to place them at the top of my list.

Another way to quickly get to Genealogy BULLETIN BOARD or Genealogy Column is to click on Jump from the bottom of any screen and type those jump words in the dialog box.

When you get to any BULLETIN BOARD on Prodigy, the opening menu looks much like the Genealogy one (see Fig. 15.4). You'll find an opening message from the leader. The small button leads to a set of small

Figure 15.2
The A–Z Index listing of genealogy pages on Prodigy.

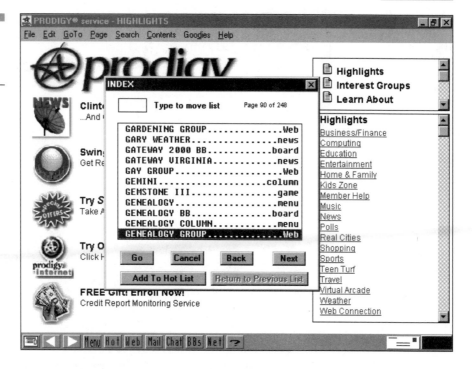

Figure 15.3
Click on GoTo | Hot List and add *GENEALOGY* to the list. Then you'll come to the Genealogy Index page quickly.

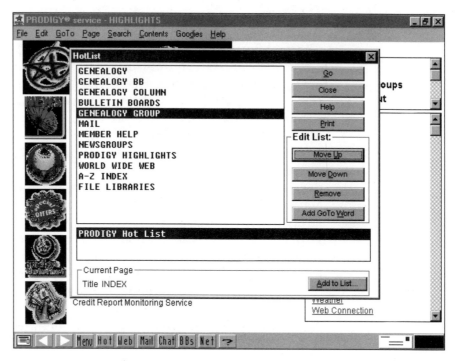

Figure 15.4
The Genealogy BUL-
LETIN BOARD (mes-
sages) opening
screen.

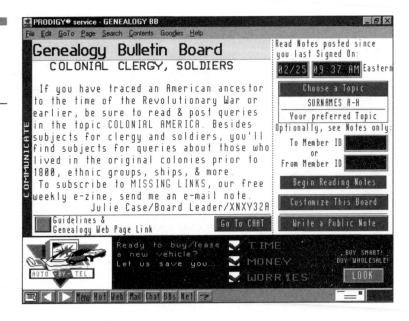

Figure 15.4
The Genealogy BUL-
LETIN BOARD (mes-
sages) opening
screen.

text files about *P BULLETIN BOARDs under Guidelines & Info and, on the right, your control panel for this session of note reading.

The date and time in Read Notes Posted Since defaults to the time of your last logon, but you can change both the time and the date. You'll Choose A Topic, then Choose A Subject, then Begin Reading Notes. However, if you wish, you can first Customize the Board. In Fig. 15.5, I have chosen to have my first Topic Surnames I–Z and Spencer subjects shown to me first. I can look at all the boards, but this is where I'll go first from now on.

Under Choose A Topic, the subjects are arranged alphabetically, and you can type in a few letters (for example, *spen*) to jump through the list to make your selection. You can choose only one topic and one subject at a time. As mentioned before, the topics include surname searches, but there are also headings for adoptions, various countries, and many others. You can click on a button to browse through the first lines of the messages by subject or topic.

To post a new message, click on the Options button in the lower-right corner of the screen. To read and reply to messages offline, you need a third-party program, ProUtil, which will be profiled later in this chapter.

Under the topic Beginning Genealogy, you'll find the subject Ask Myra. This is where Gormley answers questions from members (see Fig. 15.6). Here, Ms. Gormley answers puzzlers from where to look for records in the Panama Canal Zone to what are good genealogy books for the beginner. She even answers questions about how the bulletin board

Figure 15.5
You can customize the BULLETIN BOARD to go to your favorite Topics and Subjects first.

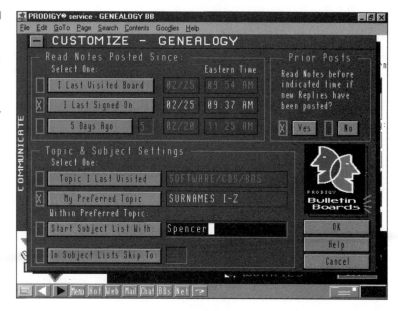

works, even though there is a separate topic for that (Software/CDs/BUL-LETIN BOARDS).

This is the sort of friendly, helpful exchange you can expect on Prodigy. The board is very busy, and it could very well take all of your monthly two-hour allotment to keep up with a week's worth of messages!

Figure 15.6
Genealogy experts answer questions in the ASK MYRA subject of the Beginner topic on Prodigy.

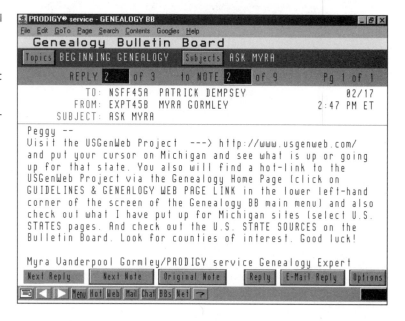

When you've read and replied to all the messages you want, Jump to GENEALOGY to get back to the index page of genealogy offerings. (Or, if you put GENEALOGY COLUMN next in your hot list, you can use that to immediately be taken to the next area, by pressing F4.) In Fig. 15.7, you see a typical column. If this were your second visit this week, and you had already visited the column, you could simply press F4 again and skip this.

Under *Tools,* you can set Copy to send text to the printer (the default) or to a file. If you want to save this column to a file, this is a good time to set that toggle, name the file, and copy the whole column to read later.

Gormley has been writing these columns every week for years, and they're online at *P for your reference. Simply go back to the column menu page and click on the button Archive and the columns appear as in Fig. 15.8. The columns, in alphabetical order, can all be found here. If you have a topic in mind, type in up to nine letters and the list will scroll to the closest match.

If you select one, when it appears on the screen you can click Copy (which will send it to the printer if you haven't selected File from the Tools button) and read it later. Clicking on Menu will return you to the list of columns. One that I heartily recommend is her discussion about the Black Dutch, which taught me some American history I didn't know.

Figure 15.7
Myra Vanderpool Gormley has a new column each week at Jump Genealogy Column.

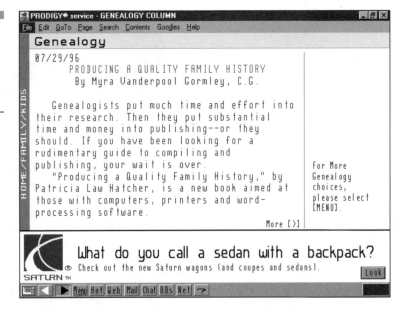

Figure 15.8
A typical list of
GENEALOGY COL-
UMN topics.

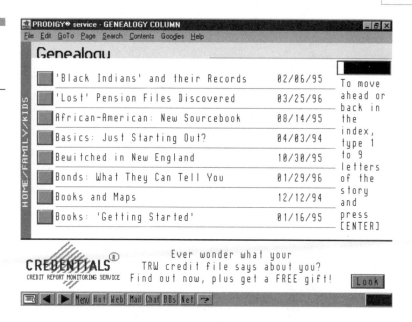

Figure 15.8 is a typical list of GENEALOGY COLUMN topics.

Prodigy Internet Access

Both Prodigy Classic and the new Prodigy Internet have Internet services, but the Prodigy Internet has better and faster software. Also, with Prodigy Internet and the right third-party software, you can telnet, finger, or use any other Internet service; with Prodigy Classic you can use the Web, Usenet, e-mail, and ftp.

Web Surfing

Prodigy Classic's Web browser has improved mightily in the last year, but although it's faster and can handle many more file types than it used to, it still doesn't have many of the advanced features of other browsers. Similarly, its Usenet news reading doesn't allow any offline reading and answering, although it does have a good search capability. The Internet services that come with Prodigy Classic (Web browsing, chat, and Usenet) are good for learning the ropes, but once you are proficient, you'll find you'll do better with a Prodigy Internet account.

The Prodigy Internet browser can be either Netscape Navigator (as in Fig. 15.9) or Microsoft Internet Explorer and includes a toolbar to the right for functions such as Chat. But beware: it won't check for existing browsers

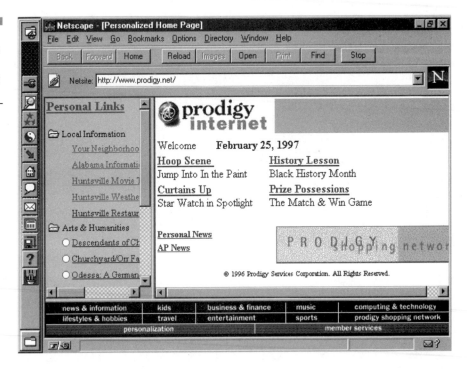

but will install its own copy. If you already had Netscape Navigator 3.0, you'll want to erase the old one to save disk space.

Prodigy maintains a genealogy Web page (see Fig. 15.10). You can get there in Prodigy Classic by clicking the Web Site button on the genealogy menu; to get there in Prodigy Internet, click HoBulletin Boardies and Interests at the bottom of the screen, then choose Pastimes, then Family History.

This page is a good place for the beginner, with some good links to get you started. You can get to the files here by following the links in the index frame of the page. You can also find an explanation of mail lists, with a special genealogy newsletter just for Prodigy Members called "Missing Links." This newsletter has news of the Prodigy Bulletin Board, member comments, book reviews, and more.

Usenet

The Bulletin Board messages are available as Prodigy-specific newsgroups, using Netscape as the newsreader. Of course, you can also subscribe to

Figure 15.10
Prodigy has a page to help you start surfing the World Wide Web for genealogy.

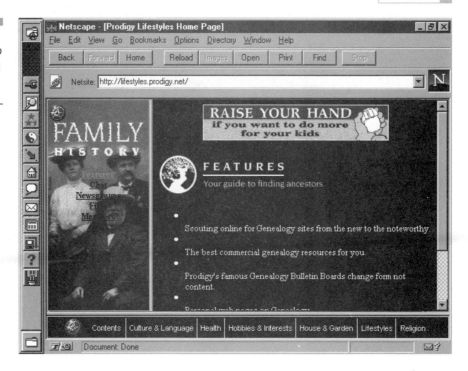

soc.genealogy.* with Prodigy Internet and the Netscape Navigator or Microsoft Internet Explorer news window (see Fig. 15.11), using the Edit|Find command to search for the surnames and places you want in the subject lines.

To read Usenet articles on Prodigy Classic, Jump USENET, you will have to assign your account names permitted to use Usenet and read some warnings about the service. Then you can choose a button called Find Newsgroups. Input *genealogy* in the dialog box and you'll be able to subscribe to any of the Usenet genealogy groups by clicking the button Add to your newsgroups. Then close out the selection boxes and your list of subscribed newsgroups is listed in the window.

Double-clicking on any newsgroup brings up the list of current articles. You can determine how far back your list of articles goes by setting the date in the newsgroup list window. Once you have a list of articles, by clicking on the Search button you can search for certain words; this is very useful in soc.genealogy.surnames.

Unfortunately, even with the companion software described later, you can't read and reply to Usenet articles offline with Prodigy.

Figure 15.11
You can read Usenet
on Prodigy Classic,
but it's better on
Prodigy Internet.

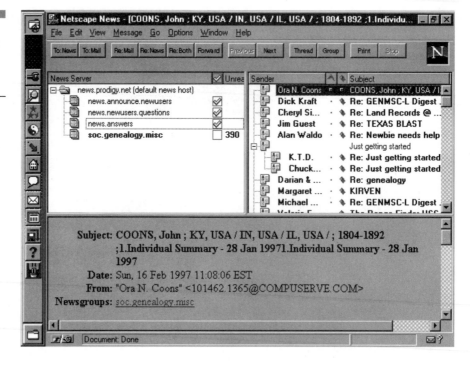

Chat

Chat on Prodigy Classic and Prodigy Internet is a very popular service. The Genealogy area has several regularly scheduled chats (see Fig. 15.12). Held in the lifesty.family chat room every Monday, Wednesday, and Friday at 10:30 A.M. (Eastern), people here discuss the following:

- *High-tech genealogy.* What you can do on the Web, on CD, in microfilm, and how to use your computer to compile and share your family history.

- *Your family tree.* Basics and beginner topics, questions and answers.

- *Family connections.* Discussions about why we love family history.

Transcripts of these chats are in the files area. To use Chat, simply click the Chat button on the Genealogy menu page in Prodigy Classic or click the chat icon on the toolbar in Prodigy Internet, and sign onto lifsty.family.

Figure 15.12
Chat on Prodigy and
Prodigy Internet is a
very popular service.

Companion Software

As improved as the Prodigy software is compared to just a couple of years ago, I still wish it had a few more functions. Fortunately, you can have them for a fee.

An older Prodigy helper is Pro-Util, a DOS-based application. Pro-Util takes about 350K of disk space, but can use less. It also takes 25 to 28K of memory, but only while you run Prodigy. It loads itself before Prodigy and removes itself from memory when you exit.

It changes the working icon to a clock, simplifies the upload and download of messages, allows you to use a word processor such as WordPerfect, includes a spelling checker for your messages, and more. "We will also have a Windows version released in a couple months with the DOS features and more features to enhance the Prodigy windows program. We will also begin work on a DOS BULLETIN BOARD off-line reader and BULLETIN BOARD manager to be released in mid-summer," said Dennis, a Royston Development programmer, in early 1994.

Pro-Util comes with over 60 pages of documentation on the installation disk, completely rewritten for version 6. You can also get online help with Pro-Util when in Prodigy.

You can order Pro-Util by jumping to Royston and selecting option 5, then selecting the Complete download. The company takes Visa and MasterCard on Prodigy or checks by mail. You can order Pro-Util 6 by mail by sending a check to:

Royston Development
4195 Chino Hills Parkway #510
Chino Hills, CA 91709

The price is $24.95 plus sales tax if you are in California, plus $3.50 for shipping and handling. Please include your Prodigy ID so they can contact you with any questions. Also, mention the disk size (3½- or 5¼-inch) you prefer.

APPENDIX A

GENSERV AND GENWEB

Would you like to search over 6 million names of genealogical research without leaving your computer? Or maybe you wish you could find a more selective source, with information on just certain surnames? Both are possible on the World Wide Web through GENSERV and the even more ambitious GENWEB.

Both are attempts to use distributed networking to share and disseminate genealogical information. But be warned: the information you find with them is only as reliable as the people submitting it. Neither project requires the information to come from a certified genealogist or to include original sources or to be proven in the way, say, DAR applications are.

GenServ

The GenServ (Genealogical GEDCOM Server) system has an extensive collection of GEDCOM databases on one computer system. These databases contain basic genealogical information such as names, dates of birth, marriage, details of family relationships, and often the details of the sources of this information and other descriptive text. This information is submitted by those wishing to participate, but none of it is checked, verified, or validated. The only authentication available is that which the submitters include in their GEDCOMs, the form of notes attached to the records.

Once you are a registered user, you can access GenServ via the World Wide Web at www.genserv.com. However, automated searches of this information can be requested by means of commands sent to GenServ by electronic mail, and the system sends you the results by e-mail. You don't have to have full Internet connectivity in order to use GenServ—just an e-mail box somewhere.

You can perform one sample search, for free, before you submit or pay anything by going to http://soback.kornet.nm.kr/~cmanis/gensspec.htm and filling out the form (see Fig. A.1). Read the instructions carefully, because you only get one try.

The GenServ database has been collected from people who donated their own family data for this project. The administrators are interested in any genealogical databases, large or small.

The data in these databases is accessible through commands sent to the system via a regular e-mail message. The system then formats the request and e-mails a report back to the user who sent the request.

The most efficient way to use GenServ, in terms of connect time, is to use your e-mail Internet access, whether that's through a commercial online service or an Internet Service Provider.

You can provide up to six GEDCOM databases to GenServ, including ones on behalf of other genealogists who do not themselves have the necessary computer and networking facilities. The rule is only those who have themselves submitted one or more GEDCOM databases can make queries, but you can query the database for other people.

Signing Up

For the first three years, GenServ was free. You can still use GenServ for free for two months by simply submitting your GEDCOM database. But as costs and time consumed rose, the administrators found they had to start charging, although they have attempted to keep it as little as possible. (See Table A.1.)

To become a user, you must follow the sign-up procedure carefully. You can submit your information by e-mail or ftp, but before you try it, you must read the latest instructions. If you wish to submit via ftp, send a message with any subject to genftp@genserv.com. But the best way is by surface mail. First, create and send a GEDCOM, as the following details, and send it to:

Cliff Manis
HHC, 18th MEDCOM
P.O. Box 579
APO AP 96205
USA
cmanis@soback.kornet.nm.kr (e-mail)

If you live in Europe you can send your disk to:

Jon Rees Church Cottage, Ringsfield, Beccles, Suffolk, NR34 8JU UK.
J.M.REES@DFR.MAFF.GOV.UK (e-mail)

Then, you send a check for the level of service you want. Make it payable to GenServ and send it to:

Cliff Manis
Attn: GenServ System
P.O. Box 33937
San Antonio, Texas 78265-3937

TABLE A.1

GenServ Costs

Yearly Cost ($)	Type	Gives You
$12	Regular sponsor	Maximum 12 requests per hour. More than one message per hour is possible, but only 12 requests. A dollar a month.
6	Over 60 (and students)	For those users over 60 years old and students attending school (verification will not be attempted).
35+	Prime sponsor	For any company, group, or individual who is willing to contribute support at a higher level. Up to 50 requests per hour while using the GenServ system.

PREPARING YOUR GEDCOM. A GEDCOM file is required for access to GenServ, but don't send off your disk willy-nilly!

Have your genealogical software compile a database with all the genealogical data you have accumulated and analyzed in your researches, including not only basic data such as names and dates, but also any Notes fields. Be sure the database is the results of your own researches, not simply one produced by automatic extraction from some other system such as the IGI CD-ROM system. (The database, in fact, remains the property of the original submitter—and will not be provided in GEDCOM format to anyone else.)

When GenServ searches, it does so on the entire set of databases that have been submitted to it. But each database remains separate and associated with the name of its author. So, if you find new or better data in the future, it is possible for you to withdraw a database that you submitted previously and replace it with an updated one. This has another implication, however: no effort is made to eliminate or merge duplicate individuals found in more than one database, and many duplicates are, in fact, known to exist.

In theory, a GEDCOM database exported from any genealogical database management system should be acceptable to any system that claims to be able to import GEDCOM. In practice, so many differences exist between the GEDCOM formats used by various systems that a GEDCOM database produced by one system may not load correctly, or at all, into some other systems.

So, once your GEDCOM has been generated, before sending it to GenServ, run a test to be sure that your GEDCOM database can be successfully imported by one of the following systems:

PAF (LDS), version 2.1 or later

GIM (Genealogical Information Manager), version 2.* or later

Brother's Keeper, any version 1992 or later

LifeLines, the UNIX Genealogical Program, any version

Three of the preceding programs are available via ftp from ftp.cac.psu .edu (128.118.2.23) from the genealogy area.

Also, it's wise to check the database with Brother's Keeper.

If you use Family Tree Maker, be sure to save your GEDCOM as a PAF file (version 4 or 5, using IBM PC character set), with no indent and with abbreviated tags before checking that it can be successfully imported into one of the preceding systems.

If you use ROOTS IV, be sure to save it as a ROOTS 3 GEDCOM file (ROOTS IV GEDCOM cannot be read by GenServ). Having performed such a check, you should send your GEDCOM database on a 3½-inch high- or low-density floppy disk (in a diskette mailer) as either an ASCII file or compressed with PKZip, in MSDOS format, to the previously listed postal address for Cliff (who is currently living in Seoul, Korea). The address for Cliff will be valid through at least August 1996 and maybe 1997.

Finally, and very important, with the disk, you must include a piece of paper on which you have typed your e-mail address, postal street address, city, state, zip, country, and your telephone number. Cliff will get your disk in less than 3 weeks and will process it and give you an access code to the user within another 7 days. In all, give him about 30 days to send you a user code; if you don't get it by then, contact him by e-mail.

SOME SPECIAL TIPS ON SUBMITTING YOUR GEDCOM

- Apple Macintosh users should use Apple File Exchange or an equivalent utility to produce MSDOS-compatible floppy disks.

- If you have a database with over 30,000 surnames, please contact Cliff for special instructions for sending your large GEDCOM file to the GenServ system. The system has databases containing over 50,000 names each, but such GEDCOMs need special handling. You can e-mail Cliff about your large database at cmanis@Soback.Kornet.nm.kr.

- GenServ is very interested in the complete GEDCOM file, with all note lines and other tags.

- The data and documents on the system are the responsibility of individual authors of the GEDCOM files. The GEDCOM files are not edited or judged for content by the operators of the GenServ System. The data belongs to the author of the GEDCOM file, and it is the responsibility of individual data providers to comply with all applicable laws and standards of what should or should not be published in their own GEDCOM files.

- Cliff Manis will not attempt to locate e-mail addresses for those sending a diskette without a valid e-mail address. If you don't include it, he can't help you.

- Updates to GEDCOM files on the system may only be sent in at six-month intervals. Don't send updates more frequently than this.

- Read the documents of the GenServ system carefully in full before you try this. You can get them in several ways:

  Download ftp from ftp.cac.psu.edu
  Download ftp.flattop.fc.net

To request the documentation by e-mail, send any message to genserv-doc@Genserv.com.

- The day you send the disk by mail, e-mail Cliff Manis to tell him it's coming! This gives him another chance at seeing whether your e-mail address is valid. This e-mail address will also be used for a message confirming that your database has been loaded and tested or for notifying you if the database you have submitted cannot be loaded. (No attempt will be made to edit the offending database in order to get it to load.)

- To update, do the same thing you did for the first submission, but label the diskette UPDATE TO <<the name of your database>>.

Using GenServ

You should get and study the latest version of HOW2DO from the GenServ site before you attempt to query the database. This file, which is updated frequently, has all the commands and error messages the system uses, with clear examples of how to do a useful search. You can get it on the Web at http://soback.kornet.nm.kr/~cmanis/how2doa.htm or by sending any message (even a blank one) to genhow2@genserv.com.

When your database is accepted to the GenServ system, Cliff will send you the user name, access code, and e-mail address that GenServ associates with your database(s). You have to include your user name and your access code in any later request you make to GenServ. The e-mail address is the address to which GenServ will send its responses to any messages from you, no matter from where they are actually sent. It is therefore very important that you notify Cliff Manis (cmanis@genserv.com) of any changes to your e-mail address.

GenServ always responds to the e-mail address that it has stored associated with your user name. If your request comes from a different e-mail address, the stored one will get the response.

All GenServ commands are processed as they are received, but there may be a small delay before the resulting reports are sent by e-mail. All valid user requests are usually processed within an hour, but it will only process up to six requests in 30 minutes for any one user. Remember that the response can also be delayed, perhaps for hours, by network outages.

Send your requests in batches of no more than six at a time. You don't have to try to get everything in one day—this system will also be available for use next week, and next year!

There's much more GenServ can do, and the administrators are tweaking and engineering all the time to improve it. For details on the reports and latest features, get the documentation. The entire list follows:

geninfo file	send e-mail to geninfo@genserv.com
genhow2 file	send e-mail to genhow2@genserv.com
genrpts file	send e-mail to genrpts@genserv.com
gedmake file	send e-mail to gedmake@genserv.com
genem file	send e-mail to genem@genserv.com
genftp file	send e-mail to genftp@genserv.com
disclaimer file	send e-mail to disclaimer@genserv.com

GENWEB

The idea behind the GENWEB project is to make all genealogical databases searchable and available on the Web. Now this requires the skill of a genealogist to gather the data, the skill of a programmer to make the information searchable and to create the search program, and the skill of a Webmeister to put it all in HTML format. Despite these hurdles, a great deal of progress has been made in 1996 toward making this wild-eyed dream a reality. New sites are going up all the time, so you'll have to use Lycos or Infoseek or some such to keep up with the new ones, and go to the official USGENWEB site at http://www.usgenweb.com/ to find out what's new (see Fig. A.2).

In March and April 1996, a group of genealogists organized the Kentucky Comprehensive Genealogy Database Project. The idea was to provide a single entry point for all counties in Kentucky, where collected databases would be stored. In addition, the databases would be indexed and cross-linked, so that even if an individual were found in more than one county, he or she could be located in the index. Now dozens of such sites exist, for states and for particular family names. By the end of 1997, the number of sites may reach in the hundreds. Together they are the USGENWEB project, which hopes to promote the linking of online genealogical resources by putting up resource home pages for each U.S. county or governmental subdivision. This is an all-volunteer effort. If you have knowledge of a particular county, you, too, can be part of the project!

To begin your search, go to http://www.gentree.com/, the home page of the GENWEB project. As surname-searchable databases are put on the

Figure A.2
You can find historical
and genealogical
information by loca-
tion at USGENWEB.

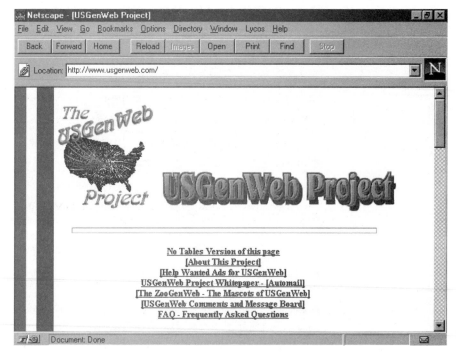

Web, they register here, with the proper URL. Tim Doyle is keeping an alphabetized list of such family databases. So, for a very specific surname search on GENWEB, start here.

But suppose you need a geographical search? Then, you need to start at the USGENWEB site, http://www.usgenweb.com/. Here you can click on a map and be transported to a page in that state. Now, some of these offer names and dates; others simply addresses to contact for information. The whole project is very much a work in progress.

For example, the Kentucky GEBWEB site (http://www.dsenter.com/ ~trice/ky/) has a list of all 120 Kentucky counties. Some have a blue ball next to them, meaning they have yet to find a volunteer to put all the information on the Web. Each county that has been adopted by a volunteer will have as much information as available: a query page, where you can post and reply; a place where you can describe what you're willing to look up for someone else or request such a look up yourself; and pointers to pages with more information about that county.

How much information about specific people will vary from county to county. But as the project progresses, it is hoped some real, original source material will find its way onto the Web this way.

APPENDIX B

TINY TAFEL MATCHING SYSTEM

Many local BBSs carry a message base called the Tiny Tafel Matching System, or TTMS. This attempts to match people searching similar lines through an abbreviated data file called a tiny tafel.

Like a GEDCOM, a *tiny tafel* is a way of expressing what data you have to share. Unlike a GEDCOM, however, its primary use is not to exchange that data, but to alert people to its existence and show how to reach you to exchange data. A tiny tafel is to indicate interest, to let people know what you have and what you need in a quick, standardized way. Though computers read tiny tafels to make these matches, once you learn the format, you too can read and understand what the TT has to say.

Paul Andereck proposed the tiny tafel format in 1986, as an alternative to the numerical Ahentafel. The advantage would be a shorthand for the data: instead of listing every known ancestor in a particular surname line, the TT would instead show a range for the surname, in dates, location, and Soundex code. An entire surname line would be summarized by one line in a tiny tafel. The top of the file would have contact information for exchanging the actual data. The data fields in a TT would be fixed, making it easy for various computer programs to read the files, and making matches easier.

The tiny tafel standard format was first used in Commsoft's Roots program, but now several genealogical data programs either have built-in or add-on utilities to output a tiny tafel from your data. As the format is very rigid and unforgiving of typos, you should probably have a program prepare your tiny tafel rather than try to do one by hand. However, you do need to know how to read them and what each column and line means.

Computers can read tiny tafels easily and build databases of them, looking for matching entries among the many files. Many bulletin boards carrying the National Genealogy Conference have such databases, and the FidoNet itself has a program to look at such databases all over the world and report the matches back to you. This is the Tiny Tafel Matching System.

Tafel is German for *table,* and the tiny tafel is a table of data pointers. Each line and column has a specific meaning.

Anatomy of a Tiny Tafel

The first few lines are information about the tiny tafel's originator. *N* starts the line with the name of the person. As many A lines as necessary can be used for the surface mail address of the person. *T* is the line for voice phone contact. *B* is the line for the BBS the person uses, *C* for the communications setup of that board. The S line lists commercial online services, with user id, for e-mail contact; there can be up to five of these lines. The D line describes what sort of floppy disk this person can use to exchange data: 3½-inch, for instance. F, the format line, describes the software format for the person. Several R lines may follow with Remarks such as, "I may have some erroneous data." Of these introductory lines, only the N line, the first one, is mandatory. The other mandatory line is the last one of this introductory section, the Z line. This line has the total number of data items (lines). If the number of lines does not match the number in the Z line, the TTMS program assumes some error has been introduced into the file. This is one reason it's best to let the computer do your TT; if you add or delete lines between the Z and the terminator line (W), but forget to change the number in the Z line, your TT will be rejected by the system.

So the top of a typical TT may look like this:

N   Elizabeth P. Crowe

A   619 Mountain Gap Road

A · Huntsville, AL 35803

T   205-555-5555

S   etravel@delphi.com

S   LibbiC@aol.com

S   lcrowe@iquest.com

C   28.8K/O/Zmodem

D   3/1.4M/DSDD

F   BK for Windows

R   I also can exchange data via fax

Z   ********

The Z line will hold the final count of the data lines.

Now comes the fun part: the description of the data. Here, each column in each line is significant. Each line is considered a record, and fields of different but usually specific lengths are assigned to the columns of the line.

The data are divided this way:

Column	Description
1–4	Soundex code for the name with the highest interest level.
5	A blank space.
6–9	Birth year of earliest ancestor.
10	Interest flag for the ancestor line. The interest flags are one character each: a space for no interest, . (period) for low interest, : (colon) for moderate interest, and * (asterisk) for highest interest level.
11–14	Latest descendant birth year.
15	Interest flag for the descendant end of the family line.
16–16+	The surname string area, which can be variable. Up to 5 surnames can be added per line from 16 on, but you want to save some room for the place names, too.
16+–PL	Place names for the birth of earliest ancestor and latest descendant. A backslash indicates the ancestor place and a forward slash the descendant place.

So, a typical TT line could be:

K530 1770*1996 Kennedy\IR/Boston MA/St. Louis MO/San Francisco CA

The Soundex code is K530. The submitter is very interested in this line in the 1770s but not interested in the present generation. The Kennedy came from Ireland to Boston, Massachusetts; the family migrated through St. Louis to San Francisco. Once you get used to it, it's very easy to read.

Some tips and rules: you must enter valid dates, and dates are required. The matching system cannot work without dates. If listing the first and last of a line hides some migration, you can break the surname into two lines. Remember this is a shorthand version of your research, and so you render the information as best you can. If you are not sure about the exact location of a place, put something there, even if it's just a continent. The more information you give, the better chance you have of finding someone with similar interests. If you have to edit a program-generated tiny tafel, remember to change the Z line if your total number of data lines changes.

Using the Tiny Tafel

There are lots of places and ways to share your tiny tafel. The first thing many people do with them is to post them to the Usenet newsgroup rec.genealogy.gendata (the corresponding FidoNet group is GENDATA.) These are for posting only, discussions of the tiny tafels take place in other newsgroups and echoes or by private e-mail. On the Internet, at http://emecee.com, you'll find Michael Cooley's archive of tiny tafels. You can submit yours and search the ones that are there. The ROOTS-L archive (at the moment residing at http://infobases.wia.net/roots-l/) also has information in a format very similar to a tiny tafel.

But the most fun is to find a bulletin board system near you that participates in the Tiny Tafel Matching System. This task is not as daunting as it sounds; the BBSs listed in the National Genealogy Society's list of genealogical BBSs will be a good place to start. Look for boards that list DA as one of their echoes. You could also ask around at local computer user groups and genealogy clubs for the nearest one.

TTMS is free. Any BBS offering the TMS service must provide it for free, although many sysops require that you first post a tiny tafel of your own to qualify for the free access. Submitting the tiny tafels is just one of the three main functions of the TTMS software. The other two are *instant searches,* where you search only those tiny tafels on the BBS you are using, and the *offline* search, wherein you submit a query and receive a report on the results several days later. The query will be sent to all the other TTMS boards before the report is generated. This is a way to do a nationwide search with just a few keystrokes.

Generally, this is done through a *door* program (a program that takes over while the BBS software steps aside except for communications). An example is shown in Fig. B.1. This is the screen from Genealogy SF in California, profiled in Chap. 2. After logging on, as described in Chap. 2, you can do an instant match. This is the less-efficient way because you must do it while online and because you can only search one board at a time. But it will do for practice. As the illustration shows, you answer a few questions, and then matching lines from tiny tafels are shown. If one looks close enough to be interesting, you can get the contact information by typing the line number of the entry (see Fig. B.2).

Once you enter your tiny tafel into TMS (and remember, only do that one time!), you will be able to choose the M)atch option. Just as with instant match, the software will ask you the questions, and you specify name (or Soundex code), dates, places, and interest levels. You can also

Figure B.1
In Instant Match you
check tiny tafels on
just one BBS. Simply
enter the surname
and close or exact
matches will be
listed.

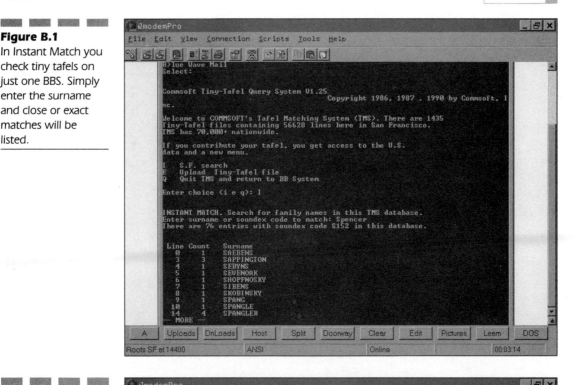

Figure B.2
If you find a match,
the tiny tafel line
matching your search
will be displayed. You
can get contact infor-
mation by entering
the line number of
the one that interests
you.

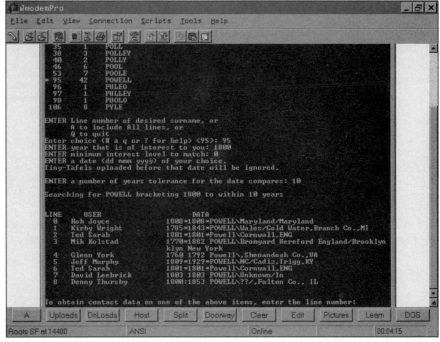

limit the search by date of tiny tafel, so that you can search only those that are new since your last search.

In a few days, you will start getting reports from other TTMS BBS. To retrieve your report, go back to the TTMS, and it will tell you which reports are waiting. You can read the report online or download it to your computer to read offline. I recommend the latter; this report has much more information than instant search and can run up to 100 pages.

The TTMS report will first remind you of the criteria and then list the matches by BBS. Names, contact information, and the TT line that matched will be listed for each hit.

Submitting a Tiny Tafel

You can submit a tiny tafel by calling a TTMS BBS directly. You can also e-mail your TT to Brian Mavrogeorge at mavrogeorge@sfo.com. Include with your TT four surnames and other information for your search (dates, interest level, locations) and Brian will get the results back to you. You can also post your TT onto the FidoNet National Genealogy Conference, in soc.genealogy.surnames or alt.genealogy.

APPENDIX C

FORMS OF GENEALOGICAL DATA: AHNENTAFELS, TINY TAFELS, AND GEDCOMS

One of the reasons to get involved in the online genealogy world is to share the information you have, as well as find information you don't have. To do that, standards have been set up for transmitting that information: ahnentafels, tiny tafels, and GEDCOMs. They are all designed to put information in a standard format. The last two are readable by many different genealogical database programs, and many utilities have been written to translate information from one to another.

Ahnentafels

Ahnentafels are not big tiny tafels. The word means *ancestor table* in German, and the format is more than a century old. It lists all known ancestors of an individual and includes the full name of each ancestor as well as dates and places of birth, marriage, and death. It organizes this information along a strict numbering scheme.

Once you get used to ahnentafels, it becomes very easy to read them, moving up and down from parent to child and back again. The numbering scheme is the key to it all. Consider this typical pedigree chart which follows. Study the numbers in the chart. Every person listed has a number, and there's a mathematical relationship between parents and children. The number of a father is always double that of his child's. The number of the mother is always double that of her child's plus one. The number of a child is always one-half that of its parent (ignoring any remainder).

In this example, the father of person no. 6 is no. 12, the mother of no. 6 is no. 13, and the child of no. 13 is no. 6. In ahnentafel format, the chart reads like this:

1. person
2. father

```
                                            8.   great grandfather
                    4. paternal grandfather, |
                       |                      9.   great grandmother
          2. Father,   |
             |         |                     10.  great grandfather
             |         5. paternal grandmother, |
             |                               11.  great grandmother
1. Person,   |
          |
             |                               12.  great grandfather
             |         6. maternal grandfather, |
             |         |                     13.  great grandmother
          3. Mother,   |
             |                               14.  great grandfather
                    7. maternal grandmother, |
                                             15.  great grandmother
```

3. mother
4. paternal grandfather
5. paternal grandmother
6. maternal grandfather
7. maternal grandmother
8. great grandfather
9. great grandmother
10. great grandfather
11. great grandmother
12. great grandfather
13. great grandmother
14. great grandfather
15. great grandmother

    Notice that the numbers are exactly the same as in the pedigree chart. The rules of father = 2 × child, mother = 2 × child + 1, child = parent/2, ignore remainder, and so on, remain the same. This is an ahnentafel chart.

    In practice, ahnentafels are rarely uploaded as text files, but it's one way to show what you do know about your tree, quickly and in few characters. Just clearly state that it's an ahnentafel.

▬ ▬ Tiny Tafels

Despite the similar name, a *tiny tafel* (TT) is a different animal. It provides a standard way of describing a family database so that the information can be scanned visually or by computer. It was described in an article entitled "Tiny-Tafel for Database Scope Indexing" by Paul Andereck in the April-May-June 1986 issue (vol. 5, no. 4) of *Genealogical Computing*.

The concept of TTs was adopted by CommSoft first in its popular program, Roots-II, and later in Roots-III. It has since been adapted by other genealogical programs, such as Brother's Keeper and GED2TT.

A TT makes no attempt to include the details that are contained in an ahentafel. All data fields are of fixed length, with the obvious exceptions of the surnames and optional places. A TT lists only surnames of interest (with Soundex) plus the locations and dates of the beginning and end of that surname. Tiny tafels make no provision for first names, births, marriages, deaths, or multiple locations.

The format of the tiny tafel is rigidly controlled. Here's the specification as released by CommSoft:

```
Header:
Column                    Description
, , , , , ,                 , , , , , , , , , ,
1      Header type
2      Space delimiter
3 - n  Text (n < 38) (n + 1) Carriage Return
Defined types:
Header
 Type      Description                      Remarks
 , , , ,        , , , , , , , , , ,              , , , , ,

N Name of person having custody of data    Mandatory first record
A Address data                             0 to 5 address lines
                                           Optional
T Telephone number including area code      Optional
S Communication Service/telephone number   0 to 5 service lines
  (MCI, ITT, ONT, RCA, ESL, CIS, SOU, etc,  Optional
  e.g., CIS/77123,512)
B Bulletin Board/telephone number           Optional
C Communications nnnn/X/P                    Optional
     nnnn = maximum baud rate
     X = O(riginate only), A(nswer only), B(oth)
     P = Protocol (Xmodem, Kermit, etc.)
D Diskette format d/f/c                      Optional
     d = diameter (3, 5, 8)
     f = format MS-DOS, Apple II, etc.
     c = capacity, KB
F File format                               Free-form, optional
   ROOTS II, ROOTS/M, PAF Version 1, etc.
R Remark                                    Free-form, optional
Z Number of data items with optional text   Required last item
```

In the CommSoft tiny tafel, the name of the database, the version of the database, and any special switches used when the tiny tafel was generated are shown on the Z line. The definitions of the special switches are as follows:

D—DATEFILLDISABLED. Tiny tafel normally suppresses the output of data for which the birth dates necessary to establish each line of output are missing. When this switch is on, the tiny tafel generator has estimated missing dates. The tiny tafel program applies a 30-year per generation offset wherever it needs to reconstruct missing dates.

N—NOGROUPING. Tiny tafel normally groups output lines that have a common ancestor into a single line containing the most recent birth date. Descendants marked with an interest level greater than zero, however, will have their own line of output. Alternatively, when this switch is enabled, one line of output is created for every ultimate descendant (individual without children).

M—MULTIPLENAMES. Tiny tafel normally lists a surname derived from the descendant end of each line. Specifying this option lists all unique spellings of each surname (up to five) separated by commas.

P—PLACENAMES. Tiny tafel will include place names for family lines when this switch is enabled. Place names will be the most significant 14 to 16 characters of the birth field. When this option is enabled, the place of birth of the ultimate ancestor and the place of birth of the ultimate descendant of a line of output, respectively, are added to the end of the line.

S—SINGLEITEMS. Tiny tafel normally suppresses lines of output that correspond to a single individual (that is, in which the ancestry and descendant dates are the same). This switch includes single-person items in the output.

#I—INTERESTLEVEL. Tiny tafel normally includes all family lines meeting the preceding conditions no matter what their interest level. An interest level may be specified to limit the lines included to those having an interest level equal to or greater than the number specified. For example, with the interest level set to 1, all lines which have an ancestor or descendant interest level of 1 or higher will be listed.

See Table C.1.

The Soundex code for any given line is obtained from the end of the line that has the highest interest level. If the interest levels are the same at each end, however, the name at the ancestor end will be used. If the application of these rules yields a surname that cannot be converted to

TABLE C.1

Tiny Tafel Data

Col	Description
1 through 4	Soundex code (note 1)
5	Space delimiter
6 through 9	Earliest ancestor birth year
10	Interest flag, ancestor end of family line (note 2)
11 through 14	Latest descendant birth year
15	Interest flag, descendant end of family line (note 2)
16 through 16+	SL, surname string area (SL = total surname length) above + PL, place name area (PL = total place name length) above + 1 Carriage return

Soundex, however, the program will attempt to obtain a Soundex code from the other end of the line.

Interest flag: the codes for interest level are

[space]	No interest (level 0)
.	Low interest (level 1)
:	Moderate interest (level 2)
·	Highest interest (level 3)

Up to five surnames can be on one line where surname has changed in that line. If more than five surnames are found in a line, only the latest five will be shown. The inclusion of additional surnames is enabled by the M switch.

Place names for the birth of the earliest ancestor and the latest descendant may be included by using the P switch. If a place name is not provided for the individual whose birth year is shown, the field will be blank. The place for the ancestor is preceded by a backslash (\) and for the descendant by a slash (/).

Terminator: *W* is the date tiny tafel file was generated, in the DD MMM YYYY format.

That's how you build one manually. Most genealogical software packages now have a function to create and accept either a TT or GEDCOM or both from your information in the database. Always be certain a downloaded GEDCOM or TT has verified information before you load it into your database, because taking it back out isn't fun.

The best way to use computers is to take some of the drudgery out of life, and the best way to use tiny tafels is to compare and contrast them with as many others as you can. Thus, the Tiny Tafel Matching System was born. It's a copyrighted software program from CommSoft and is on many BBSs, which have to be on The National Genealogy conference (FidoNet) to carry the program. You have to be a qualified user of a BBS and submit your own TT file to be allowed to use TTMS to the fullest. Your file can have more than one tafel in it.

To find a TTMS near you, call the CommSoft BBS at 707-838-6373, register as a user, and look at the Files section under genealogy-related files. You can also get a description of the system there. Or call Brian Mavrogeorge's board Roots (SF!) at 415-584-0697. He also has an eight-page article about the system. Send him an e-mail message at brian.mavrogeorge@p0.f30.n125.z1 .fidonet.org to ask for a copy.

The TTMS system has three main functions:

- Collecting and maintaining a local database of TTs
- Presenting instant matches on the local database
- Allowing batch searches of all other databases on the NGS

In this context, *instant* means while you sit waiting at your keyboard, hooked onto the BBS, which could take some time, with you and your line tied up. For this reason, some BBSs will limit the time of day you can try this. A *batch* search means that your query is sent out on the NGS and, in a few hours or days, you'll receive messages about other TTs that match yours. Then you can contact the persons who submitted the data.

Anyone who can sign onto a BBS can look for instant matches, but you have to submit a TT file of your own to do a batch search. The searches can be limited by dates, Soundex, interest level, and so on to make the hits more meaningful.

Your TTs should be machine-generated (by Brother's Keeper, for example) to avoid formatting errors. Keep the TT as concise as possible and submit to only one board; for the batch system to be most efficient, redundancies have to be minimal. And be sure to experiment with the date overlap features to keep the reports short. As you find new information, you can replace your old TT file with new information; this is especially important if your address changes.

GEDCOMs

In February 1987, The Church of Jesus Christ of Latter-day Saints (Mormon church) approved a standard way of setting data for transfer between various types of genealogy software, including its own Personal Ancestral File, or PAF. The standard has been adopted into most major genealogical database programs, including MacGene, Roots, Family Roots, Family Ties, Brother's Keeper, and so on. The standard is a combination of tags for data and pointers to related data.

If data from one database doesn't fit exactly into the new one even with GEDCOM's format, the program will often save the extraneous data to a special file. A good program can use this data to help you sort and search for whether it has what you're looking for. Which is why so many people upload GEDCOMs to BBSs; perhaps someone somewhere can use the data. But, as GEDCOMs tend to be large, many BBSs have a policy against uploading them. Instead, you upload a message that you're willing to exchange it for the price of the disk, or some other arrangement.

As a practical matter, it's often easier to turn a GEDCOM into a TT for uploading, although some details won't go through. Then, you can exchange GEDCOMs when someone's TT matches yours at some point.

APPENDIX D

INTERNET ERROR MESSAGES

The information superhighway is full of potholes, dead ends, and wrong turns. You know you've hit one of these when you get something that says, "404 not found" or "Failed DSN lookup." Scratching your head, you wonder, "40what? Failed who? What do those cryptic messages mean anyway?"

They mean the Internet is trying to tell you something. Here's a short guide to some of the most common ones, their probable cause, and what you can do about it.

Browser Error Messages

403 forbidden. The Web site you're trying to access requires special permission—a password at the very least. No password? You'll probably have to give up or find out how to register for the site. Your browser has made it as far as the remote host computer, but it can't find the page or document you want.

404 not found. Your browser found the host computer but not the specific Web page or document you requested. Check your typing, make sure you have the address (URL) right, and try again. If this doesn't work, shorten the address, erasing from right to left to the first slash you encounter. For example, if *http://www.benchley/pub/dottie* isn't working, try *http://www.benchley/pub/*. If that doesn't work, keep erasing the address back to the first single slash.

Bad file request. The problem: you're trying to fill out an on-screen form, and you get this message. Cause: either your browser doesn't support forms or the function isn't turned on. Another possibility: the form you filled out or the HTML coding at that Web site has an error in it. If you are sure your browser isn't the problem, send e-mail to the site administrator and surf on.

Cannot add form submission result to bookmark list. A script—say, from a WebCrawler search—returns variables, such as the results from a query. You can't save the results as a bookmark because they are not a permanent file on the Internet. They are just a temporary display on your computer at this moment. You can save only the address of a page or document that's stored on some computer on the Internet. You can, however, save the result of a search to your own hard disk and create a bookmark that points to that.

Connection refused by host.   See *403 Forbidden.*

Failed DNS lookup.   The Web site's address couldn't be translated into a valid IP address—the site's officially assigned number. Either that, or the domain name server (DNS) was too busy to handle your request. What does this all mean? Well, the vespucci.iquest.com site I visit is also known as 199.170.120.42. The computer that translates the site's name into that number is a *domain name server.* If I see this message, the DNS couldn't take the word-based URL and translate it into a IP address (numbers). First, check your spelling and punctuation. If you still get the message, try to ping the site. Or, assume the DNS was busy and try again later.

File contains no data.   The browser found the site but found nothing in the specific file. If you typed in a URL and got this message, check your spelling and punctuation. If you got this message after using an interactive page, perhaps you didn't finish the form, or the script on the page is faulty. Try again, at least once.

Helper application not found.   Your browser downloaded a file that needs a viewer (such as a video clip), and it can't find the program to display it. Go to your browser's Option menu (or similar menu) and make sure you've properly specified the necessary helper program, its correct directory, and executable file name. Then try again. *Note:* You can usually ignore this error and download the file to view it later.

NNTP server error.   You tried to connect to your Internet Service Provider's newsgroup server, the computer that handles messages going to and from all newsgroups supported by your ISP. The problem: your browser couldn't find it. This could be because the server is down or because you typed in the wrong server. Be sure you entered the news server correctly in the Preferences or Options dialog. Try again.

Another cause could be that you have tried to access one Internet Service Provider's news server from your account on another Internet Service Provider. You can't use CompuServe's network to read Usenet off Prodigy Internet and vice versa.

Not found.   The link to a page or document or some other site no longer exists. Shorten the URL back to the first single slash and try again. If you still can't find the site, access a Web search program such as WebCrawler or Lycos and see if you can find the site's new address.

TCP error encountered while sending request to server.   Some kind of erroneous data got in the pipes and is confusing the easily confused Internet. This could be due to a faulty phone jack, line noise, sunspots, or gremlins.

Try again later and if the problem persists, report it to your system administrator.

Too many users.   Many servers, especially ftp servers, have a limit on the number of users that can connect at one time. Wait for the traffic to die down and try again.

Unable to locate host.   Your browser couldn't find anything at the URL you specified. The address could have a typo, the site may be unavailable (perhaps temporarily), or you didn't notice that your connection to the Internet Service Provider has dropped.

FTP Error Messages

There are probably hundreds of ftp programs for the PC and Mac, and the error messages will vary. Nevertheless, here are some errors, their causes, and resolutions.

Invalid host or *Unable to resolve host.*   This is ftp's equivalent to *404 Not found.* It doesn't mean the site isn't there, it just means your ftp program couldn't find it. First, check your syntax and try again. If you still run into a brick wall, run a ping program and see what's going on. Most ISPs have a ping program on their servers; Windows 95 comes with one. Just type *ping* <<sitename>>. If the site exists, ping will tell you how long it took a signal to travel there and back. If ping couldn't get through, then assume the site is down, at least temporarily. Try another day.

Another way to find out if a site exists is to run *nslookup,* a program available from many ISPs. It looks up a server's IP address in a master Internet directory. When you are logged on to your ISP, just type *nslookup* <<hostname>>.

Your ftp program connects then suddenly freezes.   If this happens shortly after you log in, try using a dash (-) as the first character of your password. This will turn off the site's informational messages, which may be confusing your ftp program.

Too many consecutive transmit errors.   This means line noise has confused your ftp program and it can't continue.

It could be your modem. If you got a bargain 28.8 Kbps modem for $99, it's possible that modem has less configurable options and cheaper interface circuits between the modem's real guts, the chipset, and the phone line. Modem connections above 9600 bps require real care in these circuits, and cheaper modems cut corners. Call your manufacturer to see if it has some workarounds.

Another possibility is you're choking Windows, the communication program, or the modem by setting the COM port's speed to higher than 38.4 or 57.6 Kbps. Even though most 28.8 Kbps modems claim to handle communications at speeds up to 115 Kbps, something in the link may not be able to. Reset the COM port speed and try again.

This could also be a problem with the command string sent to your modem before dialing. Check with your vendor and be prepared to supply the model number; the current initialization string sent to the modem; and settings for hardware flow control, error correction, and so on.

Usenet Error Messages

Reading and participating in newsgroups is one of the Internet's oldest and most enjoyable pastimes. But to avoid glitches and online faux pas, read some FAQ files first. You can find a good set at http://www.cs.ruu.nl/wais/html/nadir/usenet/faq/part1.html.

Usenet error messages are usually specific to your newsreader, but there are some common traps.

Invalid newsgroup. This jarring note can appear for various reasons. You may have spelled the newsgroup name wrong. It's easy to put periods in the wrong places. Or maybe the newsgroup no longer exists. This is very common with the alt.* groups. Search your provider's list of all newsgroups. You can also find a list of active newsgroups at http://www.cis.ohio-state.edu/hypertext/faq/usenet/active-newsgroups/top.html.

If you try to add a newsgroup but get the address wrong, you'll get this message. Finally, your news server may not carry this group. Talk to the sysop about adding it or find the archived messages of the group via ftp at rtfm.mit.eduin the /pub/usenet, /pub/usenet-by-group, or /pub/usenet-by-hierarchy directories. If all else fails, search for the newsgroup (or its archives) with DejaNews (http://www.dejanews.com) or the Excite searcher (http://www.excite.com/).

No such message. Sometimes, especially if you are using a browser, you'll get a list of messages that is out of date. The message you wanted to read is still listed in the index, but it has *scrolled off* the server. This means it has been erased to make room for newer messages. Go to DejaNews or one of the archive sites to search for that message. Some archives are

ftp.uu.net/usenet/news.answers

ftp.seas.gwu.edu/pub/rtfm

Could not connect to server. Either the news server is busy (you can try again later), down (you should notify your ISP), or you are not allowed access to the news server. Another possible cause is you have set up your browser or newsreader client incorrectly. Check your typing in your configuration screen.

A Usenet message looks like gibberish. This isn't really an error. It is a binary file, such as a picture, sound, movie, or program, that has been uuencoded into ASCII characters. You can copy that message to a file and use a uudecoding program to restore it; however, the newest and best newsreaders come with automatic decoding. Read the instructions for getting coded messages for your newsreader.

E-Mail Error Messages

E-mail is what the Internet was originally designed for and it's very dependable. Most mail errors are user syntax errors. When addressing a message, you must get the syntax exactly right. Commas and spaces are never allowed in e-mail addresses. The first thing to do when an e-mail you've sent is bounced back is to check your typing.

Unknown user. Usually you have typed the name wrong. Sometimes you have the wrong address. Call the person and ask for the correct e-mail address.

Mail from a mail list stops coming. If delivery from one of your favorite mail lists suddenly stops, it could be caused by a temporary glitch in that site or the Internet. If you are not getting mail from anywhere else, the latter is probably the case. If you are, you may have been involuntarily unsubscribed by the mail list program at the site. (The usual reason is because mail it sent you was bounced back with an error.) The solution is to resubscribe.

Another possibility is the list may have been discontinued and you weren't reading the messages closely. If you suspect this, send an e-mail to the site with just this in the body of the message: *review* <<listname>>, with *listname* being the name of the list. You should get back the list's current status including the address of the owner, who you may query.

Message undeliverable Mailer Daemon. You've just met the mail program that parses all messages. If something is wrong, the header will try to tell you what. Read the whole header and you'll probably find the problem. Usually, it's spelling.

WARNING: Message still undelivered after xx hours. Sometimes the Internet is kind enough to warn your when you mail isn't getting through. This message is typically followed by one saying the mailer will keep trying for so many hours or days to deliver the message. You don't have to do anything about this message, but you might want to call the recipient and tell him or her the e-mail will be delayed.

GLOSSARY

Ahnentafel The word means *ancestor table* in German, and the format is more than a century old. It lists all known ancestors of an individual and includes the full name of each ancestor as well as dates and places of birth, marriage, and death. It organizes this information along a strict numbering scheme.

anonymous FTP (file transfer protocol) The procedure of connecting to a remote computer as an anonymous or guest user in order to transfer public files back to your local computer. Anonymous FTP is usually read-only access; you often cannot contribute files by anonymous FTP. *See also* File Transfer Protocol (FTP) *and* protocol.

Archie An Internet program for finding files available by anonymous FTP to the general public.

backbone A set of connections that make up the main channels of communication across a network.

baud A measure of speed for data transmission across a wire. It is not equivalent to bits per second, but to changes of state per second. Several bits may go across the wire with each change of state, so bits per second can be higher than the baud rate.

Bitnet Originally, a cooperative computer network interconnecting over 2,300 academic and research institutions in 32 countries. Originally based on IBM's RSCS networking protocol, Bitnet supports mail, mailing lists, and file transfer. It eventually became part of the Internet, but some colleges restrict access to the original Bitnet collection of computer.

browser An Internet client for viewing the World Wide Web.

bulletin board system (BBS) A set of hardware and software you can use to enter information for other users to read or download. In this book, a BBS is usually a stand-alone system that you dial up with the phone, but many are now reachable by telnet. Most bulletin boards are set up according to general topics and are accessible throughout a network.

chat When people type messages to each other across a host or network, live and in real time. On some commercial online services this is called *conference*.

client A program that provides an interface to remote Internet services, such as mail, Usenet, telnet, and so on. In general, the clients act on behalf of a human end-user (perhaps indirectly).

compress   To make a file, whether text or code, smaller by various methods. This is so that it will take up less disk space and/or require less time to transmit. Sometimes the compression is completed by the modem. Sometimes the file is stored that way. The various methods of compression go by names (followed by the system that used the method) such as PKZIP (DOS), ARC (DOS), tar (UNIX), STUFFIT (Macintosh), and so on.

conference   A live, online chat or a forum or echo (which see) of e-mail messages.

CREN   Computer Research and Education Network is the new name for the merged computer networks, Bitnet and Computer Science Network (CSNET). It supports electronic mail and file transfer.

database   A set of information organized for computer storage, search, retrieval, and insertion.

domain name   The Internet naming scheme. A machine on the Internet is identified by a series of words from more specific to more general (left to right), separated by dots: microsoft.com is an example. *See also* IP address.

domain name server (DNS)   A machine with software to translate a domain name into the corresponding numbers of the IP address. *No DNS entry* from your browser means a name such as first.last.org was not in the domain name server's list of valid IP addresses.

door   A program on a BBS that allows you to perform specific functions, e.g., download mail, play a game, scan the files, and so on. The BBS software shuts down while you are in a door, and the door's commands are in effect.

downloading   To get information from another computer to yours.

echo   A set of messages on a specific subject sent to specific BBSs that have requested those messages.

e-mail   An electronic message, text or data, sent from one machine or person to another machine or person.

flame   A message or series of messages containing an argument or insults. Not allowed on most systems. If you receive a flame, ignore the message and all other messages from that person in the future.

file transfer protocol (FTP)   Allows an Internet user to transfer files electronically from remote computers back to the user's computer.

forum   A set of messages on a subject, usually with a corresponding set of files. Can be on an open network, such as ILINK, or restricted to a commercial system such as CompuServe.

gateway Used in different senses (e.g., mail gateway, IP gateway), but most generally a computer that forwards and routes data between two or more networks of any size or origin. It is never, however, as straightforward as going through a gate; it's more like a labyrinth to get the proper addresses in the proper sequence.

GEDCOM The standard for computerized genealogical information that is a combination of tags for data and pointers to related data.

Gopher An Internet program to search for resources, present them to you in a menu, and perform whatever Internet program (telnet, FTP, etc.) is necessary to get the resource. *See* Veronica *and* Jughead; all three are read-only access.

host computer In the context of networks, a computer that directly provides service to a user, in contrast to a network server, which provides services to a user through an intermediary host computer.

hot key When a BBS system responds to one-keystroke commands, without the Enter or Return key, that option is called a *hot key.* Some BBS software enables it with no option to turn it off; others let you set your user configuration to choose this or not. Without a hot key, to make a command take effect you must press Enter or Return; also without a hot key, some systems let you string together several commands on one line.

HTML Hypertext Markup Language, a coding system to format and link documents on the World Wide Web and intranets.

hub A BBS that collects e-mail regionally and distributes it up the next level; collects the e-mail from that level to distribute it back down the chain.

Internet The backbone of a series of interconnected networks that includes local area, regional, and national backbone networks. Networks in the Internet use the same telecommunications protocol (TCP/IP) and provide electronic mail, remote login, and file transfer services.

Internet service provider (ISP) A company that has a continuous, fast and reliable connection to the Internet and sells subscriptions to the public to use that connection. The connections may use TCP/IP, shell accounts, or other methods.

INTERNIC The company that has contracted to administer certain functions of the Internet such as maintaining domain names and assigning IP addresses. Its home page is at HYPERLINK http://rs1 .internic.net/ http://rs1.internic.net/

Intranet   A local network set up to look like the World Wide Web, with clients such as browsers, but self-contained and not necessarily connected to the Internet.

IP (Internet protocol)   The Internet standard protocol that provides a common layer over dissimilar networks, used to move packets among host computers and through gateways if necessary.

IP address   The alphabetical or numeric address of a computer connected to the Internet; also called Internet address. Usually the format is user@someplace.domain; but also seen as ###.##.##.##

Jughead   An Internet program that helps Gopher build menus of resources by limiting the search to one computer and a text string. *See* Gopher.

list (Internet)   Also called mail list. listserv lists (or listservers) are electronically transmitted discussions of technical and nontechnical issues. They come to you by electronic mail over the Internet using listserv commands. Participants subscribe via a central service, and lists often have a moderator who supervises the information flow and content.

lurk   To read a list or echo without posting messages yourself. It's sort of like sitting in the corner at a party without introducing yourself, except it's not considered rude online; in fact, in some places you are expected to lurk until you get the feel of the place.

mail list   Same as list.

MNP   Data compression standard for modems.

modem   A device to modulate computer data into sound signals and to demodulate those signals to computer data.

moderator   The person who takes care of an echo, list, or forum. This person takes out messages that are off-topic, chastises flamers, sometimes maintains a database of old messages and sometimes handles the mechanics of distributing the messages.

NIC (network information center)   A NIC provides administrative support, user support, and information services for a network.

NREN   The National Research and Education Network is a proposed national computer network to be built upon the foundation of the NSF backbone network, NSFnet. NREN would provide high-speed interconnection between other national and regional networks. SB 1067 is the legislative bill proposing NREN.

offline   The state of not being connected to a remote host.

online   To be connected to a remote host.

OPAC   online public access catalog, a term used to describe any type of computerized library catalog.

OSI (open systems interconnection)   This is the evolving international standard under development at ISO (International Standards Organization) for the interconnection of cooperative computer systems. An open system is one that conforms to OSI standards in its communications with other systems. As more and more genealogical data becomes available online, this standard will become increasingly important.

PPP (point-to-point protocol)   A type of Internet connection. An improvement on SLIP, it allows any computer to use the Internet protocols and become a full-fledged member of the Internet with a high-speed modem. The advantage to SLIP and PPP accounts is that you can usually achieve faster connections this way than with a shell account. *See* SLIP.

protocol   A mutually determined set of formats and procedures governing the exchange of information between systems.

remote access   The ability to access a computer from outside another location. Remote access requires communications hardware, software, and actual physical links, although this can be as simple as common carrier (telephone) lines or as complex as telnet login to another computer across the Internet.

search engine   A program on the World Wide Web that searches parts of the Internet for text strings. It may search for programs, for Web pages, or for other items.

shareware   Try-before-you-buy concept in microcomputer software, where the program is distributed through public domain channels and the author expects to receive compensation after a trial period. Brother's Keeper, for example, is shareware.

shell account   a method of connecting to the Internet. You dial an Internet service provider with regular modem software and connect to a computer there that is connected to the Internet. Employing a text interface, usually with a menu, you use the Internet with this shell, using commands such as telnet. In this system, the Internet clients do not reside on your computer, but on the ISPs.

signature   A stored text file with your name and some information, such as names you are searching or your mailing address, to be appended to the end of your messages. Should contain only ASCII characters, no graphics.

SLIP (serial line IP)   A system allowing a computer to use the Internet protocols with a standard telephone line and a high-speed modem. Most ISPs now offer PPP or SLIP accounts for a monthly or yearly fee.

Spider   A program that gathers information on Web pages for a database.

sysop   The system operator of a BBS, forum, or echo. The sysop sets the rules, maintains the peace and operability of the system, and sometimes moderates the messages.

tagline   A short, pithy statement tagged onto the end of a BBS e-mail message. Example: *It's only a hobby, only a hobby, only a . . .* Taglines are rarely seen on commercial networks such as AOL, MSN, and CompuServe.

TCP/IP (transmission control protocol/Internet protocol)   A combined set of protocols that performs the transfer of data between two computers. TCP monitors and ensures correct transfer of data. IP receives the data from TCP, breaks it up into packets, and ships it off to a network within the Internet. TCP/IP is also used as a name for a protocol suite that incorporates these functions and others.

telnet   An Internet client that connects to other computers, making yours a virtual terminal of the remote computer. Among other functions, it allows a user to log onto a remote computer from the user's local computer. On many commercial systems, you use it as a command, e.g., telnet ftp.cac.psu.edu. Once there, you are using programs, and therefore commands, from that remote computer.

terminal emulation   Most communications software packages will permit your personal computer or workstation to communicate with another computer or network as if it were a specific type of terminal directly connected to that computer or network. For example, your terminal emulation should be set to VT100 for most online card catalog programs.

terminal server   A machine that connects terminals to a network by providing host telnet service.

thread (message thread)   Discussion made up of a set of messages in answer to a certain message and to each other. Sometimes very worthwhile threads are saved into a text file, as on CompuServe's Roots Forum. Some offline mail readers will sort by thread, that is, according to subject line.

tiny tafel (TT) A TT provides a standard way of describing a family database so that the information can be scanned visually or by computer. All data fields are of fixed length, with the obvious exceptions of the surnames and optional places. Many TTs are extracted from GED-COMs.

TN3270 A version of telnet providing IBM full-screen support, as opposed to VT100 or some other emulation.

upload To send a file or message from one computer to another. *See* downloading.

Usenet A set of messages and the software for sending and receiving them on the Internet. The difference between Usenet and a mail list lies in the software and the way you connect to them.

V.32 Data compression standard for modem.

Veronica A search program for gopher.

World Wide Web (WWW or the Web) A system to pull various Internet services together into one interface called a browser. Most sites on the WWW are written as pages in HTML.

Z39.50 Protocol Name of the national standard developed by the National Information Standards Organization (NISO) that defines an applications level protocol by which one computer can query another computer and transfer result records using a canonical format. This protocol provides the framework for OPAC users to search remote catalogs on the Internet using the commands of their own local systems. Projects are now in development to provide Z39.50 support for catalogs on the Internet. SR (Search and Retrieval), ISO Draft International Standard 10162/10163, is the international version of Z39.50 protocol.

Smileys (Emoticons)

Because we can't hear voice inflection over e-mail, a code for imparting emotion sprang up. These punctuation marks used to take the place of facial expressions are called smileys or emoticons. Different systems have variations of these symbols. Two versions of this unofficial smiley dictionary were sent to me by Cliff Manis (Internet: cmanis@csf.com; Roots-L mailing list administrator), and I have edited and combined them. Several versions are floating around, but I think this one sums up the smileys you are most likely to see.

:-)	Your basic smiley. This smiley is used to show pleasure or a sarcastic or joking statement.
;-)	Winky smiley. User just made a flirtatious and/or sarcastic remark. Somewhat of a "don't hit me for what I just said" smiley.
:-(	Frowning smiley. User did not like that last statement or is upset or depressed about something.
:-I	Indifferent smiley. Better than a frowning smiley, but not quite as good as a happy smiley.
:->	User just made a really biting sarcastic remark. Worse than a :-)
>:->	User just made a really devilish remark.
>;->	Winky and devil combined.

Those are the basic ones ... Here are some that are somewhat less common. *Note:* A lot of these can be typed without noses to make midget smileys.

- -:-)	Smiley is a punk rocker.
- -:-(	(Real punk rockers don't smile).
;-)	Wink.
,-}	Wry and winking.
:,(	Crying.
:-:	Mutant smiley.
.-)	Smiley only has one eye.
,-)	Ditto ... but he's winking.
:-?	Smiley smoking a pipe.
:-/	Skepticism, consternation, or puzzlement.
:-\	Ditto.
:-`	Smiley spitting out chewing tobacco.
:-~)	Smiley has a cold.
:-)-	Smiley drools.
:-[	Un-smiley blockhead.
:-[	Smiley is a vampire.
:-]	Smiley blockhead.
:-{	Mustache.
:-}	Wry smile, or beard.

:-@	Smiley face screaming.
:-$	Smiley face with its mouth wired shut.
:-`	Smiley after eating something bitter or sour.
:-&	Smiley is tongue-tied.
:-#	Braces.
:-#|	Smiley face with bushy mustache.
:-%	Smiley banker.
:-<	Mad or really sad smiley.
:-=)	Older smiley with mustache.
:->	Hey hey.
:-|	"Have an ordinary day" smiley.
:-0	Smiley orator.
:-0	No yelling! (quiet lab).
:-1	Smiley bland face.
:-!	Ditto.
:-6	Smiley after eating something sour.
:-7	Smiley after a wry statement.
:-8(	Condescending stare.
:-9	Smiley is licking his/her lips.
:-a	Lefty smiley touching tongue to nose.
:-b	Left-pointing-tongue smiley.
:-c	Bummed-out smiley.
:-C	Smiley is really bummed.
:-d	Lefty smiley razzing you.
:-D	Smiley is laughing.
:-e	Disappointed smiley.
:-E	Bucktoothed vampire.
:-F	Bucktoothed vampire with one tooth missing.
:-I	Hmm.
:-i	Semi-smiley.
:-j	Left-smiling smiley.
:-o	Smiley singing national anthem.
:-O	Uh-oh.

:-o	Uh-oh!
:-P	Disgusted or nyah nyah.
:-p	Smiley sticking its tongue out (at you!).
:-q	Smiley trying to touch its tongue to its nose.
:-Q	Smoker.
:-s	Smiley after a *bizarre* comment.
:-S	Smiley just made an incoherent statement.
:-t	Cross smiley.
:-v	Talking head smiley.
:-x	"My lips are sealed" smiley.
:-X	Bow tie.
:-X	Smiley's lips are sealed.
::-)	Smiley wears normal glasses.
:'-(	Smiley is crying.
:'-)	Smiley is so happy, s/he is crying.
:^)	Smiley with pointy nose (righty). Sometimes used to denote a lie, myth, or misconception.
:^)	Smiley has a broken nose.
:(	Sad midget smiley.
:)	Midget smiley.
:[	Real downer.
:]	Midget smiley.
:*	Kisses.
:')	Smiley is drunk.
:<	Midget un-smiley.
:<)	Smiley is from an Ivy League School.
:=)	Smiley has two noses.
:>	Midget smiley.
:D	Laughter.
:I	Hmmm ...
:n)	Smiley with funny-looking right nose.
:O	Yelling.
:u)	Smiley with funny-looking left nose.

:v)	Left-pointing-nose smiley.
:v)	Smiley has a broken nose.
`:-)	Smiley shaved one of his eyebrows off this morning.
,:-)	Same thing, other side.
~~:-(	net.flame.
(-:	Smiley is left-handed.
(:-(	Un-smiley frowning.
(:-)	Smiley big-face.
):-)	Ditto.
(:I	Egghead.
(8-o	It's Mr. Bill!
):-(	Un-smiley big-face.
)8-)	Scuba smiley big-face.
[:-)	Smiley is wearing a walkman.
[:]	Smiley is a robot.
[] -	Hugs.
{:-)	Smiley with hair parted in the middle.
{:-)	Smiley wears a toupee.
}:-(	Toupee in an updraft.
@:-)	Smiley is wearing a turban.
@:I	Turban variation.
@=	Smiley is pro-nuclear war.
*:o)	Bozo the Clown!
%-)	Smiley has been staring at a green screen for 15 hours straight.
%-6	Smiley is brain-dead.
+-:-)	Smiley is the Pope or holds some other religious office.
+:-)	Smiley priest.
<:-I	Smiley is a dunce.
<:I	Midget dunce.
<|-(	Smiley is Chinese and doesn't like these kind of jokes.
<|-)	Smiley is Chinese.
=)	Variation on a theme . . .
>:-I	net.startrek.

|-)	Hee hee.
|-D	Ho ho.
|-I	Smiley is asleep.
|-O	Smiley is yawning/snoring.
|-P	Yuk.
|^o	Snoring.
|I	Asleep.
0-)	Smiley cyclops (scuba diver?).
3:[	Mean pet smiley.
3:]	Pet smiley.
3:o[	net.pets.
8 :-)	Smiley is a wizard.
8 :-I	net.unix-wizards.
8-)	Glasses.
8-)	Smiley swimmer.
8-)	Smiley is wearing sunglasses.
8:-)	Glasses on forehead.
8:-)	Smiley is a little girl.
B-)	Horn rims.
B:-)	Sunglasses on head.
C=:-)	Smiley is a chef.
C=}>;*{))	Mega-smiley. . . . A drunk, devilish chef with a toupee in an updraft, a mustache, and a double chin.
E-:-)	Smiley is a ham radio operator.
E-:-I	net.ham-radio.
g-)	Smiley with pince-nez glasses.
K:P	Smiley is a little kid with a propeller beanie.
O :-)	Smiley is an angel (at heart, at least).
O |-)	net.religion.
O-)	Megaton man on patrol! (or else, user is a scuba diver).
X-(	Smiley just died.

INDEX

Page numbers for computer screen samples are in italics.

H

Haley, Alex, and influence of *Roots* (1976) on interest in genealogy, xiv

Henderson, Thom, on advantages and disadvantages of FidoNet, 114–115

Hereditary kings, lists of, compiled by ancient civilizations, xiii–xiv

Heritage Quest Magazine, 218

Historical groups, genealogy mail lists of, 58–59

History, relevance of professional genealogical studies to, xiii

Hobbs, Darrin, on Everton's On-Line Search on WWW, 143

Host, FidoNet term, 113

Humor, in cyberspace communication, uses of and caveats concerning, 20

HyperACCESS, telnet program in card catalog search, 150, *151*

Hypertext, 69

HyperText Markup Language (HTML), 68

HyperText Transfer Protocol (HTTP), 69

Hytelnet, 73–78, 150; illustrated, *74–78*

I

InfoSeek Net Guide, 39, 83

Inheritance, importance of genealogies in determination of, xiii–xiv

Instant Relatives (Salt Lake City), profile of, 104–106, *107*

Integrated Services Digital Networks (ISDN), 15–17

International Genealogical Index (IGI), of LDS (Mormons):
copyrighted database, 168
information on obtaining CD-ROMs of, 170, 172–173

Internet:
and AOL access, through Internet Center, 178, 189–190
and CompuServe, 208
as concept, xviii–xix
and development of browsers, 68
error messages:
browser, 263–266
e-mail, 267–268

Internet (*Cont.*):
ftp, 265–266
Usenet, 266–267
more difficult to use in early 1990s, 68
MSN access to, 215–216
present limitations of sound/pictures across, 69
Prodigy access to, through Web browser, 226, 228, 235
services, introduced, xix–xx

Internet bulletin boards (*see* Usenet)

Internet news (*see* Usenet)

Internet Roadmap, 73

Internet Service Provider (ISP):
importance of selection of, 8–10
questions to ask before choosing, 9–11

Internet Tour Guide, The (Fraase), 11

Israel, tribes of, biblical genealogies of, xiii

J

Jewish genealogy, on Genealogy One, 126

Journal of Online Genealogy, on World Wide Web, 42, *43, 47,* 64

Judaic genealogy, newsgroup listing of, 35

K

KC GeneSplicer (Kansas City, Kansas), profile of, 96, *97, 98, 99*

L

Law, relevance of professional genealogical studies to, xiii

LDS (Latter-Day Saints of Mormon Church), genealogical database, 38

Library of Congress:
access to data files from:
gopher, 163–165
text-only, 165–166
Web, 161–163
extraordinary abundance of genealogical information at, 160
ftp site of, 166

ABOUT THE AUTHOR

Elizabeth Powell Crowe is the author of three books, including *Genealogy Online*, whose two previous editions were both bestsellers. She also wrote *Information for Sale* (with John Everett) and *The Electronic Traveller*, both published by McGraw-Hill. She is the twice-monthly "Net Surfer" columnist for *Computer Currents* magazine and author of numerous articles for both popular and technical publications. She lives in Huntsville, Alabama, with her husband and two children.